Let *the* Magic Begin

Opening the Door
To a Whole New World of Possibility

Cathy Lee Crosby

Simon & Schuster

SIMON & SCHUSTER
Rockefeller Center
1230 Avenue of the Americas
New York, NY 10020

Designed by Deirdre C. Amthor

Cover photo courtesy of Harry Langdon

Manufactured in the United States of America

10 9 8 7 6 5 4 3 2 1

Library of Congress Cataloging-in-Publication data is available.

ISBN 0-684-80280-5

The instructions and advice in this book are in no way intended as
a substitute for medical counseling. We advise the reader to consult
with his/her doctor before beginning this or any regimen of exercise. The author and the publisher disclaim any liability or loss,
personal or otherwise, resulting from the procedures in this book.

To my family: Francesca, Harry, Linda, Lou,
Jean, Gene, Linda Lou, Hart, Lucinda, Carey,
Corey & Maggie Rose, for surrounding me with
their unselfish love and unconditional support.

To dancing in the Bliss Zone
                    and
awakening the Magic in all of us.

Acknowledgments

There are really no words that can aptly describe the loving, selfless, and heartfelt contribution the following people have made, not only to the creation of this book, but also to the experience of magic in my life.

My grateful thanks to the Source of everything, who led me down the path and presented me with the opportunity to write this book in the first place.

To my family, please know that your love is my strength, and that I carry your spirit with me always.

To Joel, you have touched my life at the "center" of things, and there can be no greater gift. In your presence, I fell in love with the best of myself.

Sometimes we have the honor and privilege of connecting with a joyous spirit who, by his or her very presence, lights up our life. To Brooke Channon, thank you from the core of my heart for your dedication, patience, caring, humor, and unbelievably hard work—what would I have done without you?!

A special thanks to Bob Asahina for steadfastly convincing me that I had to write this book, and then making me believe that I actually could!

To Michael Korda, my editor Bob Mecoy, Sarah Pinckney, Pete Fornatale, Jackie Seow, Larry Norton, Ted Landry, Barbara Hanson, Kerri Kennedy, Anita Halton, Marie Florio, Victoria Meyer, the entire sales staff, and everyone at Simon & Schuster who worked so hard to publish a book I am extremely proud of.

To Jan Miller and Mark Seal, for the spark that lit the flame.

To James Ragan for his love, his unselfish dedication, his ability to help me find the "poetry" in my writing, and for teaching me so much about the written word.

To Brian Oxman, Maureen Jaroscak, Steve Breimer, Curt Abramson, Larry Rubin, Etta Lerner, George Short, and Richard Ross for keeping the fire going with love and caring even during the roughest times.

To Moshe Zwang and his wife Diana, Jim Channon, Sister Jane Roach, Dan Millman, Deepak Chopra, Marianne Williamson, Shakti Gawain, Paulo Coelho, John Welwood, Salle & James Redfield, Wayne Dyer, Jack Canfield, and Joan Brown (Ngeton) for your inspiration, wisdom, spirit, and patience in allowing me the opportunity to grow.

And, my love and grateful thanks to my extended family and cherished friends who have touched my life so profoundly in ways that are beyond description: Madeline, Janie, William, & Larry Cummings, Ed Viramontes, Ivan Menchell, Vicki Stuart, Dale Eldridge Kaye, Larry Otting, Lynn Thoma, Eric Edmeads, Paula Charlton, Liz Golf, Troy Garrison, Christopher Sheasby, Bob Yerkes, John Manulis, Liz Heller, Craige Citron, Dr. Duane Townsend, Gregg & Christine Champion, Leslie Moonves, Roy Rogers & Dale Evans, Ave Butensky, Leah Hanes, David & Gloria Wolper, Clare Busceglia, Byron Donzis, Wendel & Terry Wong, Alan Nierob, Kathy Buckley, Robert Caro, Rona & Luke O'Connor, Charlie Reinmiller, Ed & Lori Shipley, Sherry Geyer, Bruce Loeb, Ira Fistel, Sandy Greenland, Aaron Tonken, Steve & Elaine Wynn, Scott & Denise Miller. Your presence in my life has made "of earth, a garden."

Contents

Introduction

Like everything else in my life in the last two years, this book came about in a completely coincidental manner. When I met with Bob Asahina, at the time senior editor of Simon & Schuster, I assumed that he was interested in me writing a book on health and fitness—something I felt would be a natural. After some twelve hours of in-depth discussions stretching over two days, however, Bob gently yet skillfully elicited my agreement to write a somewhat different book—the exact one he wanted. It was a book that I felt totally unequipped to write because of the highly personal nature of the journey it was to focus on. These doubts, I might add, never left me, even up to the date of publication. But something inside kept pushing me forward in spite of all my trepidation. So, finally, I gave up trying to control the book's destiny and allowed myself the freedom, excitement, surprise, and anxiety of riding the horse in the direction it was going. I let go enough to become the vessel through which the Universe could work its creative magic.

Simon & Schuster classifies this as a motivational book. If that's true, then it's certainly one of the most unorthodox motivational books ever written. It is not a paint-by-the-numbers road map of "How to get . . . rich-beautiful-sexy-successful OVERNIGHT, in ten easy chapters." Rather, it is simply an account, in all its color and emotion, of one particular person's evolution of going through the eye of the hurricane and coming out the other side, face-to-face with the magic within. These pages are filled with the story of that journey I took to the "center" of things.

Just when I had achieved everything I had ever dreamed of, in every aspect of my life, the Universe proceeded to show me the one thing I had neglected to remember. Within a very short period of time, I lost everything I had ever worked for and achieved in such a dramatic fashion that, when I hit bottom, I landed with a reverberating thud.

The particular circumstances of my fall were really no diffferent from those of anyone else who has faced trauma in their life. We've all been there in varying degrees at some time or another. So, the essence of this book is not a tale of how I fought back from "despair," or my step-by-step journey back to the "top." It is the story of how life itself forced me back into that magical place of awe and wonder, where coincidences abound, opening the door to all possibility. It is the world of universal energy and total potentiality. I will tell you the facts of what happened, but more important, the actual process by which I gradually became aware of what "reality" really is. You will discover, as I did, the sheer joy of allowing life's inherent gifts, available to you in every moment, to endow you with a richness and joy more profound than you ever thought possible.

For those of you who have long traveled on this path and already knew . . . have a good laugh on me and just know how much I appreciate who you are.

For the rest of us, I hope this book will not only be a reminder for myself of the journey I have taken and the gifts I have received, but will also serve as a *guide* for those who have lost their map; as a *sign* for those who are about to undertake the trip; as a *door* for those who have been searching; as a *gift* for those who are against the wall; and a *beacon* for those who are in the middle of the fight.

A journey begins with courage, trust, and one small step, and I wish you magic in yours.

Cathy Lee Crosby

How many things have to happen to you, before something occurs to you.

Robert Frost

1
A Truth to Remember

"Ladies and Gentlemen, I'd like to introduce you to one of America's most recognizable faces. She's an exciting, versatile, talented actress and performer who has excelled in virtually every facet of show business. The star of numerous feature films, mini-series, television movies, and entertainment and sports specials, she first gained international fame as the star of ABC's smash hit television series That's Incredible. *This phenomenal success not only led her to New York for her Off-Broadway debut, but also to Lebanon where she entertained the armed service personnel as a guest of Bob Hope on his last Christmas tour of the Mediterranean. In addition, long before she became a household name, she represented the United States in international tennis competition and achieved a national ranking as high as number seven in singles and number four in doubles. In contrast to the bright lights of Hollywood, our honored guest has also donated countless hours to numerous charitable endeavors, including the Get High on Yourself Foundation, which she founded and then served as its Chairperson for eight years. In recognition of all her philanthropic work, the President of the United States appointed her Special Ambassador to Children for the United Nations. . . . So, without further delay, it is my honor and privilege to introduce our very special guest, Cathy Lee Crosby."*

Standing in the doorway listening to this glowing introduction, all I kept thinking was, *something's wrong.*

I'd done these speeches before, basically a quick hour accompanied by a nice fee, an interesting audience, and a few laughs. But approaching the podium in early 1994 for the annual seminar of the Green Mountain Coffee Roasters Company in Vermont, I felt strangely uneasy. My throat was dry as a bone, yet my hands were slippery with sweat. I was more than nervous, I was petrified. But why? What was so different about this particular appearance? Why was I so utterly riddled with fear?

Then I saw it. On the front wall of the auditorium, hung a huge banner on which was clearly printed the seminar's theme: *The Wisdom That Empowers.* I guess I had been unconsciously staring at it as I stood at the doorway of the auditorium waiting to make my entrance. The words on the banner seemed to penetrate right through me; not as individual words, but together as a concept. I was literally speechless. My thoughts began to scramble, and I could feel the panic swelling inside me.

All of a sudden, I had the horrifying realization that the talk I was about to give, a version of the one I had always used, just wouldn't cut it. It was about as far off the mark as possible, plain and simple.

Lord help me, I thought. *What am I going to do?*

I couldn't escape the surge of desperation rising within me as I listened to the last of my introduction.

What wisdom could I possibly give them, I wondered in the safety of my thoughts as I approached the microphone to the sound of warm applause.

A myriad of ideas started flashing through my brain, each discarded as quickly as the next. I could feel my heart pounding in my neck, as I became more and more overwhelmed by the sheer terror of my dilemma. And then, just as I opened my mouth to speak, I realized that nothing was coming out!

Good thing the audience is still applauding, I rationalized, *maybe they'll think I'm just taking a gracious pause to acknowledge them.*

After what seemed like an eternity, the ovation stopped. In that precise moment, in the midst of my resounding hysteria, I heard myself stammer, "Thank you . . . thank you for that . . . unbelievable introduction. Standing here, listening to all those accomplishments, I must say I'm overwhelmed. That person sounds pretty remarkable, doesn't she?" I stuttered, desperately grasping at straws. "She seems like a person who has it made. Someone whose life has been a piece of cake. Obviously, she has it all."

The laughter ricocheted off the auditorium walls as fifteen hundred heads nodded in simultaneous affirmation.

"Well." I continued slowly, desperately searching for something to say next.

"Well . . ." I repeated on the verge of utter despair.

Then, just when I thought all was lost, and I would surely be paralyzed in the embarrassment of this moment forever, I heard some words trickle out of my mouth into the microphone.

"Wisdom That Empowers," I began. "That phrase means . . . means more to me than just a theme for a seminar . . . or a topic for a speech, considering . . . what has happened to me over the last six years."

I was standing in front of the podium saying the words, all right, but at the same time, having the oddest sensation that some distinct "other part of me" had decided to speak up after a very long hibernation.

"You see," I continued, "prior to 1988, I felt my life was remarkably fulfilling. Self-discovery, or any search for personal *wisdom,* was simply a luxury I dabbled in from time to time. It was nothing more than a quasi on-and-off curiosity about the broad area of self-improvement and human potential. It served as little more than a psychological "booster" whenever I needed an emotional recharge. I'd read a magazine article here, or a newspaper column there, and I'd feel better. It was really just a 'quick fix' . . . like eating a psychic Twinkie.

"But in 1988, I began to reel from the effects of the first of four traumatic, life-altering events which would eventually knock me to the canvas. My entire foundation would be shattered to pieces and every one of my belief systems would be shaken to the bones.

"For the first time in my life I desperately needed wisdom—any wisdom! I needed something to empower me and to give me enough strength to survive. It was a need for survival at its very core, at a depth I could never have even imagined."

Slowly and evenly, my words began to gain momentum. They started to flow directly to the audience, coming from a place within me stripped naked of any facade.

Almost effortlessly, I began to tell the story of a California golden girl who had been given the keys to the Universe, as we all are, at a very early age. But somehow, as she grew up, this particular golden girl had forgotten where she'd put them. It was my story all right, but for the first time, it seemed like all the pieces of the puzzle were finally coming together in one inescapable presentation for my own ears to hear. The audience just happened to be there.

The entire six-year saga was pouring forth in words that even I was hearing for the first time. The story had enough drama for a nighttime soap: I was a teenage tennis champion, an "overnight" success in the entertainment business, and the star of a top-ten television series. In addition, I was an athlete in top physical condition, and was also involved in an extraordinary, loving relationship with someone I believed was the man of my dreams, Washington Redskins' quarterback Joe Theismann. To top it all off, I enjoyed the comfort of a seemingly tight-knit family, my career was skyrocketing, I had become a multimillionaire, and had even started my own charitable foundation! Everything I had ever dreamed of was coming true.

Now, as I look back, I realize that I had been so busy and preoccupied with achieving what I believed was important in life, that I had completely forgotten about a very special place deep inside my heart. A place where I used to play, and live, and dream as a little girl. I had unintentionally abandoned it, step by step, as the pace and responsibilities of my busy life took hold.

I had forgotten about this magical realm of pure possibility that I would eventually come to call *The Bliss Zone* ™. It's that inner sanctuary of pure energy and creativity where life just "flows" from and through the very core of your heart. It's living from that place of seemingly no effort, where action is taken because one intuitively knows it's right. It's connecting with that place of harmony deep within you, where generosity, trust, and love seem to naturally go hand in hand with success, instead of being its polar opposite. It's when you know you're on the right track, you feel it, and you're flying!

But Divine circumstances seem to have a funny way of leading you back to the road you're supposed to be on in this game called "life," just in case you've veered off in the wrong direction. At first, the Universe attempts to steer you back with gentle reminders. For most people, one or two nudges are enough. But in my case, for whatever reason, I just didn't get it. I'm sure the good Lord had almost run out of "nudges" trying to get my attention, because when He finally did, it was a real wallop!

I systematically began to lose everything that had held significant meaning in my life, and everything I had worked so hard to achieve. Not only that, these losses came about in the most humiliating fashion conceivable, and my fall was as dramatic and meteoric as my rise had been. Though I wouldn't be aware of it for many years, the forces of the Universe were preparing to show me exactly what I needed to remember.

Prophetically, the first of the four devastating events that triggered my eventual "crash" was a death. My beloved grandmother, Frances Mendenhall ("Francesca," "Nanny Mo," or "Grams" to her family, and "Mom" to her beloved husband, Joseph), died at the age of ninety-three. She had always been my special "champion," and a battery that could recharge my spirit in a heartbeat. She was strong, kind, loving, generous, willful, sexy, deep, and as connected to the earth as anyone I've ever known. From the moment I was born, I felt she gave me permission to be as spirited, as spontaneous, and as adventurous as I dared, simply by her presence alone. Emotionally, the death more than got my attention, it numbed my heart. I missed her terribly, but the severity of the impact of losing her had only just begun to surface.

A short time later, the second trauma occurred. I was stricken with a virus called Epstein-Barr. It zapped my once-endless energy, completely draining me both physically and emotionally. It is a disease, by the way, that even today many doctors say doesn't exist. But when you're suffering from night sweats, fevers, loss of memory, and aching bones, as well as the ensuing depression, it's hard to believe that Epstein-Barr is psychosomatic. Especially when it lasts, as mine did, for six torturous years.

Then, just as I began to show some meager signs of recovery from the virus, I was hit by a third catastrophic event. I was forced to end my seven-year relationship with Joe Theismann, the man I sincerely believed was my soul mate. It had become painfully clear that the person who stood before me was not the same man with whom I had fallen deeply in love. His behavior had changed radically, heightened by the emergence of a personality that I had never seen before and didn't understand.

After making every possible effort to find a way to heal the situation, I had no choice but to leave the man I had considered the love of my life.

It's interesting how differently each of us reacts to the same circumstances when we're wounded. After ending the relationship, I closed down and turned inward. Joe's reaction to the pain, however, was to lash out in the form of legal action.

He sued me all right—oh boy, did he sue me, asking for half of everything. The competitive fervor that he had learned and perfected on the football field took over once again and showed itself brazenly in the courtroom. So, legal actions were filed by his attorneys in several states and were vigorously pursued for some four-and-a-half years. The pain of being attacked so vehemently and so relentlessly by someone I had loved, and who had loved me so deeply, was profound. It shook every single belief I had about commitment, love, devotion, and most of all, about myself. It left me raw.

I had to part with an unbelievable amount of money to extricate myself from the situation, including almost $1 million in legal fees. I could write an entire treatise on how I feel about the legal system, how dishonorable it has become and how blatantly it nurtures the greed in society. What's honest, fair, reasonable, and just is no longer a part of the equation. What's "right" has been cast aside for a no-holds-barred game of winner-take-all maneuvering and manipulation—a carnivorous game in which everyone loses.

Unfortunately, I would have to encounter the full nightmarish spectrum of the legal system on not one, but *two* separate fronts.

The icing on my upside-down cake was a direct result of the enormous drain on my finances during my battles with Joe in court, as well as my being physically unable to work for almost three years. My coffers had become bare and I was unable to stop the downward spiral. I was advised that the only solution to getting me back on my feet again was to declare bankruptcy. After a thorough, agonizing examination of my limited options, I decided I had no choice but to comply. It's interesting to note that approximately 90 percent of every penny I owed at the time I filled out the bankruptcy papers was owed to lawyers. At any rate, thus began my efforts to survive the fourth and final traumatic blow to my psyche.

Not only that, it wasn't long before I realized I'd been out of the loop far too long to simply make one telephone call and miraculously restart my career engines once again. It became crystal clear that I would have to start over from scratch. I remember a feeling of absolute anguish and fear washing over me, an emotion I can't even begin to describe. In a town where professional idleness is tantamount to career evaporation, who would understand, or care?

I was too embarrassed to tell anyone in the "business" what was really happening to me for a long time, so I dealt with it alone. I didn't go to lunch. I didn't go to interviews or attend meetings. And I certainly didn't go to parties. Instead, I stayed within the confines of the only safety net I had at the time, my home.

To make matters even worse during this reclusive period, someone had started using my "name" professionally. They say fame is a fleeting thing, veer off the map for a second and they'll forget about you. So what could be the worst thing imaginable for someone whose livelihood depends on name recognition? How about mistaken identity? Kathie Lee Gifford hit the morning airwaves and started to use both Kathie and Lee together professionally for the first time. And coincidentally, just as my star began to head for the deep freeze, hers began to heat up. Even though I had been born with the name "Cathy Lee," and had been using it as far back as my competitive tennis days, it didn't make me feel any better at the time. Now, of course, I think it's funny and we both use our feigned "indignance" to the hilt. Today, we share a friendship as well as our name.

At any rate, for almost three years I stayed at home, trying to heal my body and soul while corresponding with the world, mainly it seemed, through law firms. At 7:30 A.M., I'd wake up to my east coast lawyers calling, and by 9:30 A.M., my West Coast attorneys would assume their positions. This was a most unpleasant way to begin each day, only to be topped, perhaps, by Friday afternoon, when my lawyers would receive another new motion from the opposition that had to be dealt with over the weekend.

I was emotionally, physically, financially, and psychologically exhausted. I had been beaten to a pulp! I had achieved fame, success, wealth, and a fabulous life, and I had lost it all!

Certainly, I had no intention of ever going public with any of this traumatic epic. But as I stood at the podium, it just began to pour out. The drama and the pain, as well as a surprising amount of humor, seemed to spring forth with an undeniable truth.

As I continued to speak from my heart, however, a curious thing began to happen. The audience seemed to surround me with their energy. I could literally feel it. I could feel their warmth and acceptance in a way that I had never experienced before in my entire career.

"Wisdom That Empowers," I said to the audience again, "what do those words really mean anyway? To be honest with you, I don't have a clue," I continued, "but the truth feels like as good a place to start as any."

I don't remember much of the rest of the body of my "speech." But I do recall telling the audience about one particular sentence that unwittingly kept repeating itself over and over in my head during the beginning stages of my epic: *Dear God, please help me regain my happy and successful life.*

Unbeknownst to me, the Universe was already at work, and that one simple, unconscious plea had been the spark. The phrase had served as a *decision* on my part. A decision that would change my life forever in ways I could never have fathomed.

Nearing the end of my ninety minutes at the podium, I stared into the audience. For the first time, I really *saw* their faces: knowing faces, accepting faces, understanding faces. How many of them had walked down the same rutted road that I had been blindly traveling on? How many of them believed that accomplishment alone could patch up the holes in their hearts as I had? How many of them had spent years relying solely on their desire and will to push them forward toward their goals as I had, only to reach the inevitable dead end that the absence of an open heart produces?

Finally, there was nothing left to say, as I didn't have any answers yet either. I only sensed that I was on a journey, the implications of which I would not begin to comprehend until much later.

My experience in the auditorium that day, however, brought to mind a question I used to wonder about when I was a child, and had obviously never answered.

Who am I? and *Why am I here?*

Delving into these two questions was certainly going take more than a ninety-minute speech. But, I felt I was headed in the right direction. That, in and of itself, seemed enough for the time being.

I ended by thanking them for allowing me the opportunity to share my experience. I had told them the truth from a place deep within me, uncensored and in vivid detail. I guess they must have connected with what I had said, because, to my astonishment, the entire audience jumped to their feet in enthusiastic applause.

I was overwhelmed. We had joined each other, the audience and I, in a truly synergistic and dramatic way. How ironic, I thought, that I was being applauded not for my performance as an actress or for anything I had achieved, but simply for who I was. I felt life was telling me, "You're doing okay, kid, you're on the right track." It was as if I was onto something—recapturing a lost part of myself in a strange way. I certainly was light years away from any *conscious* wisdom or empowerment, but something profound had happened.

Following my experience in Vermont, little by little and step by step, I began to open myself up even more. At first, it was simply a function of survival, the need to ease the pressure of the burdens facing me. But the Universe had other plans in mind.

Having no clue as to these Divine forces that were already in motion, I was totally unaware of the fact that my life was about to change forever.

At the time, I only sensed a faint light way off in the distance. A brilliance that was magnetically pulling me toward it with such a force, that I had no choice but to heed its direction. I could feel it beckoning, and the more its presence enraptured me, the deeper I delved into myself to find a way to reach it. And the deeper I went, the more I realized that, with open eyes and an open heart, I would have to sail back into the squalls of my life, at the height of their frenzy, and face them head-on.

Just as I was debating where to begin, the first thunderous wave began to swell in my memory. Oddly enough, it was one of the worst days of my entire six-year saga that occurred about halfway through my disastrous descent. This enormous whitecap, in all its wrath and fury, came in the form of a man named Haberbush.

2
Much Ado About "Nothing"

Wounding involves a painful excursion into pathos, wherein the anguish is enormous and the suffering cracks the boundaries of what you thought you could bear. And yet . . . in the Greek tragedies, the gods force themselves into human consciousness at the time of pathos. It is only at this time of wounding that the protagonist grows into a larger sense of what life is all about.

Jean Houston

"Miss Crosby, I want to inform you, that as of this moment, you are nothing," barked David Haberbush, a trustee of the U.S. Bankruptcy Court at the beginning of my 341 hearing.

It was the introductory court session that was designed to acquaint the debtor with the legal morass of going belly-up. Usually, it is scheduled sometime between two and six months after the date one files, which I did in July of 1992.

"Everything you ever worked for your entire life is now mine," bellowed Haberbush. "Basically, I own you, and you are nothing. Is that clear?"

I am nothing!?

Though I sensed this was being said merely as a legal tactic to intimidate me, the trustee's words blasted like gunfire, ripping away at any last tenuous shreds of self-esteem I might have had. I'd gone bankrupt all right: physically, mentally, emotionally, and financially. Not only that, the insidious disease had also found its way into the center of my psyche.

I am nothing!?

How could this have happened? Only a few short years ago, everything in my life seemed wonderful. I had been given so much, and yet here I was sitting in a cold, drab, musty public courtroom, listening to a perfect stranger telling me he owns me!

And if this wasn't enough, along came one final blow that broke the camel's back. Because the 341 hearing is only the first procedure in the bankruptcy process, creditors typically don't bother to appear. They're generally not allowed to speak at this point, so they don't want to waste the time and expense of attending. Accordingly, none of my creditors were present. The courtroom was empty of spectators, save for one major exception. My seven-year "soul mate," Joe Theismann, had plunked himself down a mere three feet behind where I was seated to witness the event. He also brought along his new wife (the soon-to-be-ex–number three, I guess you could say), a Canadian woman and former karaoke singer in Japan. Their presence alone, sitting so close behind me, was an indescribably painful addition to an already horrific experience.

I looked up at the clock, wishing that my desperation alone could somehow move the hands forward in time. Unfortunately, it was only 10 A.M.

In spite of myself, at the sound of Joe's voice, I couldn't stop flashing back to some of the wonderful experiences he and I had shared during our seven years together. Special moments kept popping into my thoughts no matter how hard I tried to keep them at bay. I remembered the winter night when he had driven me home from the airport to our farm in Virginia. Before I'd even set foot in the house, he led me to the outside balcony overlooking the two-hundred-yard lake below to show me a special surprise. As he turned on the backyard lights, a blanket of white was illuminated as far as the eye could see. Carefully carved out in it were the words, *I LOVE YOU ANGEL,* in three-foot-high letters extending the full length of the frozen lake. Joe had spent the entire day shoveling his heartfelt sentiment in the new fallen snow.

Again, I glanced at the clock. It seemed like the hands were literally dragging themselves from second to second—only one interminable hour had passed.

Isn't it awful how your mind goes right for the jugular at the worst possible moments? They say that extremely passionate, obsessive love can flip into an equally intense hatred, yet his presence was beyond anything I could ever have imagined. Everyone told me it was obvious that he still loved me deeply. The signs were hard to miss. They also rationalized that he clearly needed to connect with me in some concrete way to dissipate and resolve all the painful feelings he had about our relationship being over. Whatever the reason, enmeshed in the mire of all his unresolved feelings, he unfortunately chose the courtroom to make this connection.

He was an athlete inside and out; and I think as far as he was concerned, this was a football game and I was wearing a Dallas Cowboys' jersey. In his mind, I think I had become the opposing team. It took every bit of courage I had left not to run out the door, to sit there and listen to everything, including the echo of Joe's voice in my ears. To say there was a cacophony of voices inside my head is a gross understatement. The only way I could bear it was to literally overpower my internal dialogue. Thank the good Lord for my friend David Krieff, who, just prior to my courtroom appearance, told me about an ancient chant that would help me through my crisis. I was convinced that I could use anything, even something as innocuous as *dog food* as my mantra and it would be sufficient. But he assured me that if I kept thinking *nam-myoho-renge-kyo,* and writing the phrase over and over, everything would be fine. So there I was, writing and writing, page after page, these four strange-looking words, the meaning of which I had no earthly idea. It's funny what people will do under extreme pressure.

It's also funny and somewhat prophetic that I would soon be intimately familiar with the meaning of the phrase at a depth I could never have predicted. *Nam-myoho-renge-kyo:* "If you wish to free yourself from the sufferings of all that you have endured throughout eternity and attain supreme enlightenment in this lifetime, you must awaken to the mystic truth that has always been within your life. This truth is *myoho-renge-kyo.* Chanting *myoho-renge-kyo* will therefore enable you to grasp all the mystic truth within you." The *nam* of the chant signifies devotion. The *myoho* stands for "the Mystic Law" or ultimate reality. The *renge* signifies the lotus blossom, which represents prosperity and longevity. And the *kyo* is all that is eternal.

At the time the phrase was merely a syllabic cocktail that somehow kept the voices in my mind at bay. It gave me strength, and believe me, I needed all the help I could get.

Tick. Tick. Tick. Only one o'clock, I lamented.

In spite of all my vigorous efforts to the contrary, my mind still occasionally took over. Sitting at the long table with my lawyers flanking each side, I began to think about how even in the roughest moments, life seems to throw you a dose of the bizarre, just to keep your sense of humor alive and intact. Personally, it's always funnier when someone else tells me about this phenomenon happening to *them.* But, in any case, my dose of the peculiar had come that very morning, just prior to the beginning of the 341 proceeding.

For security reasons, my lawyers had requested that I be escorted from the parking structure beneath the courthouse to an anteroom outside the main courtroom. Although I knew about the request, I had no idea that it would involve uniformed officers from the Los Angeles Police Department. Needless to say, I was quite taken aback when four burly men in blue uniforms came to lead me and my attorneys from the underground garage to the appointed waiting area.

As we entered, one of the policemen began to giggle and asked if I would mind posing for some photographs.

"I'm terribly sorry for troubling you, what with everything that's going on and all. But I have every big celebrity's picture who's ever been through here, and you're my favorite of all," the big cop said.

I was mortified. If I could have run, I would have. In my stupor, I must have mumbled "yes," because off he went to find a Polaroid camera!

Upon his return, I guess for dramatic emphasis and because it would be so much "funnier," they suggested handcuffing me. Before I could utter even the slightest refusal, I heard a loud *click!,* and I was in cuffs. So there I stood, in this very plain, ultraconservative dress that my attorney had pointedly "suggested" I wear, shackled in handcuffs, making every effort to force a smile. Humiliation is certainly the "cause celebre" of a mortified soul.

I felt like I was in *The Twilight Zone* until the flashbulbs popped in my eyes and awakened me from my mortified trance. If the cringing embarrassment of my circumstances wasn't enough, all four policemen dutifully gave me an additional copy of my picture, handcuffed with each of them, to take home with me as a gift. If I hadn't been there myself, I wouldn't have believed it. Even if I'd wanted to, I didn't have enough energy to get mad. Actually, they were pretty terrific guys who were simply trying to make the best of a bad situation. They certainly didn't mean any harm, and, thankfully, the sum total of the experience definitely lit a fire under my sense of humor.

Nam-myoho-renge-kyo, nam-myoho-renge-kyo, I scribbled once again, focusing my attention on Mr. Haberbush as he continued with the proceedings. His job, according to the law, is to represent the debtor in response to his or her creditors. He is supposed to ensure that the insolvent person is protected under the law, and that the proceedings are resolved as quickly as possible so the debtor can begin rebuilding his or her life. I'm paraphrasing the legalese, but that's the gist of its meaning. In regard to what I went through personally, however, and from what I have learned about others who have found themselves in similar circumstances, bankruptcy procedures are frequently prolonged and insanely complicated. The trustee and the lawyers often seemed to take every unnecessary and superfluous action possible, including filing motions in court against the debtor. Of course, the trustee and his lawyers (who charge by the hour) are paid first, before any of the creditors can be reimbursed. So, the endless delays and machinations certainly don't hurt them.

In addition, because the debtor is deemed to be in a vulnerable position and thus unable to fight back, there seems to be an overwhelming tendency for the trustee and his lawyers to treat the debtor with extreme disrespect. In my particular case, no vulgarity was spared when it came to their rudeness and personal denigration.

Certainly, trustees and lawyers should be held accountable for all their actions, and be evaluated as to their performance and ability. In addition, strict measures should be enforced to ensure that the original *intention* of bankruptcy law and its proceedings is upheld.

Unfortunately, as I was sitting there in the courtroom, I didn't have the blessing of hindsight. I was only aware of three things: the random thoughts that periodically raced through my mind, the ticking of the clock on the wall in front of me, and the continuous grating of Haberbush's voice as it kept jarring me back to the proceedings at hand. I was struggling to survive, and it took far greater courage than I thought I possessed just to remain sitting there. If someone next to me had whispered, "this is hell," I would have believed them.

The absolute craziness of the past four years flashed through my mind. I thought about all of the law firms, and all of the attorneys and their petty motions and depositions, designed not to uncover the truth, but simply to help formulate a story that would "play well" in court. I wondered if I would ever be able to forget all the antics of these legal piranhas, who would sink to any level just to get a nip of my flesh.

I remembered the degradation that I felt at the "open viewing/pseudo-sale" of all my possessions by the trustee. The court had not even heard a motion, much less made a decision, as to whether my furniture and all my personal possessions would remain mine, but Haberbush ordered the viewing/pseudo-sale to take place anyway. He said that an independent valuation was needed, but he had already had everything professionally appraised and knew full well that, at that point, nothing could be sold. So, I felt as if the entire procedure was just an effort to embarrass and humiliate me, for what reason I couldn't imagine.

"You are nothing," echoed Haberbush's voice throughout the courtroom, bringing me back to the reality of my present nightmare.

I looked up at the clock. It was 4:45 P.M.

I became transfixed as I sat there watching the second hand ticking away, beat after beat, almost as if each second stood alone.

Suddenly, I noticed that the air in the courtroom had turned thin. I couldn't breathe. I felt like I was hyperventilating. The room began to spin, and within a heartbeat, my mind was screaming, barely able to withstand another minute.

In the middle of this panic, I vaguely heard the trustee dismiss me from the courtroom. I have no idea how I did it, but I stood up and walked calmly out the door, struggling with every ounce of energy I had left to hold my head high in some semblance of dignity and composure.

Once outside, I made a beeline for the parking lot, not waiting for the guards to escort me this time. I headed straight for my car. *"Hold on, just hold on,"* I kept repeating to myself, desperate not to lose control. But the minute I got inside and closed the door, the tears began streaming down my face. Within seconds, the tears had become sobs—real, deep, hysterical sobs, the likes of which I had never experienced before. The dam had finally burst.

Just get home, I thought, desperately trying to calm the flooding emotions within me.

I could barely focus on the road ahead. The tears began to blind my view. Down the freeway, through the interchange, off on Wilshire. *Concentrate,* I said to myself. *Just keep driving.* When I finally got through my front door at 6 P.M., I collapsed on the living-room couch in a heap. I felt like I was choking on a veritable avalanche of emotion from all the loss and pain of the last four years.

Time passed in a blur as I struggled for each breath. Then suddenly, I heard a phone ringing on the table beside me. I don't know why, but I picked it up. On the other end of the line was my sister, Linda Lou, calling from Washington, D.C. to see how the proceedings had gone.

"Hi," she said, "how are you doing?"

I couldn't utter a word. My entire body was literally racked with sobs.

"What's wrong?" she asked. "Tell me. I can't hear you. Talk to me."

No words came. Only more sobs.

"Talk to me, please."

Nothing.

In the inimitable Crosby family fashion, my sister immediately called our aunt, Gene Crowell, for help. Since it was now midnight, Washington time, my aunt assured her that she'd take over and drive straight to my house. Because she and my uncle live in Pasadena, which is a forty-five-minute drive away, she decided she'd better call first to see how I was and to let me know she was on her way. Interestingly, I would have sworn that she made that drive and stayed with me the whole time. But the truth is, she didn't. She stayed on the telephone for almost five hours, because once she had me on the line, she was afraid to hang up and lose the connection during the time it would have taken her to get to my house.

Since I only had a vague recollection of what had transpired over the phone, I asked Aunt Gene to help me remember what in heaven's name she had said during our unbelievably long conversation.

"Nothing, really," she answered thoughtfully, "I just kept repeating things like, 'nothing can kill your spirit, Cathy Lee, nothing. Even when you could barely crawl, you were always so ready for life. So delighted to be there. There was no waiting for tomorrow for you. No, you wanted to try everything *now.* You would even wake up laughing, raring to go, raring to do. Remember? Always ready to climb the highest mountain. Even though so much has been taken from you, you're still Cathy Lee. You're still you. You still have your God-given talent and all your God-given abilities. You have a family and friends who love you. You haven't even *started* life yet, believe me. Now is not the time to give up. The sun will come up tomorrow, I promise.' "

And so it went, hour after hour after hour, aunt to niece, friend to friend, and soul to soul, connecting in whatever way they could. Finally, at about two o'clock, I remember beginning to fall asleep.

Somehow, knowing I had passed the critical point, my aunt whispered, "sweet dreams Li'l Kitten," and we both sleepily hung up the phone.

My eyes were only closed for about three hours, but what actually happened during that time I wouldn't fully understand for some time. Maybe David Haberbush, in an odd twist of fate, had been right. Maybe I did become "nothing" that night. Whatever the case, I had no way of knowing that those three hours of sleep would turn out to be a gift so magical that it would change my life forever. How could I have known that every ounce of the scar tissue I had acquired during the last four years of trauma would miraculously be ripped away by the time I had opened my eyes?

By going back and purposely reliving my courtroom drama, I had sailed back into the first frenzied squall and had met it head-on. The experience was cathartic, for sure. But, buried beneath the surface of my conscious mind, was the fact that I had actually taken my first steps back into the *Bliss Zone*—back into the realm of magical harmony that I had known in my childhood.

As the harshness of the memory faded from my mind, I again became aware of the "beacon." Only this time it had moved closer, and the warmth of its light was penetrating my defenses and rendering them inoperable. The feeling was so compelling that I had no choice but to continue my journey forward in an effort to understand more.

We put thirty spokes together and call it a wheel;
But it is in the space where there is nothing that the usefulness of
    the wheel depends
We turn clay to make a vessel;
But it is the space where there is nothing that the usefulness of the
    vessel depends
We pierce doors and windows to make a house;
And it is in these spaces where there is nothing that the usefulness
    of the house depends
Therefore just as we take advantage of what is, we should recognize
    the value of what is not.

                                                        Lao Tzu

3
The Sense-Ability of "Nothing"

It takes a long time to understand nothing.
Edward Dahlberg

One's main task in life is to give birth to oneself.
Erich Fromm

When I opened my eyes the morning after my dreadful saga in the court-room and my five-hour conversation with my aunt, I remember feeling as though I had landed in a whole new world. It was as if I had been reborn on another planet. The "me" I'd known no longer existed, and I wasn't exactly sure what, if anything, had taken its place. The only thing I was sure of was that something had disappeared. Actually, to be more accurate, *everything* had disappeared! And yet, I felt strangely peaceful.

As I looked around my bedroom, I thought, . . . *this is nothing. This is what nothing feels like. Right here, in this moment, I have nothing. I am nothing!*

My reaction to this rather dramatic realization was even more peculiar. It made me laugh. I'd often heard people say that in the precise moment you truly experience having nothing, you actually have everything. Well, maybe that's essentially true, but at the time it happened, believe me, it certainly didn't feel like I had everything. No, quite the contrary. It felt exactly like I had *nothing*. No viewpoint, no opinions, no judgments, nothing. I remember being unable to grasp any "particulars," either past or present. I couldn't seem to conjure up any "scenarios" to delve into for answers. I had no desire for anything, and likewise, no need for anything either. In addition, all judgments and opinions had magically vanished. It was as if every single incident of the past had simply faded away like erased chalk on a blackboard. They were still faintly in my memory, but their importance and intensity had completely disappeared. There was *nothing* to win, and likewise, there was *nothing* to lose. All that remained was a clear, calm connection to everything. There was no longer a separation between myself and anything my eyes focused on, or my ears heard, or my mind thought.

I couldn't believe that someone like myself, who had experienced such a life of activity, energy, passion, and doing, was actually enjoying the feeling of nothingness! The magnificence of the feeling astonished me.

After remaining in bed for what seemed like hours, I thought about getting up, to do *what* I didn't know.

Should I brush my teeth? Good start. Why not?

As I slowly walked to the bathroom, I was aware of every breath I took —actually aware of the oxygen entering my lungs and filling them to capacity. It was as if I needed to breathe in every detail of what was happening to me. All of my senses had been turned up to the highest possible frequency. Everything seemed to be magnified: colors, sounds, smells, and feelings. I didn't have a specific thought or plan or attitude in mind, and yet, I felt immensely fulfilled.

It was so quiet! All the normal everyday chatter of voices in my head was gone. All the constant babbling of "shoulds" and "should nots," and "musts" and "must nots" had disappeared. The only thing remaining was a profound silence and the astounding experience of . . . *nothing*.

Even more remarkable, perhaps, was the total absence of fear. For the first time in my life, I felt that there was *nothing* to be afraid of. *Nothing* could ever stop me or hurt me or betray me or cheat me, or do anything *to* me again, because I realized that my experience of life and who I was were actually one and the same. There was no delineation. How I experienced the events that occurred in my life, had very little to do with the *facts* of those events, yet everything to do with my *interpretation* of those facts. Normally, our interpretation of anything is colored by our past, and therefore, we are never looking at life with a clean slate. When I woke up that morning, however, and realized that *nothing* was all that was left, my slate had been miraculously wiped clean. It was as if each moment of my experience was a mirror, and in that mirror, I was looking straight at myself and my connection to everything.

My journey through this *nothingness* and back onto my destined path, unblemished by the scars I had received along the way, is the essence of how I eventually reconnected with the magical realm of bliss within me.

Not only that, as I forged ahead on the path before me, I began to open the door to more and more unique and intriguing experiences. In doing so, I became aware that a distinctive "energy" was surrounding me at every moment. It was a "life force," alive with awe and wonder, that seemed to effortlessly bring me everything I needed to move forward.

Unfortunately, prior to the moment I woke up that fateful morning I was not aware that such an energy force had always been available to me at every single moment of my life. Perhaps that is why I spent a good deal of my time struggling for what I wanted and needed, as most of us do. I was attempting to control everything solely with the strength and force of my will, as I had been accustomed to doing. In fact, ever since I was a little girl, I remember being taught to "go after" what I wanted in life. If I didn't, I was just plain "lazy," and would "never amount to anything."

Later I would realize that the severity and intensity of hitting bottom prevented me from responding to life in the same old ways. Despite my attempts to use the force of my will, it was to no avail because my patterns of behavior were irrevocably broken. I had had all of the "fight" knocked out of me, and there was no choice left except to begin going with the flow.

Once I got the hang of it, I began to have a different experience of life. I became more aware of everything around me, resulting in inexplicably spontaneous behavior on my part. With no other option at hand, I began to live more of my life simply "shooting from the hip." In other words, I was acting without any structured evaluating process, willing to let the chips fall where they may. It was strangely comforting to respond to life in this manner. It was as if I had awakened that morning and found myself in a whole new world of innocence and wonder. My experience of it was nothing short of magical.

I tried to recall if I had ever felt anything like this before. Had this feeling always been a part of me and somehow I'd forgotten and lost my connection to it? Why did it seem so totally foreign to me and yet so familiar at the same time?

My curiosity was piqued, and I needed to know more. I needed answers that could help me understand what had happened. Was there a connection of some kind between my experience and the very roots of who I was? This question, in particular, was compelling, but not knowing exactly where to turn first to find the answer, I decided to go back to the very beginning of my life and take a closer look. I had a premonition that the key to the next door I needed to open would be found somewhere in those early years.

When one sees that everything exists as an illusion, one can live in a higher sphere than ordinary man.

Buddha

4
The Will to Survive

If children grew up according to early indications, we should have nothing but geniuses.

Johann Wolfgang von Goethe

We are born princes, and the civilizing process makes us frogs.

Eric Berne

Even as a little girl I had a feeling that there was something I needed to know, an answer to a question that I couldn't put into words. It was as if I had a secret life deep down inside, whose meaning was hidden even from me. I remember being very aware of it, strangely comforted by both its presence and its distance. Maybe this explains why I was on the move from the moment I was born. I wanted to go, and explore, and do, anything and everything, as if the momentum alone would somehow carry me to this answer I was seeking. I assumed, of course, that I would find it "out there" somewhere. So, if there was a limit, I pushed it to the edge. If there was a line, I crossed it. If there was a wall, I climbed over it.

It was as if God had given me the wind and told me to fly.

The word *boundary* didn't even exist in my vocabulary, physically or in any other way. This inner spirit of mine was not a result of my being merely contrary or rebellious, rather, it was rooted in a driving impulse to test and explore whatever presented itself before me. In these moments of spontaneous energy, which colored a good deal of my behavior when I was little, I became so totally immersed in whatever I was doing, that I seemed to actually "merge" with it. The activity and I became one and the same.

A particularly vivid memory of this phenomenon from my childhood years centered around my adamant desire to be a palomino colt when I grew up. Even though my mother had gently explained to me that this would most likely be impossible to achieve, I was undaunted. I spent many an afternoon galloping across the open fields near our house in Southern California "being" that young steed, simply because I loved the feeling of running free with the wind blowing through my hair. It's interesting that not once during these outdoor jaunts did I ever even consider being the *rider* of the horse; no, I *was* the horse, and that was that.

I remember feeling such ecstatic "bliss" during these times, that I couldn't wait to try the next adventure with the same wild abandon. Judgment and fear were simply not a part of my reality. I desperately wanted to tell someone how much fun I was having, but I just couldn't find the words to explain to myself, much less to anyone else.

To gain a better understanding of what had happened to me up to and during my three-hour sleep, I soon realized that I would have to delve into these early years of my life with an even more detailed eye. What I had recalled so far had merely skimmed the surface. If I was going to try to make a connection between my experience of waking up to *nothing* and the roots of who I was as a child, it was obvious I needed more information. Yet as I began to dig deeper, all the remaining pictures of my past seemed garbled, and were no longer available to me in any clear detail. Furthermore, the "story" of my life that I had been steadfastly holding on to in my mind for as long as I could remember, seemed to have disappeared. Nothing was adding up.

Out of pure frustration, I decided to sit down and write out everything that had ever happened to me in my life, in chronological order. I was going to spell out every single incident that I could remember, in full detail, *exactly* as it had occurred, without embellishment, justification, editing, or comments. To the best of my ability, I would tell the truth about everything that had happened up until the day of my "crash" after the 341 hearing.

I figured that if I wrote down the real truth about my life on a piece of paper in my own handwriting for my own eyes to see, this **Biographical Life Sketch** ™ would surely provide me the insight I was looking for.

This exercise proved to be profound. After completing it in full detail, I was amazed not only at what I'd learned from actually writing it down, but also what I had come to understand after reading it back for my own ears to hear. The process was extremely liberating because I saw in black and white that the sum of everything I had written on those pages equaled the *truth* about who I really was. I was no longer a slave to the selective memory that I had utilized most of my life. It occurred to me that we all modify our past experiences in one way or another, either by embellishing, diminishing, or omitting the facts. Obviously, this is done to protect ourselves from those memories we feel reflect negatively upon us. Unfortunately, this results in a tremendous loss of freedom and a pigeon-holing of our ability to fully realize all the possibilities in our future.

When I first sat down to write, of course, I knew none of this. I was simply compelled to complete the exercise, for reasons that weren't entirely clear.

I took out a pad of paper and began to record the facts of my earliest years, along with the observations and insights that flowered from them. . . .

I was a breech birth, entering the world fanny first. I wish I could say that this alone explains the fact that more often than I'd like to admit, I have done things rather unconventionally. At least that's the reason I have always used to explain my behavior when all other reasoning has failed.

I was the second of three daughters (Linda Lou, and Lucinda Sue, respectively) born to RKO actress Linda Hayes (née Rachel Mendenhall) and early radio pioneer and writer Lou Crosby.

The first incident I could vividly recall in its entirety was at the age of two, when I fell into the deep end of a swimming pool. My family and I were at a garden party, and I remember standing mesmerized beside the blue water, not realizing the danger that awaited below. It looked so wondrously inviting, that true to my inimitable fashion, I leaped in. My mother ran to the edge of the pool to rescue me, but before she could jump in, a family friend grabbed her by the arm and said, "wait a minute, Linda! Look what she's doing!"

Everyone ran over and stared into the water, speechless. Here was this two-year-old child walking along the bottom of the pool, then pushing up to the surface to gasp for a breath of air, and then making her way back down again to walk a little further along the bottom. I repeated this underwater "dance" until I had walked the entire length of the swimming pool!

I realize now that I must have been well ensconced in the *Bliss Zone* as I traversed that underwater cavern, but as a two-year-old, of course, I didn't understand that. Imagine, if as children, and as adults for that matter, we were able to continue to be aware of our natural connection to this magical world of intuitive impulses. How radically our lives would be changed!

At the time of the incident, however, after being helped out of the shallow end of the pool, all I wanted was another cookie after the fun I'd had in the water. To my mother and to those around her, though, I think the experience had a rather extraordinary effect. I believe, in large part, that this was simply a case of their inability to rationalize my somewhat "miraculous" pool adventure. I didn't actually hear the story myself until several decades later during my six-year saga, when mother thought I needed a reminder of my ability to survive even in the most trying of circumstances.

The impact of the next compelling series of events that I had written down on the paper in front of me was shockingly contrary to the joy I experienced around the age of two. I could plainly see that my inner world of innocence had begun to take a backseat to the "realities" of some family difficulties. As clearly as I could recall, I was around six years old when my creative connection to the magic of life in the *Bliss Zone* began to clash with the harsh reality of life. In my attempt to survive these challenges with the limited know-how of a six-year-old mind, I began to put up a protective wall around me, to safeguard my world of awe and wonder. Like most children faced with circumstances beyond comprehension, I developed what seemed to be an obligatory case of spiritual or "being" amnesia. But why did I do this? Why did I have to leave the very center of my power and joy? Was there no other choice? Had I merely accepted an unconscious pattern, passed down from generation to generation mandating that this was what life was about? What had I learned from those who were in charge of teaching me the ropes? I needed to know more. I needed to keep writing.

My mother, Linda Hayes Crosby, was one of those rare women who could do just about everything and do it beautifully. She was a talented and successful actress under contract to RKO in the forties; she was a great athlete, achieving a national ranking in skeet shooting; and, she was a fiercely independent spirit to whom family was the key to life.

My father, Clayton Louis Crosby (no relation to Bing) was a genius. His IQ, from what I understand, was close to 200. He was also extremely creative and loved to write: jingles, poems, songs, and numerous stories. His first adult job was as an announcer, first on radio, then on television. Later, he created and performed on-air pitches for a variety of successful commercial campaigns: the Dodge Boys, Maxwell House, and many others. He was also the writer/announcer/spokesperson for Dodge automobiles on *The Lawrence Welk Show* for some twelve years.

When I was growing up, times were often tough financially. Then, just prior to my entering high school, Mom and Dad began to hit it big. Money, however, was no salve to the war that all too often was beginning to erupt in our home.

Dad was a complicated man; intelligent, handsome, self-doubting, creative, and yet desperately controlling. He also would become consumed with anger at the most unexpected moments. And, when he drank, his rage expressed itself in extreme physical violence, which focused primarily on my mother and me, for reasons that were never clear. Whether this behavior came from his own upbringing, or from his problems with alcohol, or can be attributed to the path he was put on this earth to travel, I don't know. But, whatever the reasons, he could be relentlessly demanding, overbearing, and abusive, both physically and emotionally. When I was little, I kept trying to understand the situation, as I had no concept of such adult complexities. It was particularly difficult for me to balance his anger and abuse with the wonderful, creative side of his personality.

A perfect example was the game I remember our family playing that centered around a story Dad had made up. It was the tale of Annie Garfinkle and her father who owned and lived in a junkyard. Several nights a week we would all sit on the floor in the living room and take turns creating the next adventure. It was a continuing yarn with each installment sparked by the discovery of another unique article (secret maps, keys, strongboxes, airline tickets, etc.) that the two characters had found in the midst of their mountain of refuse.

At the same time that my imagination was being nourished by the creative aesthetics of storytelling, however, there were also many occasions on which I had to stay awake long into the night, listening and praying for the fighting between my parents to stop, so I could finally go to sleep in peace.

The rest of our family stuck close together during this time, but it was difficult growing up with a man who was so creative and brilliant on one hand, yet so consumed with anger and self-loathing on the other. It was as if he was festering from a soul long untended. As for myself, once again my survival instinct took over. I remember saying to myself over and over, *no matter what you do, Daddy, you will never destroy me,* as his hand or belt or switch came down hard across my body.

It was evident from what I had written that even during this difficult period, I was unconsciously aware of an inner sanctuary in my heart. Though another stone had been placed in the wall separating me from the world, I could see that my soul was alive, well, and intact, and I was determined to ensure that it remained unscathed. This was evidenced by how I dealt with the beatings when they became particularly fierce. To lessen their impact, I would mentally picture myself up on a cloud, where it was soft and comfortable and safe. I literally created a place in my mind where I felt secure, because in the world of my imagination, my father's hand couldn't reach me. Up on that cloud, I could mentally heal my wounds, take a needed breather from the turmoil, and, once again, allow myself to play in the wonder of the *Bliss Zone,* I so loved.

After completing this first section of my *Biographical Life Sketch,* certain pieces of the puzzle were becoming more and more clear. I was beginning to get a picture in my mind of who I had really been as a little girl, and how that picture was connected to the magical morning I woke up and experienced *nothing.* It wasn't at all difficult to understand from my new written perspective why my will had to emerge as strongly as it did. My very survival depended on it. Yet, I still wondered why it ended up separating me from my ability to experience life in the *Bliss Zone.*

Curiosity had the better of me, so I took out another sheet of paper and continued with my historical journey.

5
The Comeback Kid

It's not whether you win or lose, but how you play the game.
Grantland Rice

Even before my teenage years, I discovered that tennis was a much-needed outlet for the pain and frustration I was experiencing at home. My introduction to the game occurred one Sunday afternoon while Mom and Dad were playing doubles at a country club near our home. In an effort more to keep us occupied than anything else, they enrolled my sister, Linda Lou, and me in a group tennis lesson. From the moment I first picked up one of the racquets that had been provided for our class, I knew I could play the game. I loved it! I was fast and naturally coordinated. And within six months, my ability had improved to such a degree that I was playing in my first tournament.

When I was on the court, I remember *feeling* like I was in the *Bliss Zone* again. I could actually "see" where I needed to place the ball, and I could "see" where my opponent was going to return it.

However, upon further review of my *Biographical Life Sketch,* I could see that there was a big difference between being "in the zone," an experience familiar to many athletes, and actually *living* in the *Bliss Zone,* as I had as a child. When I merely "in the zone," in order to stay there, I had to concentrate with all my might and focus my determination toward a goal outside myself. On the other hand, when living in the *Bliss Zone,* it seemed that all I had to do was to join in and utilize the natural rhythm that was flowing through my heart, allowing the momentum to invigorate my entire body. This energy naturally propelled me forward toward whatever I wanted. All I had to do was enjoy the ride.

This sheer joy of "playing" and "going with the flow," however, began to be replaced by a feeling that life was a struggle. And the stronger this feeling took hold of me, the more my life became just that. My determination to withstand the trauma with my father at any cost, began to solidify and permeate other areas of my life. Consequently, I developed an intense fighting spirit which, before long, had become a habit. In addition, as I became more and more skilled at my sport and began winning more and more tennis matches, my relentless pursuit of victory became vastly more important than the joy of playing the game. Plain and simple, my will was in the driver's seat.

Though cultivating my dogged persistence did help me to survive at this stage of my life, I could see that it nevertheless reinforced the wall that I'd unwittingly put up between me and the magical world I'd once played in. A perfect example was my first official tennis tournament.

My mother and I were waiting in line to check in at the prestigious Southern California Tennis Association's Annual Championship, when out of my mouth popped a rather curious question.

"Mom," I began with a decidedly serious tone, "how does someone get to be ranked number one?"

"Honey, you can't expect so much of yourself on your first time out," she said, "because, you'd not only have to win this tournament, but five or six more over the rest of the summer to be number one. There are one hundred twenty-eight contestants entered here," she continued, pointing to the names of all the entrants in the thirteen and under division that were posted on a twenty-foot high wooden board, "so theoretically, you'd have to beat every single one of them!"

Her statement seemed to trigger my will, and I interpreted her words as a challenge. What I heard was that something I wanted to do was impossible, and that was tantamount to a personal decree for me to go for it.

As mother continued to stand in line, I turned on my heel and headed straight for the girls' locker room. Once inside, I proceeded to the nearest vacant stall where I sat down cross-legged on the cold tile floor. With my eyes closed, I began to play each and every contestant in my mind, none of whom I'd ever even met! If I visualized losing a point, I'd simply play it over and over again until I'd won it. After beating every single faceless entrant in my head, I left my inner sanctum and went out on the court to play my first match.

Over the course of the week, true to my calculated imaginings, I kept advancing to the next round until I'd finally won the championship! Mother was shocked. I was shocked. By the end of the summer I was ranked number one and *everyone* was shocked!

In six short months, I had gone from a tennis neophyte to the number-one player in my division. This meteoric rise certainly couldn't be attributed to my tournament skills, in view of the short amount of time I'd been playing. Another factor was obviously in the mix. Making up for whatever I lacked in actual ability to play the game was an unshakable tenacity in my need to be victorious.

I could be behind six-love, five-love, forty-love, and it wouldn't matter. Something in my brain would just click, and I would *decide* to win. I would "see" the victory, and once that happened, there was no stopping me. During that first summer of tournaments, one of my matches even took an astounding seven hours over the course of two days to complete. My opponent in this momentous contest was ranked number one in Southern California in the thirteen-and-under division at the time, and was a much better player. But, that didn't matter to me. I literally *willed* myself to victory.

This determination rapidly became second nature and I capitalized on it as often as I could. So much so, that within a few short years after that first tennis tournament, I had built up a reputation as "The Comeback

Kid." My opponents knew that if I thought I had even the slightest chance of winning, no matter how far ahead they were in the match, at some point I would make up my mind to win and will the winds of fate to my point of view.

Sitting at my desk, with the facts in front of me, it was obvious that I truly loved the sport and that my years of international tennis competition afforded me numerous benefits. I gained a sense of achievement, the habit of discipline, the value of hard work and the importance of self-esteem. But, I could also see that competing in the sport had been an impediment to my staying in touch with my heart. When determination took over the reins of my life not only did my will become synonymous with *winning, but winning became synonymous with success.* Before long, this pattern of behavior had taken over to such a degree, that no other quality could surface with enough energy to balance it.

So, even though I had traveled the world, was relatively self-sufficient, was powered by the tenacity of a champion, and buoyed by a strong dose of self-confidence, most of the other elements of my personality had been swept aside. Zeroing in on the material in front of me, I saw clearly that my heart had taken a backseat to my backswing.

My indomitable fighting spirit which had been such a necessary part of withstanding my relationship with Dad, would turn out to be one of the biggest obstacles to my rediscovering the *Bliss Zone* as an adult. The zone I was in on the court was certainly enjoyable in its intensity and control, and I truly loved being immersed in the world of the competitive quest. But the pure unencumbered joy and exuberance of experiencing life in the *Bliss Zone,* requiring no opponent to overcome, nor any specific goal to be achieved in order to breathe in its riches, was nowhere to be found. At the time, I wasn't consciously aware that this magical realm had disappeared from my experience. Nevertheless, I had relinquished the natural freedom of this blissful place in exchange for the struggle of the "real" world.

Though the insights I had become aware of thus far were certainly informative and eye-opening, they still weren't enough to allow me to complete the entire puzzle. Something was missing. I couldn't put my finger on it. The mystery of it spurred me on. It enticed me to continue my linear diary, knowing that more compelling and illuminating insights were almost within my reach.

6
From Role Playing to Playing Roles

No trumpets sound when the important decisions of our life are made. Destiny is made known silently.

Agnes De Mille

In my late teens, life's harsh realities intensified my battle for survival on the home front. While I was taking a break from my homework, a family conference escalated into a horrible confrontation. Dad became enraged and true to his pattern, he advanced toward me. As I stepped back into the kitchen, trying to avoid the situation at all costs, he came straight at me with a smoldering, trancelike look on his face. I was petrified. He kept coming. Finally, with my back against the counter, unable to retreat any farther, I spun around in total panic and picked up the first thing I saw: a twelve-inch bread knife. I stood there shaking, with the knife raised, unable to utter a sound. We both knew that if he stepped one inch closer, I would strike. He stood there for what seemed like an eternity, glaring into my eyes. Then, slowly, he backed up and turned around. Without uttering a word, he walked out the front door and drove away.

I knew my father would return to the house in a few days, but his absence from my day-to-day life would soon be permanent. Though my mother and father would not officially end their marriage for several years, I finally realized that I needed to protect myself emotionally and physically by moving away. I left for good a short time later. As painful as it was for me at the time, I knew I had to let my mother figure out her own way through her relationship with Dad. I had to give up feeling responsible for protecting her, and physical separation seemed to be the only viable answer.

Although I was still competing on the tennis circuit, I moved onto campus to continue my studies at the University of Southern California, where I was majoring in premed.

After arriving home from my last world tennis tour, in the late summer between my junior and senior years at USC, I quit the sport on the spot. Just like that, I decided my tennis career was over. I'd achieved everything I had set out to accomplish, and I knew in my heart that the sport wasn't what I wanted to pursue for the rest of my life.

After graduating *cum laude* a short time later, I was at a crossroads in my life. I knew I didn't want to be a doctor, nor a professional tennis player, but what my next step should be, I wasn't sure. So, I did what a lot of women do at this particular stage in their life when faced with the uncertainty of their future.

I got married.

My husband, Alec, was the only man I'd ever seriously dated. He came from a very traditional family, and though I felt I was in love with him at the time, I think I fell equally in love with the idea of living within the safety net of peace and security that he and his family offered. Besides, I had grown up believing marriage was every girl's dream. You find your prince, get married, have a family, and live happily ever after.

Alec was a great guy and the picture of reliability and stability. He was my "8:00, 12:00, and 6:00 man," I used to tease—breakfast at eight, lunch at twelve, and dinner at six, right on the button. I followed right along, becoming the perfect housewife. I cooked, cleaned, made furniture, took flower-arranging classes, in addition to playing an active role in all the normal family occasions and activities.

Including the two years we dated, everything went smoothly in our relationship for six years. Then one afternoon, I saw a stranger in the mirror. I was attending Alec's sister's bridal shower at the Huntington Hotel in Pasadena, when I happened to glance in the powder-room mirror and saw something shocking. Before me stood an unnerving apparition: a girl dressed head-to-toe in baby pink—pink dress, pink shoes, pink purse, pink everything!

I couldn't believe it! I was staring at a budding Junior-Leaguer bound for an evening at the country club—certainly a far cry from the palomino colt that had lived within me as a child. The adventurous, energetic, off-the-wall rebel that I'd always considered myself to be, was nowhere to be found.

Something happened in that instant reflection. Perhaps I woke up from an unconscious "nap." In any case, I stood staring at this obscure vision of myself in "costume." I was frozen in the sorrowful realization that somehow I had missed the boat. Who was this person I saw reflected in the mirror? I didn't recognize her at all. The image I was looking at was no one I was familiar with, and it produced an overwhelming need to separate myself from what I was looking at. But, I had no idea how to extricate myself from the vision without leaving my marriage. The answer to my dilemma was not clear, so I simply put a lid on my feelings. I was unaware, however, that the pot was still simmering and rapidly coming to a boil.

Glancing back on the pages I had written, it seemed difficult to comprehend the turn my life had taken. But the further I delved into the material in front of me, the more I realized that my marriage had actually given me a chance to heal. It provided me with the strength I needed for the next step in my life's journey. I don't mean to trivialize my marriage to Alec, or my relationship with his family in any way. They all gave me an extraordinary amount of nurturing, kindness and love. And they gave it unselfishly. Destiny, however, was to take me in another direction, and our journey together was not to be forever.

Coincidentally, it was during this time that a friend of mine, Craige Citron, invited me to visit his acting class. My reaction was almost the same as when I had started playing tennis. I felt immediately at home. *I could do this! I loved it!* The territory felt familiar, and there was a similar focus on immersing myself in what I loved. But once again, I was looking outside myself to find "the rush." And, the further I went "out" in search of it, the further away I got from the center of my being, and life in the *Bliss Zone.*

I began attending the class on a regular basis, and before long I knew I wanted to give acting a serious shot.

Alec's parents and his aunt and uncle, however, three of whom are doctors, adamantly opposed my decision.

"Actors and actresses are *never* happy!" they reasoned. "Their lives are always tumultuous and unfulfilled."

Alec wasn't far behind in his feelings on the subject as well. This was not the direction in which he had intended his life to go. He saw himself living a much more conventional lifestyle, as opposed to what he presumed was the spontaneous and unpredictable world of show business. He was certainly right on that account.

I, on the other hand, had found something I was passionate about and wanted the opportunity to give it a try. This philosophical difference began to divide us, and there seemed to be no way to turn the tide. A short time later, we filed for divorce. Ending my relationship with this good, caring man and his loving family was heart-wrenching. But, I think we both knew there was no other option. I'm sure they know by now that the direction both of our lives took was the way it was meant to be. But I also hope they realize how much they gave me. They will forever be in my heart.

Following my new direction to pursue a career in the entertainment business in earnest, I decided to break the ice and delve into a more serious study of my craft. I "broke" in all right. *Literally.* I had heard that the renowned teacher, Lee Strasberg, (famous for bringing "The Method" to the Actor's Studio), was holding a California workshop. The tuition, however, was something like six thousand dollars! There was no way I could afford that kind of fee, so I did the natural thing a girl of strong will and unbridled spirit would do. I parked in the alley behind the theater where the class was being held, and climbed up the fire escape outside the building. After crawling through an open window, I snuck behind the stage and found a little nook where I could hide. I watched the entire workshop through a hole in the backdrop while I filed away every word on my trusty tape recorder. It was such an exciting class, and I soaked up everything like a sponge.

After about four weeks of the six-week program had been completed, Lee Strasberg's wife, Anna, happened to catch me sneaking back down the fire escape one night after class.

"Who are you and what are you doing?" she asked.

Caught in the act and scared to death, I gave her my name and told her the truth.

She took a long pause. Then finally, as a faint smile appeared on her face, she said, "Well, let's just say I didn't see anything," and walked away.

I finished the program as I had begun it, watching through a hole in the backdrop, taping away.

Some months later, I graduated to studying acting in a more conventional fashion—through the front door. As for the craft itself, I loved everything about it. I thoroughly enjoyed the process of connecting with a character and losing myself for twenty to thirty minutes in whatever fantasy world the scene depicted. It was exciting, and I loved the challenge.

It wasn't long before I began to actively pursue my acting career. Did I subconsciously believe that this was the answer I'd been searching for, that certain something that would bring me the meaning and intensity my soul so craved? Did I hope the applause and the accolades would fill the void I felt deep down inside? Probably yes, on both accounts, as I look back at it now. But at the time, I just went for it. Whatever came my way, I took it. There were no judgments or questions on my part about my ability or what I was supposed to do. I just forged ahead, straight toward my goal.

I began with all kinds of jobs: modeling, singing, interviewing, appearing in commercials, as well as acting. Soon I was auditioning for movie and television roles as well, and within a year, my career had taken off in earnest. I pursued my acting with vigor, just as I had my tennis. I knew where I was headed and I was determined to reach my destination.

Looking back, I could see that I had heard the song before, and was familiar with the territory. Once again, I got blinded by ambition, searching outside myself for the salve to heal the hole inside my heart. Consequently, as I steadfastly focused on my path, my *next* job and my *next* level of achievement became paramount to the joy of acting itself. The momentum of my success blinded me, and I couldn't see that I had moved even further away from the essence of who I was. This additional loss of connection to the core of my being allowed my success free reign to run wild, and the chaotic results landed me in a place even I couldn't believe.

7

Incredible, but True

Life is what happens while you're busy making other plans.
John Lennon

It's funny how careers often choose us, though we think it's the other way around. Certainly, I pray that it was true in my case. I was attracted to the entertainment business because it centers around the creation of something from nothing. It is a field wherein one's vision can be interpreted in an exciting and dynamic way for all the world to see. Because of this, the business is a magnet for many of us who prefer to live and work in the world of our dreams. This is both the good news and the bad.

On the good side, nothing is more exhilarating than the process of creating one's vision on paper, on tape, on the stage, or on the screen. The spirit is filled to capacity, satiating all of our needs. Not surprisingly, this incredible high is quite literally addictive.

On the negative side, the business is filled with dramatic lows. Promises are not kept. Projects get put on hold for years and years. Money is raised and then lost, or worse yet, can't be raised at all. This multitude of variables comes into play from the time you pursue a role or a project is conceived until, or if, it is realized. The fragility of working in any form of the business is overwhelming. Therefore, it is a form of competition of a completely different sort. The only opponent in this case is the challenge of surviving the business itself. And surviving it with dignity, honor, integrity, patience, knowledge and skill intact, is a feat few ever achieve.

At the time I began seriously pursuing the acting business, I had no way of understanding this, of course. I was simply embarking on an activity that I loved. I was willing and eager to accept whatever came my way. But once I began to work at my craft on a regular basis, my once freewheeling attitude was overpowered by the desire for more and more success. I was hooked. I'm not even sure what succeeding meant to me at the time, but the desire drove me just the same. Again, my heart took a backseat to my will.

Reviewing the details of my experiences in print, I noticed several things. First, after "Wonder Woman," I segued right into feature films, cast opposite such stars as Walter Matthau, Bruce Dern, Louis Gossett, Jr., and Michael Biehn. A buzz was in the air, and my star was rising. Secondly after having completed six films in a row, I was invited to the Cannes Film Festival in France. Two of the pictures I was starring in were showing there, albeit outside of the major competition. But it was a very big step in the right direction. My timing was auspicious. With the help of an amazing public relations woman in Paris named Yanou Collart, the word spread. Overnight, my face was in every European newspaper and on every European television channel imaginable. They were calling me *The New American Sensation!* Not bad for a girl who, fourteen days earlier, was virtually unknown on the entire continent! Yet here I was in Cannes, riding on yachts with John Huston, and attending movie premieres with the likes of Elizabeth Taylor, Michael Douglas, Richard Gere, and Steven Spielberg!

All the public relations hullabaloo that Yanou had orchestrated for me created such a sensation at the Festival that it caught the eye of the ABC network executives. Soon, they were hot on my trail, offering me a television series called *That's Incredible*. It was to be a weekly cavalcade of everyday people doing unreal, outrageous, unbelievable and/or incredible things. At the time I thought, *you've got to be kidding, this is the worst job I could possibly accept if I want to be considered a serious actress!* So, I graciously turned down the pilot, and ABC filmed it with someone else. Evidently, they weren't happy with the results, because they came back and offered me what seemed like the sun and the moon in terms of salary, as well as the chance to shoot the entire twelve shows in just twelve days! *Hey,* I thought. *How bad could it be? I'll do twelve shows, make enough money to hold out for a major film break, and be done with it. Nobody will ever hear of* That's Incredible, *and that will be that.*

Riiiiiiight.

I truly believed that the series would never go beyond those original twelve shows, so I was confident that my feature film career would remain right on track as planned. I soon learned a very valuable lesson: "If you want to hear God laugh, tell him your plans." I didn't know anything about television ratings, but boy oh boy, did I get a quick lesson.

I was filming a miniseries called *Roughnecks* the night the show aired, and I remember someone coming on the set the next morning to announce that *That's Incredible* had snared a "thirty-nine" national share. I breathed a sigh of relief. I figured ratings were like school grades: 100 was the best and a 39 was about an F. *Thank goodness that's over,* I thought to myself.

But a thirty-nine share was to die for in the world of television. Nowadays, a high number like that is almost nonexistent, except for the occasional championship sporting event. At any rate, *That's Incredible* was a smash! It blazed away on ABC (mostly in the top ten) for some five years, and still plays in worldwide syndication.

Unfortunately, the tremendous success of the show had a negative effect on my feature film career. I couldn't buy a movie role if my life depended on it, as there were no successful crossover performers (from television to film) at the time. On the other hand, I had finally become a household name—a star.

I became a star all right, the star of the weirdest show on television! I'm sure the producers didn't have to view much of the original footage before they came up with the name *That's Incredible.*

It certainly was. But if you thought the show was wild, you should have been backstage with me.

I'm not exactly sure how to put this delicately, but I was "peed and shat" upon, literally, by every creature known to man in the animal kingdom. No matter where I stood, somehow they'd find me—lions, elephants, snakes, tarantulas, Komodo dragons, everything. Putting any of God's critters near me was as good as an open invitation for the beast to release its bladder or sphincter. It became the running joke of the show: What animal have we got for Cathy Lee today?

"Gosh," the trainer would apologize. "He/she *never* does that!"

The audience would howl. The crew would howl. The producers would howl. And John Davidson and Fran Tarkenton, my cohorts and friends, would be on the floor in hysterics. Thanks a lot, guys! Everyone loved the playful interplay between the three of us: It was two guys against the girl, and of course, I was always the odd one out when it came to a vote on who would have to handle the next oddity. Additionally, the producers tried not to let me know ahead of time what outrageous guests awaited behind the curtain. That way, they felt, my reaction would be funnier. No kidding!

Also, I began to experiment with the different styles of clothes I wore on the show. I had more "looks" than Madonna in a house of mirrors. Each week, I'd waltz out in a new creation of my own design, complete with a matching "do." We used to get tons of mail about my hair alone. Some viewers were positive and others wondered if I'd lost my mind.

The ABC executives had a more serious concern, however. Included in the first reports that came in from the network to the producers of the show, lovingly referred to by the cast and crew as *The Nipple Reports,* was the suggestion that if by chance, I didn't want to wear a brassiere, it would be totally "acceptable" to them. The producers of the show, shocked and repulsed, darted off a stinging reply saying that they felt it was important to our "family" audience that a brassiere (meaning "no nipples") *definitely* be a part of my attire. If you can believe it, this earth-shattering argument went on for almost four days!

Finally, I'd had enough. I took things into my own hands, so to speak. "Guys," I said. "You choose the guests and the stunts, and I'll choose my underwear." No one ever mentioned it again.

I also wish I would have had at least some input in regard to the guests that appeared on the show as well. Some were truly beyond the realm of taste by anyone's definition. Others simply left me frightened to death—either by who they were, or by what they were attempting to do. In the latter category, I particularly remember "The Tarantula Lady," a rather sweet-looking, gray-haired woman from the midwest who brought with her about twenty members of one species of the animal kingdom that leaves me beyond petrified. I had carefully explained to her, prior to our taping the show, that I was deathly afraid of spiders—any spiders. I thought I had made myself perfectly clear. In fact, I couldn't have been *more* clear.

"I will be happy to do *anything,* but please don't put a tarantula anywhere near me," I pleaded pointedly.

Nervous about being on national television for the first time, she must have completely forgotten my request. Because, in her excitement of being on camera, she began to pull out her army of fist-sized hairy brown spiders from their aerated boxes, and placed them all over my arms and shoulders.

"And here's Henrietta . . . and Thelma . . . and here's Milton . . ." The tarantulas may have loved it, but I broke out in a cold sweat. I was paralyzed.

The audience, of course, thought this was hysterical. The more terrified I became, the harder they laughed.

What a way to make a living!

And how about the man from Australia? Just your normal everyday guy, with whom John and I were going to have dinner—on camera. As we were sitting there, at a beautifully set table, with silver and crystal placed neatly on white linen, I turned to the guest of honor.

"So what do you have to show us tonight?" I inquired.

"That I'm not a real good cook," he replied, as he carefully lifted the silver dome covering his dinner plate and placed it on the floor beside him. On the plate in front of him sat a *live* crab, about a foot across. Nothing else—just the crab. Still unaware of what was about to happen, I watched in horror as he proceeded to pick the critter up in both hands.

"First, you have to chew off the eyes," he said chomping away, "that way they can't see what's happening. Then, you eat the brain."

He bit into the shell, in an area I assumed was the crab's cerebral gray matter. Throughout the feast he continued to answer my questions with crab guts hanging out of the corners of his mouth and sliding down his chin. I repeatedly slashed my hand across my throat in a frantic signal to the producers to *cut tape* and end this misery. I couldn't believe that this man was actually eating a live crab! Not only that, they were filming this crusty scenario for national television!

Despite my pleas, the cameras kept rolling.

And to think I traded a movie set for this!

Another unbelievable incident occurred right in the middle of one night's taping. I was reading the TelePrompTer in front of me, when I introduced "The Incredible Albinis," who, of course, I'd never met. The studio doors opened and there, standing in order from the tallest to the shortest, wearing matching red plaid shirts, blue jeans and boots, was a family of seven white-haired, white-skinned, pink-eyed albinos! I couldn't believe the sight before my eyes. They stared at me. I stared at them. The fact that the entire family of seven people had albino characteristics was incredible enough, but I couldn't believe that the producers had added to the macabre by dressing them in matching outfits! The overall visual was like a cross between something out of the backwoods of Appalachia, and a *Saturday Night Live* sketch of the Coneheads!

Trying desperately to maintain my composure, I cleared my throat and made an effort to begin my on-camera interview. Not five words into my first question to them, I could feel the corners of my mouth begin to tremble. The laughter was uncontrollably building inside me. *The Albinis? The albinos? The Albini albinos?* I was about to come apart at the seams. *What am I going to do?* I thought. The more I tried to remain the consummate professional so I wouldn't embarrass the Albini family, the more I began to lose it. Within minutes, the audience began to roar, and soon, the situation was more than I could bear.

I glanced over at the production table for help, but the producers had lost all sense of shame and were laughing right along with everyone else.

Fran and John were no help either. They were hiding over in the corner of the stage, practically doubled over. Even the crew had abandoned their positions and had headed for the hills.

I turned back to the Albinis, and that sight was the final straw. Laughter had now permeated my entire body, and tears began to run down my cheeks.

Realizing that somehow I had to make a quick exit, I stuttered something to the Albinis like, "I'm terribly sorry, but I just need to take a break for a few minutes. I'm so sorry. Please excuse me."

I ran off the stage, leaving the family standing there.

Amidst their convulsions, the producers motioned to Fran and John to take a stab at finishing the interview. They gave it an earnest try, but fared no better than I had. As it turned out, the family never got to say a word. I'm not even sure if we ever finished the segment at all. It was one of those moments where you could just die of embarrassment, but at the same time can't stop laughing for the life of you!

To the Albinis, wherever you are, I sincerely apologize.

Or how about the guy who ate an entire car? That's right. He ground it up, and over the course of about a month, we filmed him eating the seats, dashboard, tires, hubcaps, carburetor, *everything*. If I hadn't seen it for myself, I wouldn't have believed it. I kept wondering how anyone ever realized they had a talent for this in the first place! What, did he start with compacts and move up the food chain to Cadillacs?

And then there were those special guests who didn't quite make the show. Take, for example, the man who showed up in an extremely vivid turquoise tuxedo, complete with turquoise shirt, turquoise bow tie, turquoise vest, turquoise cummerbund, and to round it off, turquoise socks and shoes. His "expertise" was to balance ten card tables, one on top of the other, in his mouth, while dancing. Naturally, the producers insisted I sit on the top table to heighten the effect. So there I was, in my very short skirt, sitting on the top of these ten tables while the "turquoise tornado" was dancing and spinning around with me hanging on for dear life.

Was it my karma? Was I being punished for my television sins in a former life?

Looking back on it, of course, I could see that the show was a tremendous gift. But I still wondered why *That's Incredible,* out of all the shows on television, was the vehicle that fate had chosen to propel me to fame in the eyes of the world.

In all fairness to the show, however, in addition to all the crazy episodes, there was another side of the series that wasn't really played up in most of our advertising. It consisted of what I called the *value* segments. They involved incredible medical wonders, new inventions, valiant rescues, recoveries of long-lost family members, and the like.

One such segment was the unbelievable discovery of a young man living in the back country of China, whose mother had literally hidden him for all of his twenty-four years because he was disfigured—a disgrace for a rural Chinese family. Research revealed that similar situations in older tradition were usually handled by death. The boy had two faces: one normal, facing forward, and the other, consuming one-half of the right side of his head. The show assembled a team of twenty-six doctors who were willing to donate their services to reconstruct the boy's disfigurement. These doctors spent eight months planning the procedure: One half of the team would be responsible for completely removing the second "face," while the other half would rebuild his frontal face to look normal again. The producers, at their own expense, flew him and his mother to the United States and taped him before, during, and after his surgery.

At the moment the bandages were removed and the doctor showed the young man his new face for the very first time, the boy sobbed uncontrollably.

Through an interpreter, his mother said that she had known all along that someday, somehow, someone was going to come along who could fix him. I will never forget the picture of that boy's face, looking at his mother telling her story. Such faith, such love, such reverence. Shows like this should be repeated as a reminder to us all that pure love is alive and well in this world of ours, in spite of all we hear to the contrary.

When you have a top-ten show, however, the network wants to keep it there, and therefore tends to push those segments that are the most sensational: the guy who water-skied behind the plane, the horse that drove a truck, the rabbit that surfed, the six-foot tall Frenchman who got into a glass box measuring twenty-two inches square, as well as the guy who shot a bullet into his partner's mouth at fifty feet. The network figured we were averaging a thirty-five share, were one of the top five shows in America, and were number one in a lot of the countries around the world, so why argue with success? I couldn't really blame them, they certainly had logic on their side.

The show brought out the playfulness among the entire cast and crew, which naturally started expressing itself in the form of practical jokes. One day we were shooting seven shows back to back. This required seven costume changes, seven hair changes as well as seven makeup redos. During one of these quick changes, I decided to take a shower. The bathroom was right across from my dressing room. When I stepped out of the shower stall, I noticed MY CLOTHES WERE GONE! I couldn't believe it. I was sopping wet, stark naked, and about ten yards from my dressing-room door. I looked at the clock, and saw that I only had twelve minutes to be fully dressed, remade up, and back before the cameras. I called for help. No one answered. With the clock ticking away, I decided I had no choice but to try and make a mad dash for my dressing room. I grabbed a handful of paper towels from the dispenser to cover the essentials. Then, I stuck my head out the door, looked both ways down the hall and, when I was sure the coast was clear, bolted across to my dressing room. I tried the handle. It was locked too! I couldn't believe it! It was never locked! My only choice was to go back where I'd come from, so I darted back to the bathroom. As I reached for the door I realized, to my horror, that somehow it was locked too! There I was, trapped naked in the hallway! I was frantic. Suddenly, I heard the muffled sound of uncontrollable laughter from inside John's dressing room. I couldn't believe it! My pals, my buddies, Fran and John. They'd gotten me again.

The show was a lot of laughs for everyone involved and it certainly left an indelible impression in the hearts and minds of America. But it was a far cry from the grown-up film career I had envisioned for myself. It was obvious that my life had gone in a direction I had not planned on. And yet, as I reread my notes, I could see the role that the show had played in my life. It had served as a constant reminder of what life could be when living it in the realm of total possibility.

Unfortunately, I was not privy to this knowledge at the time, but it was certainly true. Because of *That's Incredible,* my career had taken off and was soaring. For nine years, I hardly stopped to breathe. I was an "overnight" sensation. I was on the cover of hundreds of magazines and on all the talk shows. *People* magazine even chose me for their annual cover, "Hottest of the Hot." Life was fantastic, and I was enjoying every minute of the fame and fortune my career was blessing me with. I was grateful and I was happy. It was not the pure, innocent joy that I had known at age two at the bottom of the pool, but I was definitely riding the wave. What more could I have possibly wanted?

8
Once Upon a Time . . .

The loss of primary attachment permits the entry of the Gods.
Jean Houston

As little girls, many of us hold on to a very particular fairy tale, carrying in the deepest regions of our hearts the idea that "someday my prince will come." He will sweep us off our feet, protect us from all harm, and, together, we will live happily ever after. Where does this come from? From the stories that are read to us at bedtime? Is it something inherent in our nature? Is it an unspoken tradition passed on from mothers to daughters? Whatever the cause, it is a powerful, emotional force that runs through us. We seem to have this natural desire to want to form a bond with someone, so that we can take on the journey of life in partnership.

On the outside, my childhood promoted independence. I was brought up to believe that I was the one responsible for my life as well as my livelihood, and was actively pursuing a career by the age of twelve. This independence was contradicted by my unconscious "story-book" longing for a life partner. This feeling was further intensified by my relationship with my father, and the dissolution of my marriage to Alec. It was becoming more and more evident as I read over my *Biographical Life Sketch* that my unconscious, yet overwhelming, desire for nurturing and love, tended to blind my ability to see beyond the surface of male/female relationships. So, in May 1983, when Joe Theismann began pursuing me with all the intensity of a fourth-down blitz, I was swept off my feet before I even realized what had happened.

My Cinderella journey began when I was invited by producer David Marmel, to be a presenter at the prestigious Victor Awards in Las Vegas, a thirty-year-old nationally televised awards show honoring athletes in every field. I was at one of the rehearsals grabbing a bite of lunch with my assistant, when Ed Marinaro, the football-player-turned-television star, came over to my table with another man I didn't recognize. Ed and I had known each other for quite a while, so we proceeded to catch up on the latest news. After a short time, the man who was standing beside Ed joined in and introduced himself.

"Hi, I'm Joe Theismann, and I just wanted to come over and say how thrilled I am to meet you," he said.

I was somewhat taken aback. There was an instant surge of electricity between us, but it soon passed and I replied, "Well, thank you. Nice to meet you, too."

Joe came over to me again during the awards ceremony while I was waiting in the Green Room. We didn't talk about anything in particular, but I do remember asking him if he was married and had any children.

"Yes, to both questions," he replied.

I spoke to him a few more times that evening, but as far as I was concerned, that was that.

During the next nine or ten months, he would call periodically, just to check in and say hello. Then one day, out of the blue, he called and asked if I'd like to go out to dinner.

"Listen," he stated right off the bat, "I've moved out of my house and I'm getting a divorce."

I was too stunned to reply.

"I know you probably think I'm out of my mind," he continued, "but I really want to take you to dinner."

"Listen," I began carefully, "You seem like a terrific guy, but I'm perfectly happy being unattached right now. And besides, you need some time to figure things out and enjoy being single."

As far as I was concerned, that was that, again.

But he persisted. He kept phoning and phoning and phoning, so much so, that his persistence made *my* will look like an old dishrag. He was absolutely relentless.

Each time he called, I'd say something like, "Look, I'm flattered but I just don't want to go out with you."

Relentless in his pursuit, he kept hounding me, and humoring me, and cajoling me, and if that wasn't enough, he sent gifts, cards, and flowers by the dozens. All the attention was hitting its mark and beginning to invade my armor.

After months of his tireless onslaught, in spite of my resolve to stand my ground, the final flame that caused my meltdown came with his next phone call.

"Look, I'm going to sit on your doorstep until you agree to go to dinner with me. If after that you never want to see me again, then fine. I promise I won't call. But in terms of having dinner with you, I'm not taking no for an answer."

Somehow I knew he wouldn't, so, out of sheer exhaustion, I finally agreed.

We met as planned, and in spite of my initial trepidation, I found him playful, charming, and charismatic. Though there was an obvious energy and spark between us, I did the best I could to protect myself from his overwhelming persistence. When the dinner was over, he walked me to my car, maintaining the posture of a total gentleman. I drove away strangely confused. I knew I wanted to see this man again, but at the same time, his immense intensity scared me.

At seven-thirty the next morning, the phone rang. It was Joe, asking me to go to the beach for a picnic. He said he had something important to tell me. I had no idea that that day at the beach would be the beginning of an all-encompassing, unwavering, passionate, seven-year long relationship. In every respect, it would prove to be one of the most poignant and prophetic experiences of my life.

At the end of the beautiful, romantic day at the beach, as we were watching the sun setting over the Pacific, Joe looked at me with absolute assurance and said, "I want you to know that I'm going to spend the rest of my life with you."

I didn't answer. I couldn't answer. I was overwhelmed with an emotion I didn't understand. Was my girlhood fairy tale coming true? Was this the love I'd always dreamed about? The moment that I embraced the idea that the answer was "yes," I buried any lingering awareness I had of the *Bliss Zone*. I was about to take the final leap outside of myself to find the answers I was looking for. A move that would cause a separation between me and the joyful world I had known as a little girl, for almost nine years.

As far as our relationship was concerned, I was drawn in more and more with each passing day, flattered by his endearing pursuit of me. The calls. The flowers. The letters. The poems. The gifts. He would even fly from Washington, D.C. to L.A. and back in the same day, just to see me for two hours. And he did this numerous times. His gallantry was breathtaking, and I inhaled the pure richness of it as if I had been waiting to experience the feelings for a long time.

I put down my pen and sat quietly for quite some time pondering the thought. Slowly, I began to realize that when we are so desperate to fill an emotional need we feel is "missing" within us, we often enter a relationship and project the fulfillment of that need onto our partner. It's the rose-colored glasses syndrome, so to speak. In my case, I could see from my notes that the little girl in me felt she needed to heal her aching heart, so she created a relationship and then endowed her partner with those attributes that made him look and feel like everything she'd been searching for. She painted her version of the perfect mate on top of what was actually there. This self-fulfilling fantasy just happened to come in the form of an explosion called Joe Theismann, and he played into the fairy tale with gusto.

He was irresistible, and his love knew no bounds. He called me his "angel" from heaven, and promptly named our 108-acre farm in Leesburg, Virginia, "Angel Acres," in my honor. We were simply mad for each other, and recklessly, hopelessly, passionately in love.

Spending much of our time in Washington, D.C., we were not only regulars at the Redskins' football games, but on the political and social circuit as well. We became a seven-course meal for the media, and they dined at every opportunity.

Joe begged me to marry him every day for almost six and a half years. He meant it. But, I had been married once before, and was convinced that the romance of a relationship ended once two people got married. Joe was insistent, however, that we *would* be married. And he didn't keep it a secret. He took every opportunity he could to tell people that I was going to be his wife, including announcing our supposed wedding date several times on radio and television. Again, his persistence was overwhelming, but I continued to stand my ground.

To the surprise of both of us, he finally wore me down, albeit only in a manner of speaking. It happened one night at a charity event at The Mirage Hotel in Las Vegas, when Joe and I were seated at a table for eight with my friends Mirage owner Steve Wynn and his wife Elaine. Steve happened to ask, "So, when are you two getting married?"

Before I could reply, Joe looked straight at me, "Go on, tell him," he said. "When *are* we getting married?"

This was the final straw. I had no more strength to resist. So I decided I would simply call his bluff, absolutely certain he would back down.

"You wanna get married? Okay, fine. Not a problem," I blurted out.

I should have known. Never challenge someone who thrives on it. Playing along, he immediately grabbed someone's pen and began to write out our own personal "marriage certificate" on the back of two party invitations, complete with signature lines for the other people at our table to be witnesses. I couldn't believe it; he had returned my bluff in spades! He signed both invitations and placed them in front me, waiting for my signature. With nowhere to turn, I finally gave in and signed. Everyone else at the table joined in the fun, and signed as well. I figured the antics would appease him for awhile, and we would continue on in our relationship as we had. Marriage, Las Vegas-style? Not in actuality, but it sufficed for the time being.

However, the relationship continued on, as it had, in full blossom. The cards, letters, poems, gifts, and flowers kept coming, even into the fourth, fifth, and sixth years. There were also wonderful trips to exotic places, exciting work-related opportunities for us to share, as well as quiet evenings snuggled up together in the normalcy of an everyday life. The connection was sound. The experience was compelling and immensely romantic. I felt loved and adored beyond my wildest dreams.

In addition to everything else that was flourishing in my life, I now thought my imagined fairy tale had come true, and, as in all good stories, I fully expected to live "happily ever after."

As I read aloud everything I had written in my *Biographical Life Sketch,* my emotions ran the gamut.

First of all, I felt relieved. Everything, once and for all, had been written down in black and white for the first time in my life. Nothing had been edited, nothing had been defended, and no corners had been rounded to ease their truth. There was no effort to try to color and shape the facts to ensure that my memories wouldn't call attention to my imagined inadequacies.

I also felt a deep sense of shame for those incidents where I had clearly wronged others, particularly when I had defended my position knowing full well that I was in the wrong.

I missed the heart of the little girl I used to be. I missed the freedom of being the palomino colt, running wild across a field of knee-high grass. I missed the unquestioning trust it took to make my way across the bottom of that pool. That child seemed so far away, and I wondered if I would ever see her again. I longed to feel her pure, innocent sense of joy.

Additionally, I felt anger at the times I had not communicated my feelings honestly, or taken action when it was called for. I wished I could have confronted my father when he raised his hand or voice against my mother and me, even though it surely would have meant another beating. Doing nothing had only hampered my freedom and courted disaster.

Perhaps most important of all, I realized that the truth had set me free. Once I saw my entire past on paper and then heard the story with my own ears, an amazing thing happened. All of the emotions, all of the incidents, and all of the realizations seemed to blend together in a truly magical way. The good and the bad, the strong and the weak, the happy and the sad, and the success and the failure, no longer stood apart. They were accepted and necessary parts of the whole picture. I finally felt there was a resolution between the past incidents of my life and the "me" I was beginning to know. We had merged, and gratefully so. Who I had been was perfectly clear.

But who was I now? I was still facing the continuing effects of the Epstein-Barr virus, my grandmother's death, Joe's suits against me, and my bankruptcy. How was I going to deal with the daily trauma of my present predicament? How was I going to find the necessary money to survive, reawaken my career, and successfully navigate the immediate pragmatic concerns still facing me? I needed help. In the midst of these realizations, I instinctively reached for the phone. I reached out for the support of the familiar, soon realizing that it was only a veil for the unfamiliar.

9
Home Is Where the Heart Is

A deep image of family, residing effectively in our hearts and imaginations, can help us work and live together in ways that no rational principle can.

Thomas Moore

Ask and you will receive. Seek and you will find; knock, and it will be opened to you.

Matthew 7:7

The mountain of practical issues requiring my immediate attention was overwhelming, and I realized I couldn't face them alone. I desperately needed some support. So, who do you reach out to when you're up against such oppressing circumstances? Who do you call at three in the morning, when you've reached your absolute limit in dealing with the calamities that life has thrown your way? You reach out to your "family," whether that involves people you are biologically connected to, or simply those individuals you've chosen as your intimate support group.

Scattered across Southern California, my biological family was threaded together by a strong underlying, matriarchal force. We also shared a powerful common bond that none of us had ever really analyzed. It was something deep, unspoken, and almost tribal in its raw state. And yet, at the same time, it was so indefinable and delicate, that it seemed taboo to discuss it in depth.

We had always been close, seeing each other as a group at least once every couple of months for birthdays, and holidays. Celebrating together had become our tradition. Furthermore, if one of us got sick, we all took turns at the bedside. If one of us was victorious, we all vicariously enjoyed the thrill. And, if one member of our clan happened to mention a problem they were having to another member, in no time at all, everyone knew about it and was offering help. So much for keeping secrets.

This was my family.

So, during the height of my crisis, the first person I reached out to for help was a family member, in this case, my mother, Linda Crosby Walker. I remember being totally panicked at the very thought of calling her. I stared at the phone.

What should I say? Where should I begin? I didn't have a clue. Why was I agonizing over such a simple phone call? I was numb with the realization that I didn't really "know" her at all. I was shocked. I had no idea what my own mother would say to me when I told her that her "successful" daughter had lost everything. It seemed incredible, but I just couldn't figure out a way to ask her for help.

I began to think about mom and me. Who was this person I was calling *Mother?* I flashed back to a vision of her as a young wife and mother, standing over my bed when I almost died from pneumonia at the age of six. I had a temperature of 105, and for two solid days, she sat on the side of my bed massaging my back and putting cold compresses all over my body to bring my temperature down.

I also saw her as an athlete, teaching me to excel at sports and imbuing me with her contagious spirit of victory.

I saw her sitting at the dining-room table, hunched over a used sewing machine late into the night, making Linda Lou's and my tennis dresses for the next day's matches—in spite of the fact that she had never sewn anything in her life! At the time, tennis clothes were very expensive, and we needed many of them, especially after the number of matches we were playing each week dramatically increased. She simply went out, bought a used sewing machine and a couple of patterns, and figured it out. Here was this talented actress, this gifted athlete, this dynamic woman, with pieces of cut material spread all over the living-room floor just so her girls could have what they needed.

I saw her sitting courtside at every one of my tennis matches, cheering me on to victory. She would drive my sister and me to every location, sometimes two or three hours each way, and then sit on the sidelines sweating out each and every point of our matches with us.

I thought about the rage I experienced when I watched her inability to stand up for herself or for me in the face of Dad's abuse. I couldn't understand how she could just take it, never fighting back and setting him straight. I was angry, hurt, and confused that anyone would allow themselves or their child to be beaten and abused to such a degree.

How could I forget the blank expression on her face the day I finally left home for good, fearing for my own safety?

I marveled at all of her efforts to keep our family together—cooking, decorating, preparing for, and hosting so many of our group celebrations.

I recalled the period in her life after Dad had left, when she was struggling to provide for her three daughters in any way she could, never once letting on as to how bad things really were. Not only that, during this financial struggle, she still gave a good portion of her time to run a charitable foundation.

Here was this remarkable, caring woman in so many respects, yet my present experience of her seemed to have been frozen predominately in the memories I had of her, prior to the day I left home. The years had gone by in a flash.

Who was she now? I wondered. *What had happened in those seemingly lost years?*

I was aware only of the basics. This was my mother, and yet I really didn't know her at all. The veil of familiarity had cloaked my experience of really knowing the woman who had given me life.

"Mommy," I said on the phone, struggling to find the appropriate words. Then silence. I couldn't talk. I began to cry.

"What's wrong, sweetheart?" she asked immediately.

Where should I start?

"Just talk to me, honey, tell me what's the matter," she continued.

My mother and I were certainly not strangers, but I felt like one now. We were probably typical of many mothers and daughters in that we had this unspoken, undeniable connection, yet we were still locked into the dynamics of our old parent-child relationship. She was still the mom, and I was still the daughter. We sorely lacked the intimacy and depth of an adult interaction. I realized that we were stuck in a habitual pattern of behavior in which each of us was simply playing out our designated role. She would put on her mother's "hat," assume the demeanor, and I followed along.

"Mom, I don't know what I'm going to do," I began.

She knew that things hadn't been going well over the last year and a half, but I'd kept most of the gory details from her—from all of my family for that matter. I didn't want them to worry.

Besides, I kept thinking, *I'm a survivor. I can do it myself. I'll bounce back and everything will be okay.*

But for the first time in my life, I hadn't bounced back. I was down for the count.

Suddenly, the precarious tether I was clinging to gave way, and I began to tell her everything. I couldn't get the words out fast enough. I was alternating between speaking and sobbing, desperately trying to get the whole story across. When I'd finally finished, there was a short pause and then she began to speak.

"It's going to be all right, sweetheart," she said simply. "You'll make it. You always do. If you need money, I'll sell some stock. Do you know when you might be able to pay it back?"

"I don't know, Mommy," I said.

"Don't worry about it then, we'll figure that out later," she answered.

The money arrived within the week.

After I hung up the phone, I was overcome. I knew my mother was financially secure, but certainly not independently wealthy. The money she was giving me was part of her life's savings, and it must have been frightening for her to dig into what she was counting on to sustain herself for the rest of her life. But there was no question in her mind. She would get me the money. I was so moved that I couldn't say much to her at the time except for a simple quiet "Thanks Mom, I really appreciate it." But inside, I remember being blown away.

It took courage for her to give me that money, and it took courage for me to ask for it. I had grown accustomed to the role of a provider in my family, having relinquished that of being provided for almost entirely. This was certainly understandable. My early adventurous spirit, coupled with my early determination to rise above my relationship with my father, helped me develop a very strong survival instinct. By necessity from my point of view, I had no choice but to do a lot of things on my own, and I proceeded to do just that. It didn't seem bad or unusual, it was simply what I had to do, and I did it.

As I became more successful in the entertainment industry, I began to feel that my family was relying on me, to a certain extent. If they needed something—money, assistance, psychological support—I would provide it. If anyone needed a job, I provided it. If someone was in a financial jam and needed a fast loan, I gave it to them. This was a comfortable position to be in for someone who had learned to do things on her own. It was natural progression.

They never took advantage of me or my generosity. Quite the contrary. But it set up a certain dynamic—a shield that separated me from them. However unconscious on everyone's part, it became a one-way flow. Don't get me wrong, I loved doing it and I loved being able to do it. But, as the person doing the giving, I never recognized the experience, much less developed the knowledge, of how to receive.

Conversely, my family did not have the chance to, nor the experience of, being able to give to me in any meaningful way. This produced not only a lack of any real connection between us, but a certain resentment on all fronts. If someone feels they cannot contribute to your life in a significant manner, they don't feel they are of value to you. And if they don't feel of value to you, they withdraw—it's a natural reaction.

It was perfectly clear after my conversation with Mother that I had no idea how to deal with her, adult to adult. I had not learned how to engage in meaningful dialogue with this person I was calling Mother.

My older sister, Linda Lou, on the other hand, a brilliant, caring, balanced, earth angel, who writes, produces and directs films and videos for the U.S. Navy, had been very successful at connecting with Mom. Maybe she had some ideas about how I could handle the situation. Curious, I called her. Although she didn't say it at the time, I'm sure she wondered where my opening question came from.

"How did you learn to deal with Mom?" I asked. "You know, really deal with her?"

"In the beginning," Linda Lou replied, "I just communicated everything I'd been holding back. I told her how I felt, and I demanded that she tell me the truth about how she felt as well. There were a lot of fireworks in the beginning, but after the initial ruffled feathers, I realized that the key to my having a great relationship with Mother was simply to love her exactly the way she is. I still tell her how I feel, but not in an effort to change her. It's not my prerogative to love my mother based on my judgment of her. This is the card game we're in together, she and I. She's my mother, I'm her daughter, and we're also adult friends. I love her for giving me life, and I love her for exactly who she is."

Hmmm, I thought. It seemed like miles away from where I was. I realized I did have judgments about Mother. There were things I wanted to change about her behavior, and it was inhibiting my ability to communicate with her openly and freely. But what could I do? Where should I start?

I remembered that one of her biggest complaints was that I never called enough. Even if I called once a week, or once every two weeks, it was never enough! So as a first step, I decided I would change that. I would call her every Sunday, no matter what. Even if I had talked to her during the week, Sunday was my day to call Mother. My first time out, I had no idea what I was going to say, but I was going to make the call anyway.

Sunday came.

"Hi, Mom," I began.

"Cathy Lee?"

She was surprised I was calling her for no particular reason. Our conversation, if you could call it that those first few Sundays, felt like a visit to the dentist: slow, painful, and somewhat numb. It only made matters worse that I was also carrying the burden of my preconceived plan. But after a couple of months, I started hearing from my sisters and other relatives about how excited mother was now that I was calling her "all the time." I had never realized how important it was for her to receive a simple telephone call from me on a consistent basis. After a short time, our conversations grew longer and more interesting. If you talk to somebody every single week, you begin to have to ask more in-depth questions. At first, out of sheer necessity. But, the result was that I was beginning to know my mother again and taking an active participation in our relationship.

Little by little, she began to open up too. She told me all kinds of things —what she loved about me and what she didn't. She told me all the things that had disappointed her in life, times when I'd hurt her feelings, her opinions about her husbands (Lou Crosby, then Frank Walker), and how much her acting career had meant to her. What do you know? We were having real, deep, interesting adult conversations for the very first time.

I realized that the dynamic we had set up in the past had produced a natural barrier to any real intimacy. That barrier not only affected the closeness we felt for each other, but it also had an impact on each of us individually.

As the months passed, however, I began to feel more comfortable, to feel more in tune with those parts of her that were like me, as well as those parts that weren't. Some I liked, some I didn't like. But I was gaining insight and it felt good.

I realized I didn't have to take care of her anymore. I didn't have to change her diet and I didn't have to insist that she stop smoking or drink less. These issues had seemed like reasonable sources of worry to me, but regardless, they had been affecting my ability to love her unconditionally. Like my sister said, I could express my concerns, but her choices in life were her own. She had given me life, and it was my job, not hers, to find a way to love her in spite of any judgments or opinions I might have put between us.

For years, I remember hiding her cigarettes, secretly cleaning out her refrigerator of all the unhealthy foods, and pouring water into her liquor bottles to dilute the strength. None of these actions had any lasting effect, except to make her extremely angry and even more steadfast in her point of view. I was trying to "fix" her into the person I thought she should be. Mother was aware of this as well, and drove the point home during one of our weekly telephone calls. She told me that I had been so keen on trying to change her, that I would occasionally resort to outright criticism. Case in point, she reminded me of a time I supposedly told her she was "too fat" and "wore too much makeup," just to get her attention.

"What?" I protested. "I said that? No way! When?"

"Don't you remember?" she said. "It was fifteen years ago. We were in the car driving too . . ."

My God! mothers remember everything, don't they!? They have the memory of an elephant. I truly don't recall saying those words and I can't imagine myself blurting out something as critical and cruel as that to my mother. But, it was definitely real to her, so it didn't make any difference if I had said it or not. I apologized right then and there, and assured her that I did not feel that way today.

Slowly but surely, deep, honest caring began to blossom. I actually looked forward to our Sunday calls. Sunday became synonymous with Mother. At the same time, her eating habits improved considerably. She began to limit herself to one drink a night and no longer was smoking! All, without a lick of help from me!

My new connection with Mother began to influence my relationships with my entire family as well. I started reconnecting with all of them anew, making a special effort to reach out and really listen to what they had to say. I realized that I needed to develop new ties with them based on these present interactions, and to use the opportunity to strengthen our familial bonds.

Who was this family of mine? It consisted of my Uncle Gene (Crowell), my niece Carey (Marvin), her husband Corey (Marvin), and their daughter Maggie Rose, my sister Lucinda Sue (Crosby), my other sister Linda Lou (Crosby), and her husband Hart (Broesel), my Aunt Gene (Crowell), and my mother. The names were clear, but who were the people behind those names?

For as long as I can remember, my grandmother, Francesca, was the leader of our biological tribe. When she died in 1988, the basic structure of the family was unintentionally, yet significantly, altered. The void she left was as profound as her indomitable presence had been. Her quiet beauty, her feisty spirit, and her unconditional love were missed by everyone, more than any of us realized. Whether it was watching her adopted family of wild skunks walking across the backyard, riding on a merry-go-round in Griffith Park, dining at the most expensive restaurants in Rome, hiking with me in the hills behind our house, or just sitting around the family table enjoying our traditional poker game, Francesca's spirit and love of life never faltered. She was the glue that had energetically held our family together.

Her death led to in-house bickering, and all sorts of little issues between family members became sources of friction. Mother-with-daughter, sister-with-sister. . . . Turf wars erupted on all fronts.

This infighting began to take its toll. We still got together every month or two for holiday and birthday celebrations, but there was an underlying current of uneasiness. Gossiping, much of it with a negative bent, further divided all the parties as well. I realized our family was falling apart. Everybody could feel it. But I guess no one knew what to do about it. It was as if our beloved Francesca's passing had unintentionally brought all of our familial ties into question.

The final straw came during a telephone conversation I had with Mother, interestingly enough, not on Sunday. She was telling me about a new disagreement that had surfaced, and for some reason I just flipped out. I'm not sure where all the anger came from, but I guess my uncommunicated feelings in regard to other family members had finally boiled to the surface. Whatever the reason, this time I let it all out.

"That's it, Mom. I've had it. I'm sick and tired of everybody tearing each other apart, and I'm not going to take it one minute longer! It's time we fixed this family."

In this heightened state, I called every member of the family over the course of the next six or seven hours, and repeated the same thing. I told them it was stupid and inane to continue this kind of behavior and that we needed to stop it immediately. I raised holy hell. I shouted and yelled. I said it all and then some. I told them I didn't want any more talking behind anybody's back. If someone had something to say to someone else, they should say it to that person's face, or keep it to themselves. If they tried to defend their actions, I stopped them in their tracks. I shocked everyone with the mere volume of my displeasure. I was adamant: No more backbiting, no more gossiping, and no more fighting. Period.

They couldn't believe that all of this was coming out of my mouth, I, who never lost my cool or my control of a situation. As I look back, I know I was over the top. But at the time, I didn't care. I was determined to keep going until I'd said everything I needed to say, no matter what anyone thought of me. Having resolved my own relationship with myself in minute detail, and having seen the benefits of telling the truth on a personal level, I was willing to deal with all of them in the same manner. I was free and eager to let them see who I really was. This process was the first step toward tearing down the walls that had come between all of us. It was the truth. I knew it and so did they.

After the last of these family phone calls, which happened to be to my niece, Carey, I noticed it was three in the morning. But, despite the hour, I felt totally invigorated. I was beginning to understand the real significance of the statement "the truth shall set you free!" My conversations were not simply about releasing anger. I had spoken from my heart, relied on my intuition, and had mustered the courage to communicate it. I felt closer to each member of my family than I had in years.

Personally, the process was an even more profound event. I felt like I had taken a real risk. I had gone out on a limb and accepted responsibility for my family, rather than just accepting the situation as it was. It's funny, in regard to our careers, we know we have to have good, communicative relationships. Otherwise, our day-to-day lives would be miserable and our livelihoods would be imperiled. But in a family, whether it's biological, adopted, or chosen, if you don't continuously address the issues, cultivate the connection, and keep the love flowing, you will never receive the tremendous gifts that the support of a family can give you.

There are situations where an individual shouldn't reach out to a particular family member or members. Especially if it's for their own protection, physically or psychologically. If that's the case, simply choose another person or group of people who love and support you, and are willing to be your family of choice. No matter what the circumstances are, when you reach out, new doors open. In my case, purposefully reconnecting gave me a degree of strength and connectedness I had never experienced.

Another piece of the puzzle had fallen into place. It was abundantly clear that my feeling of being separated from, or not close to my family, was just a symptom of my untended relationships. It was not the "truth." My connection with them had been there all along. Unfortunately, I had relied on my childhood and adolescent connection to my family to dictate the depth of my adult relationship with them.

It seems that we learn lessons when we least expect them, but always when we need them the most. And, the true "gift" inherent in these lessons, always lies in the learning process itself.

For example, my mother provided me with untold wisdom from her volumes of life experience, in ways I could not have imagined had I not delved beyond my petty judgments and opinions of her. After all, she is my maternal connection to "all time," and I needed to recognize that.

I'm so grateful that I healed my relationship with my mother before her unexpected death on December 19, 1995, and that she was able to feel the strength of her family once again bonded solidly around her. All ten of us were together at her bedside for her final moments. I know without a doubt, that she died with peace in her heart fully aware that her family circle had been reconnected. I only regret that she didn't have the chance to read this book so she could have seen in print the indelible contribution she made to each and every one of her family, including me. I love you,

Mom, and rest assured that you will *always* be my loving connection to all time.

In reconnecting with my family, I also learned that my sister, Linda Lou, had lessons to teach me that only an older and wiser sister could. Besides introducing me to the finer points of "motherology," she is always there to remind me that life is about having fun. There is so much to learn from her that now I listen with open ears. I take in her sense of justice, her connection to the earth and her undying love for our family. I watch her balance perfectly the needs of each member in relation to the whole. I also watch her achieve, without giving up who she is; and I marvel at the way she expresses her love for the life she has created. I am blessed to feel her walking beside me, always just a little bit ahead to clear my path.

I realized that my sister Lucinda Sue, a gifted writer and entertainer, is a reminder that life is truly what you make it and exists only as you see it through your eyes. She sees the lyrics of her songs as a voice for her own experiences, and in doing so, has taught me that each of us is responsible for his or her own happiness and well-being. She continues to teach me that the freedom to make one's own choices is the fruit of one's personal growth.

I learned an amazing thing about aunts. They're really backup quarterbacks you see. They may not start the game, but they're always ready to go into the lineup at a moment's notice. One summer, when Mother and Dad were working, my aunt and her girlfriend, Meg Young, offered to take Linda Lou and me on a week's vacation in Laguna Beach. We were both at that particular age (between ten and fourteen), when questions begin to arise regarding a girl's eventual initiation into womanhood. Simply stated, for months we had been begging Mother for bras. This was certainly not out of necessity on either of our parts, but we were undaunted. This became our primary focus, and it was clear to Aunt Gene that the matter had to be settled if we were going to be able to get on with our vacation. Being the good sport that she is, she took us straight to the nearest department store to remedy the situation. Realizing that we were on a roll, I must confess that my sister and I took advantage of the shopping spree by bringing up the fact that since we were now wearing bras, we should also get some lipstick and nylons to go with them. After all, what was a girl to do without lipstick, nylons, and a bra!? Whatever the circumstances, I am grateful for what gentle, kind-hearted mothering looks like through the eyes of a loving aunt. Her concerns for us are certainly not her responsibility, but obviously her joy.

I discovered that my niece, Carey, was rooting for me in a way I had never even considered. I had spent a lot of time taking care of her as she was growing up, and I noticed how she would study me and try to emulate everything I did, from the type of clothes I wore to the style of my hair to the way I interacted with friends. It was almost as if she was taking notes and filing them away for future use. It was flattering at the time, but it never occurred to me what effect her actions would have. Simply put, she taught me that life is a circle: You receive wisdom from those who precede you, hopefully enrich what you have learned, and then pass it on to those who follow. In following this principle, she shines her light back on me just by being who she is. How grateful I am that this unique, sensitive, loving soul is open to sharing all that we both have learned and will learn.

My Uncle Gene was always an enigma to me because of his strong, silent nature. Though I could always count on his generosity, kindness, and level-headed advice, I had never known how to reach out to him on anything more than a superficial level. I began to connect with him during my traumatic struggle, at first by seeking his advice regarding financial matters. In doing so, I realized the value of someone who stands for what is right and good without so much as a spoken word on the subject. I revel in his ability to "walk his talk" and to live his life in accordance with the simplistic, ethical values he was taught as a child. How refreshing it is to be in his company.

My nephew, Corey, epitomizes the perfect balance between intelligence, kindness, honesty, and simplicity. I marvel at his appreciation for merely being alive, and the easy manner in which he makes the responsibilities in his life seem like a privilege.

As for my relationship with my brother-in-law, Hart, the rugged cowboy rebel, I realized that kindred spirits can connect in spite of all outward appearances to the contrary. Viewpoints, opinions, and politics aside, it is so rewarding to watch and partake of his ability to share life at a level untarnished by surface trivialities.

And then there is Maggie Rose, the five-year-old mirror image of myself as a child. I watch in amazement as she literally flings herself at life with reckless, joyful abandon. Just in case I forget about the palomino colt of my early years, Maggie Rose is ever available to remind me what life looks like through the eyes of a freewheeling, blissful child.

Having taken the time to appreciate my family at a deeper level, free of any past judgments, I was able to experience them in a whole new way. I was not so quick to form an opinion concerning their actions, and therefore had the chance to understand and value the distinct life path each of them was on. I realized how important it was to cherish and support them, whether they were doing what I thought they should be doing or not. I enjoy the conscious feeling that I am a part of all of them, and likewise, that they are all a part of me.

Healing my family connections was more than just a sense of no longer feeling alone. The strength of these new unions allowed me to accept all of the biological and emotional elements that had helped shape my personality. I was no longer traveling alone. Actually, I had never been doing so, but I had to go through the experience, and purposefully reconnect with them in order to realize it on a conscious level.

Strengthening my family bonds was absolutely necessary in light of what would turn out to be the next steps of my journey back into the magical realm I had enjoyed as a child. Soon, I would be encountering something even tougher than the tidal rift that had divided my family, and I would need the buffer of my ties with them to keep me strong. With misfortune still as my unwitting first mate, before long, I would be plunging head first into another blustering wave of the storm.

Unaware and unprepared for this dive, I was going to need all the physical strength I could muster. Coincidentally, the Universe knew exactly what was needed and presented it, in the reflection of a mirror.

10
Mirror, Mirror, on the Wall . . .

The human body is the best picture of the human soul.
Ludwig Wittgenstein

Someday you're gonna have to face that deep, dark, truthful mirror.
Elvis Costello

The next step toward my eventual understanding of how to let the magic begin in my life came quite unexpectedly. As I started to get dressed one morning, I inadvertently caught a full length picture of myself in the mirror. I stood there for a moment in utter shock. I couldn't believe the apparition staring back at me. Though I had only gained about nine pounds in the four years since 1988, when I had been officially diagnosed with Epstein-Barr, what struck me more than the added weight, was that my naturally long, lean body, always trained for optimum performance, had suddenly morphed into a shape somewhat resembling a pear. I had become a victim of the "north-south-east-west spread."

That can't be me! screamed a voice inside my head.

But there was no denying it, the mirror wasn't lying. Obviously, the inactivity from my bout with Epstein-Barr had taken its toll.

I first noticed the effects of the virus in late 1987, when I arrived in Japan for a promotional tour. A group of us had gone to a sushi bar for a late-night dinner on our first evening there, when suddenly the most unbelievable fatigue I'd ever experienced washed over me. I was literally falling asleep at the table. I told my friends I had to go back to the hotel —immediately. I couldn't even finish my meal.

The next morning I felt better, so I wrote the experience off to a bad case of jet lag. When I returned to Los Angeles, however, things went from bad to worse. I was struggling to stay awake for even two hours at a time. I was also having terrible difficulty remembering my lines when I was filming, and suffering from an on-and-off fever, and a severe case of aching joints.

Since I had been an athlete for a good portion of my life, my body was geared to tolerate a certain amount of discomfort, and therefore, I was not one to complain easily. But at the time, behind my competitor's facade, I felt like I was hanging on by a thread. I did my best to hide it from everyone for almost a year, sneaking catnaps where and whenever I could. Finally, I realized I had no choice but to go to a doctor. I was lucky to find a physician who was able to diagnose the cause of my malaise within a week.

He explained that I had Epstein-Barr, a virus that is actually a member of the measles and mumps family. He told me that everyone has the virus in their system, but that no one really knows why it becomes active in one person and not another. Furthermore, he told me that a lot of doctors didn't even believe the disease existed, that there was no known cure, and that the virus would eventually just run its course, which could last any-where from eight months to eight years!

My own battle with the virus affected every aspect of my life. Forget playing tennis, I couldn't even hold the racquet. I didn't feel like going out with friends, or socializing at all for that matter. I just didn't have the strength. I couldn't work for any appreciable period of time, so I ended up taking jobs that only required my participation for a few days in succession, like a commercial or a cameo appearance in a film.

As I stood in front of the mirror, it was painfully clear that no matter what the cause, the result was dramatic in regard to how much my body and my health had been altered. The mirror was telling the whole story, and there was no question in my mind that I had to take some drastic action.

Let's face it, if this were truly a perfect world, every woman would be able to take a pill before she went to sleep and wake up in the morning a perfect size six, thin, strong, and full of vitality.

Unfortunately, this is not a perfect world, and my only option was to find a method of *eating, breathing,* and *exercising* that would be simple to begin, easy to do in light of my fragile physical state, time efficient, and yet one that would allow me to once again feel healthy, vital, and physically fit.

It's interesting that in many aspects, my body had become the physical manifestation for what my life had become, weak and off-track. I realize that my body was reflecting on the outside, what was going on inside: "weight" gain, lethargy, "weak" muscles, "sore" back, and the like. Most of us don't pay attention to these symptoms until life intervenes and forces us to wake up. In my case, it was the mirror screaming reveille!

I had to start somewhere, and when you have nowhere else to go but up, you might as well start at square one. And that's exactly what I did.

As horrifying as it sounds, the first thing I did was take another good look at my body in the mirror. Only this time, I wrote down what I saw, *everything* I saw. Next I began keeping a food diary. Then I wrote down everything I was putting in my body, and how I felt immediately after consuming it. These two exercises provided the first clue to finding the solution to my problem.

The body is the vehicle which carries us through life and the structure that supports our mind as well as our soul. I had never given much thought, however, to the idea that the body is a uniquely designed, intricate machine, and therefore must be cared for as such. Nor did I give much credence to the concept that what you consume affects everything you do, think, and create. Obviously, from what I had written down, and from my diminished physical state, I had a lot to learn.

I was aware that we eat for many reasons other than hunger, (sadness, happiness, frustration, comfort, joy, pain), primarily because, as children, we got into the habit of comforting ourselves with food, and never broke that association.

The question was how to break my own pattern of dysfunctional eating. How was I going to find out which foods made me feel the strongest, and then incorporate the habit of eating them on a consistent basis? I personally didn't have to search very long or hard to find one of the primary sources of trouble in my eating habits.

The evidence was in my refrigerator.

I took a look inside, and believe me, the truth awaiting there was eye-opening. I'm almost embarrassed to say what I found, and I had always considered myself a relatively healthy eater.

In addition to the normal staples and condiments, the predominant feature was, believe it or not, burritos.

A plethora of burritos, from shelf to shining shelf. And these were not just any burritos, but bean-and-cheese burritos. And not just any bean-and-cheese burritos, but only the ones from 7-Eleven. Only the ones with *lard* in them.

Because of the lingering effects of the virus, I just didn't have the strength to go to a regular market or out to restaurants for other food choices. I rationalized that even if someone else did the shopping, I wouldn't have enough energy to prepare the food at home. And even if someone offered to do the cooking, it probably wouldn't have mattered, because the pull toward my favorite bean burritos had become a well-ingrained "habit" during my battle with Epstein-Barr. I loved Mexican food anyway, the burritos were easy to heat up, and they seemed inexplicably comforting to my body. Eventually, their emotional hold on me had become too strong to resist.

Now I'm sure the bean part of this 7-Eleven burrito, has some minute amount of protein left in it, sandwiched, of course, between the additives and the lard. But, when the strange-looking processed cheese is added to the mix, undeniably, I couldn't have chosen a worse meal. I look back in amazement at how I, the athlete, could possibly have succumbed to this severe case of dietary amnesia. At the time, however, I felt miserable and wanting to eat anything was a blessing. Consequently, whenever I was hungry, I would simply reach for one or two burritos from my stockpile in the freezer, put them into the microwave, and chow down.

If I had to limit myself to only one food, I suppose bean burritos weren't the worst food I could have chosen, but they were certainly close to it. In terms of the fat grams alone, they were horrendous—about twenty-five grams per burrito! Multiply that by three meals a day and, well, you get the picture. I should have just taken the one hundred fifty grams of fat and injected it straight into my thighs.

With the help of the mirror, I began to see that my eating patterns were not only inhibiting my healing process, but were also ensuring the future degeneration of my body. I couldn't get well or in shape eating in this manner. I had to find a new way to think about food—and a new way of eating, in spite of what my taste buds were demanding. Although I dreaded the idea, I had to educate myself about nutrition.

The first place I looked was my own bookshelf and I found one dusty volume on the subject, which my doctor had recommended I purchase at the time of my diagnosis. It was *The Immune Power Diet* by Dr. Stuart Berger.

Not all of his nutritional principles were appropriate for my particular situation, but I learned some extremely valuable information about the immune system and how to fortify it for optimum health. Dr. Berger's philosophy opened an important door to my awareness of the subject and of nutrition in general.

I began reading other books and articles on the subject as well. From magazines like *Health and Fitness, Prevention, Life Extension,* and even *Cosmopolitan,* I soaked up everything I could. I had no choice but to become my own teacher. My life depended on it.

The first thing I noticed was the amazing number of conflicting "facts" on the subject: calories count, calories don't count . . . eggs are bad, eggs are good . . . too much fat, not enough fat . . . food combining is important, food combining means nothing. . . .

I soon realized I needed someone who could help me gather the information necessary to design a specific eating plan that I could incorporate into my life. I needed a qualified nutritionist. Trial and error would be a natural part of the process, but I was determined not to get discouraged.

During my search for a professional, I began to experiment on my own. I started writing down specifically what happened to my body immediately after I ate different kinds of foods. Did I feel invigorated? Did I feel sluggish? Did I get a headache? Did I get a stomachache? Did I feel bloated? Did I feel more alert? I kept an active list of the results, and soon I began to eliminate foods that did not produce the physical results I wanted.

I also started keeping a small notepad in my purse to jot down an article or piece of information that seemed helpful. In other words, I was developing my own personalized list of nutrition tips. (See page 232).

When I began to venture out to restaurants once again, it was obvious that I couldn't just order straight from the menu. The foods there were often cooked with sauces and other additions that were contrary to what I knew I should eat. Besides, it was too easy to fall back into my old patterns of choosing a meal based on how I was feeling at the moment, as well as my tendency toward going on automatic pilot in terms of ordering. I also found that certain foods actually triggered my hunger pangs beyond control. I decided the only solution was to choose exactly what I was going to eat *before* I entered the restaurant. It was imperative for me NOT to look at a menu. *Menus,* when pronounced phonetically, have the same pronunciation as the word menace. Menus = Menace. This is a great tidbit to help instill the idea permanently.

The satisfaction of these important first steps spurred me to search for more information. I went to health food stores, yoga classes, and gyms, and began to ask questions. I kept my eyes and ears open for any new helpful hints that crossed my path.

One spark of inspiration hit me while I was taking a walk on Venice Beach. Standing about twenty yards away was one of those beefy bronzed bodybuilders that you see in muscle magazines. He was a solid mass of brawn without an ounce of fat on his rippling body.

He must know the secret to nutrition and a lean healthy body, I thought, so I approached him.

I introduced myself, explained my plight, and after giving me a few tips on the spot, he suggested I go over to Gold's Gym to learn more.

I'd been there several times in the past, working out with some of my friends like Marcus Allen, Arnold Schwarzenegger, and Carl Weathers. When you step inside the door, it's immediately evident why it has gained its reputation as the "muscle capital of the world" not only for bodybuilders, but for professional athletes as well.

As I walked inside, it all came back. This was a gym! No frills. No fancy decor. There were only men, women, and machines, and the smell of sweat permeating the air.

Several people asked me to join them in a little workout session, but I could not have pumped iron if my life depended on it. So I politely declined, and instead turned to the man at the reception desk and asked if he knew anyone who was a specialist in the area of proper eating habits for optimum body tone and vitality. He told me about Cathy Sassin Smith and her husband Billy, the team that handles nutrition for the gym itself.

They were located adjacent to the main building, so I decided to pay them a visit. Their office was businesslike, simply furnished, yet literally crammed with every conceivable piece of material regarding nutrition: books, products, pamphlets, and videos. I'd struck a gold mine of information.

I introduced myself and explained that I was absolutely determined to get my body well again, and that I had to start from scratch.

"I want to know everything. In particular, what you do to prepare for a bodybuilding show, what foods you eat, what supplements you take, *everything.*"

Since bodybuilding and athletic competition are their lives, they were more than sympathetic when I explained my plight. After three hours in their office, I had almost filled a notebook with facts, nutrition tips, shopping lists, and menu ideas. In particular, they gave me a specific eating plan that a bodybuilder uses during the thirty days prior to a competition. This diet is specifically designed to minimize one's percentage of body fat, while maximizing the percentage of lean muscle mass. (See page 246.) Obviously, no one should undertake this or any other eating plan without the consultation of his or her doctor, but for me, the plan seemed ideal.

Now that I had learned the bulk of what I needed to know concerning proper nutrition, I decided I wanted to find someone who could teach me how to prepare relatively nonfat, high protein, healthy meals.

My friend, Larry Otting, introduced me to Jean Louis and Lynn Cowan, a couple who specialize in preparing dishes for serious bodybuilders and ardent fitness buffs. I made an appointment, and they came over to my house for what I thought was going to be an explanation of what they did. Before I knew it, however, they were going through every inch of my refrigerator and cupboards, showing me why certain foods were healthy and certain foods were not. Without any warning, they started tossing all of the unhealthy items into several large garbage bags that they had brought with them. I was too shocked to say anything, but they certainly had my attention.

I thought I had a reasonably healthy kitchen, but that was exposed as a myth when Jean Louis and Lynn began collecting any food item, spice, or condiment that contained chemicals, additives, high levels of fat, or sugar. I stood there gaping as they tossed bottles, cans, and packages into the large plastic receptacles: Into the garbage went the ketchup (loaded with sugar), the mayonnaise (high fat), the entire frozen-food section (too many chemicals), even the whole-wheat bread (sugar) and the diet hot chocolate (chemicals).

They were working their way from one end of my kitchen to the other. In addition, they made me read the label of each particular item that had to be tossed out. Before long, the cupboards were bare. My refrigerator looked brand new . . . and totally empty.

"If you don't know what you're eating, how can you have any control over your health?" Jean Louis asked.

Good question, but I had a strange urge to reach up and put my hands firmly around his neck.

Finally, they had finished. All I could do was watch in amazement as they proceeded to put *three* bulging garbage bags of cans, bottles, boxes, and other discarded foods into the trunk of their car. They wouldn't even leave them in my trash cans.

"We've tried that before," they said, "but people get pretty desperate, and we've seen them dig through the trash to retrieve their favorite goodies."

"That's unbelievable," I replied, covering the fact that I would have done exactly the same thing.

As Jean Louis and Lynn left, they told me they'd return at the end of the week.

"We're going to take you shopping to replace everything we've taken out of your kitchen. We'll substitute them with *healthy* alternatives," Jean Louis said as he climbed into his car. "But we're booked until Friday, so we'll see you then."

"Wait a minute!" I called after them as they drove down the street. "What do I do until Friday? I'm starving!"

I was so ravenous, that I was willing to do anything for a taste of any of my beloved goodies. Isn't it funny that when you're told you can't have something, you want it even more? I'm glad I didn't have anything left to eat at that moment, or believe me, I would've reached for the nearest comfort food and been proud of it!

Walking back into my kitchen, I began searching for any little morsel to appease my emotional as well as physical hunger. All I could find was one small tin of cinnamon and several bottles of sparkling mineral water. Not exactly a feast.

I decided I had to go grocery shopping immediately, at least to pick up enough things to last me until Friday. After my encounter with the food police, however, I knew healthy foods were my only option.

Heading down the first aisle, I happened to pass by the baby-food section. Suddenly, I got an idea. Since I needed to lose nine pounds anyway, why not try some healthy baby food with no additives, preservatives, or sugar? Seemed reasonable and easy to me, and thus was born the Baby Food Diet!

I figured that if it's good enough for an infant, it certainly was good enough for me. I would know exactly what I was putting in my mouth, and furthermore, eating puréed food would give my entire digestive system a chance for some much-needed rest. After all, what could be easier on a body than baby food? The amount I consumed would be easy to control, and I could travel with my meals in my purse. It sounded like such a swell idea: start simple, eat nothing but baby food, begin to heal the body. I proceeded to buy fifty little jars representing every major food group: baby carrots, baby peas, baby veal, baby chicken, baby pasta, baby plums, baby pears, and, of course, baby desserts (sugar-free).

Back in my empty kitchen, I proudly lined up my little bottles in preparation—vegetables in one line, carbos in another, fruits in another, proteins in another, and desserts in the center. Then I settled down to enjoy my first totally healthy baby food lunch. My choice: baby carrots, baby veal, baby peas, and a dessert of baby bananas. It sounded so good! I was excited. I was starving. I opened the first jar, spooned out a mouthful, and dove in.

Ahhhhhhhh!

All I could think was, *maybe it's just the veal that tastes suspiciously similar to puréed cardboard.*

Quickly, I replaced the top on the veal and moved over to the jar of carrots. I even heated them up and added a little cinnamon.

Egads! This is awful, I thought. *Maybe it's not the choice of food, maybe it's just the first spoonful.*

I took two more bites. No, it was awful. I grabbed the baby bananas. I was positive that they would resemble some food I'd eaten before.

First spoon, second spoon, third spoon . . . I sat there dumbfounded. It suddenly became perfectly clear why children grow up dysfunctional. It has nothing to do with society or the breakup of the American family. It has everything to do, however, with the taste of the baby food that they're forced to eat in their early life. It is definitely the seed of all the rebellion that magnifies as they grow older. I have a whole new empathy for juvenile delinquency, because this food could absolutely change the personality of anyone for life. It was more than intolerable. It was disgusting!

But I was desperate, I was famished, and the mirror was still screaming. So believe it or not, I stuck with this infantile-sorry-excuse-for-food regimen until Friday. All I can say is, when Friday finally came, I had never been so excited about going to the market in my life! As for anyone who's even remotely considering trying this diet, *do not,* I repeat, *do not try this at home.* Starting a baby-food regimen without the express written consent of both your doctor and a good psychiatrist is hazardous to your health.

On Friday, Jean Louis, Lynn, my friend Madeline Cummings, and I were on our way to Ralph's grocery store. Jean Louis had picked what he considered a normal market so he could show me what was healthy and available in any average, everyday supermarket.

We began our search in earnest, aisle by aisle, can by can, and bottle by bottle, reading every label and discussing in detail the specific food that was to be accepted or rejected.

First stop: the frozen pizza section, where I stared longingly at a fourteen-inch vegetarian pizza with all the trimmings.

"Take a look at the label," instructed Jean Louis.

Of the fourteen-inch label that appeared on top of the pizza wrapping, approximately eleven inches were devoted to a list of ingredients, most of which I had never even heard of. Basically, three-fourths of that pizza consisted of ingredients that could just as easily have been used in making chalk for all I knew. Other than tomatoes, spice, and veggies, there were at least sixteen different chemical names that I couldn't even pronounce. Now I knew that this was not the optimum health food, but I must admit that I had no idea of the amount of nonfood substances that were added to something as simple as a frozen pizza.

I was amazed that we found a great tasting, healthy alternative to not only the pizza, but also for about 95 percent of what had been trashed from my kitchen earlier in the week. From spices without salt, to twelve-grain bread with no sugar, to nonfat, no-sugar ketchup, to eggless mayonnaise, to sugar-free, all-fruit jam. The array of alternatives was amazing. (See pages 234–238 for shopping list.)

Try this in a grocery store near you. If they don't have the foods you need, talk to the manager and make some specific requests. Soon, you will realize that eating healthy foods, and eating with the intention of creating the maximum benefits for your body, is a lot easier than you ever imagined!

As we continued our market survey, I felt as though I was back in college. I was taking notes as fast as I could write. I jotted down how to make the best waffles in the world with four freshly ground grains that can be bought anywhere. Simply mix the flours together in a bowl with a little soy or rice milk and cook them in the same amount of time it takes to toast a frozen waffle. Best of all, I was even able to go back to eating burritos! Only this time, I learned how to make healthy ones: Rosarita nonfat refried beans with green chilis, rolled in nonfat tortillas with a little fresh salsa—absolutely delicious. I found a substitute for my beloved pumpkin pie: Take the uncooked pumpkin pie mix, add all the spices, use low-fat milk, egg whites, and bake it in a low-fat graham cracker crust. Pretty soon I realized I didn't even need the crust at all. I could simply eat the pumpkin pie mix cold from the refrigerator, right out of the can. You wouldn't find it on the dessert menu at Spago's, but it's absolutely fantastic. It's low-fat and loaded with fiber.

Little by little, I was beginning to substitute all of my negative food choices with healthy alternatives, and soon had found replacements for every food I'd ever loved. Now, of course, eating this way has become a part of my everyday lifestyle, and I can't imagine living any other way.

Not only that, as I changed my eating habits, my thoughts about food changed as well. I began to see food as a "gift" that was provided for my well-being. As a champion shopper from way back, I figured why not shop for food the way I shop for clothes. Now I seek out the best of the lot at whatever price I can afford. Eating is no longer about satisfying unconscious patterns or emotional cravings. It's about fortifying my body with as much "live" food as I can get. In other words, I eat food that once grew in the ground, has a high water content, and inherently cleanses me, rather than clogs me. I ask myself if the food is going to give me energy, and if it will provide the optimum fuel for my machine. Put simply, in regard to eating food, I developed the new habit of demanding the very best for myself.

I also picked up several more tricks of the trade.

First, I learned to ban the knife and fork from my table and use chopsticks instead. They limit what I can eat, and force me to take my time. Also, using a knife and fork, the same utensils we have used all our lives, tends to put me on automatic pilot during a meal. With chopsticks, I am forced to think about each and every bite.

I also learned to use pepper and other spices instead of salt. For some reason, pepper made me feel full more quickly. Some people might think this is simply a matter of mental deception. But I know it works, so I don't argue. I just do it. (See pages 232–233 for Nutrition Tips).

After this first stage of realigning the amounts and types of foods I was eating, I was still bothered by headaches and lethargy. Sometimes, even though we're eating the best possible foods in terms of caloric intake, proper vitamins and minerals and a low-fat, high-fiber, and high-protein content, we might still be eating some foods that do not agree with us. The body could be allergic, so to speak, to certain items you're eating, regardless of their nutrient value. I learned this from Dr. Murray Susser, a wonderful M.D. and natural health practitioner. He told me about the Meridian Valley Clinic Lab in Kent, Washington, which is reputed to be one of the premier laboratories in the country for the purpose of testing for possible food allergies. The process is simple: Any lab takes your blood, and then your doctor instructs them to mail it to the Meridian Lab. The complete package of results is returned to your doctor within two to three weeks. I figured it was worth a shot, and that the proof would be in the results.

Dr. Susser was not talking about allergies in the normal sense. He was talking about reactions to certain foods that produce adverse physical symptoms in your body such as indigestion, fatigue, headaches, muscular aches, irritated skin, and brittle hair. These conditions are generally not permanent, so if you abstain from eating those particular foods that are causing the reactions for a period of time, the body has a chance to heal and the offending foods may be reintroduced. What the lab does is rate about five hundred different types of foods from zero to three thousand as to the degree, if any, you are allergic to that particular food. There are four categories: no problem, eat not more than once or twice a week, eat sparingly, and never eat.

My own results showed I had been indulging in some foods that ranked very high in my never-eat category: mustard, mushrooms, kale and casein (a milk protein found in cheese, yogurt, milk, and ice cream). Although I had never eaten kale to the best of my knowledge (unless it was on that frozen pizza), the other three culprits had been a regular part of my daily menu!

Slowly but surely, I continued to discover not only what my body would or wouldn't tolerate, but also what made it run at its optimum level. I noticed that shortly after I began excluding the culprit foods, my headaches and indigestion disappeared. I wasn't as tired, and I could concentrate longer. The texture of my skin changed, and my hair became fuller and more lustrous. I didn't seem to crave those foods that had been causing the problems in the first place. I was nourishing myself back to wellness and full strength.

I continued to work hard to ensure my freedom, once and for all, from the vicious cycle of unhealthy eating habits. Did I slip? Of course, but very seldom, and never unconsciously. Do I slip now? Of course. But certainly less often, and never unconsciously. This is important, because once you become aware and in control of what you put in your mouth, you will have a big head start on the road to a long, vital life.

In addition to everything I'd learned, however, I needed to address one final element. With the unbelievable demands made upon us in our busy lives, not to mention the pollution everywhere around us, I felt I also needed a good-quality, totally natural, multivitamin/mineral supplement. There were also some new, natural substances, that according to current research, were anti-aging, immune boosting, and extremely beneficial to the body. I chose those I felt were important for my particular health needs, and added them to my daily regimen as well. (See page 238–245.)

To ensure I get enough protein on a daily basis, I also make a drink every morning which includes: two heaping tablespoons of vegetable protein (twenty-six grams), fresh juice, a ripe banana, ice, two tablespoons extra-virgin *cold-pressed* olive oil (alleviates dry skin), and fresh or fresh-frozen (without syrup or sugar) raspberries or strawberries—all blended together. It's a great way to start the day, without the bloat of a large, high-fat/high-carb breakfast, or the hunger pains which result from eating nothing. If you eat something in the morning, fruit in particular, with the addition of an easily digestible protein source, your body begins its cycle of digestion immediately, rather than waiting one or two hours after your noon meal. It felt great to get my body moving first thing in the morning, both inside and out!

To round out my nutritional program, I also included a vitamin B-12 shot every week or so, as a natural energizer and immune-system builder.

When you've lost your health as I did, and are desperate to regain your vitality and strength, you seek all the information possible to assist you in healing. My search also brought me in contact with what is often called the other side of medicine, or *alternative medicine.*

From everything I've learned regarding both sides of the medical question, it makes sense to me to have conventional medicine and alternative medicine working hand in hand as a mutually beneficial force.

Alternative medicine is more of a preventative measure—a way of looking at your body as an engine that needs to be kept in top mechanical (physical) shape. It also is a resource for solutions to health problems seemingly unsolvable by more conventional medical means.

Conventional medicine, on the other hand, plays an important role in diagnosis, surgery when needed, and acute medical emergencies.

It's unfortunate that most medical schools do not include the study of nutrition or alternative healing methods as part of their curriculum. I'm sure many conventional physicians would love to have information to give their patients that would help keep them in optimum health—information that would enable their patients to better guard against the need for more drastic measures down the road. Alternative medicines have been around for thousands of years in various forms, and personally, I have found them to be particularly helpful in preventing problems before they start.

After a few short months of healthy eating and taking supplements, I not only began to notice a remarkable difference in my health, but perhaps even more important, I had the desire to move again. I actually wanted to exercise, and I wanted to shake off the remaining shackles of my illness. I was ready and willing, but was my body able?

11
The Birth of a "Natural" Athlete

I hear and I forget.
I see and I remember.
I do and I understand.
                Aikido saying

When one is willing and eager, the gods join in.
                Aeschylus

Although my body was responding amazingly well to the change in my eating habits, and I seemed much stronger, I still felt like a cross between the Tin Man of Oz and the Pillsbury Doughboy. My joints were beyond rusty and my bulges were definitely still bulging. I needed to get moving again, no matter what. I had been a highly trained athlete, but I had never really paid attention to physiology or the specifics of proper exercise. Now, I had no choice.

Since I wasn't yet able to tackle a full-blown physical program, none of my previous regimens were appropriate. Somehow I had to find a different way of exercising. I had to redefine for myself one of the most cursed words in the English language: E-x-e-r-c-i-s-e.

It's amazing how these eight little letters can conjure up such pronounced images of drudgery and pain for all of us. No wonder we don't want to do it. And, in light of my present physical condition, I didn't want to do it either. If I were going to get back on track physically, it was obvious I would have to create a new understanding of the word that was consistent with what I felt I could actually do. I had no choice but to erase everything and start over.

Shortly after this realization, an amazing coincidence occurred, the significance of which I wouldn't fully realize until further down the road. I was out to dinner with some pals at a local restaurant, when I noticed a book sticking out of my friend's backpack. I pulled the paperback out because the title, *The Warrior Athlete* by Dan Millman, caught my attention. I was curious and began to leaf through the pages. Noticing my interest, my friend, Jackson Sousa, told me to take it home, which I did.

The book opened the door to a whole new understanding of exercise and what it really meant to be an athlete. It was a road map geared toward reaching full potential as a "natural" athlete. The author felt there were four attributes that had to be developed by anyone wishing to attain physical health in this natural manner: strength, suppleness, sensitivity, and stamina. But Millman's approach to these four areas, however, was unique because it incorporated the laws of nature. In that regard, he stressed the importance of incorporating nonresistance, accommodation, balance, and moving with the natural flow of life, in order to achieve the full benefits of any exercise endeavor.

It made sense. If you look at a baby learning to walk, you see that he or she stands up and falls down over and over and over. But, he keeps repeating the process because his desire to move is natural to him. There's no specific technique the baby uses, he just knows that he wants to get up and move and proceeds to accomplish that task in any way he can.

I decided I would begin in precisely the same manner. I would forge ahead with no specific structure or routine, relying solely on my desire to get moving again. I took a deep breath and started in.

Funnily enough, the first thing I noticed was how good it felt to take that deep breath! I guess I'd never paid attention to, or had any reason to pay attention to, breathing before. Was it a key to my physical recovery?

I wasn't sure, but I wanted to find out more about the connection breathing had to one's overall health.

I discovered that the basic underlying "food," in terms of our health and physical fitness, is the air we breathe. Oxygen circulating throughout the body is what nourishes and cleans the blood. In turn, that blood nourishes and cleans the organs and muscles in our body. It is also a crucial unifying link between the mind and the body. Dan Millman writes that "*inspiration,* in addition to its usual connotation, also means 'to breathe in.'" *Inspiration* is what it takes to start anything, including your path toward ultimate physical fitness. And though breathing is relatively simple to do, of course, learning to do it correctly is what makes the difference. (See page 247.)

As I began to practice this natural breathing, not only did it feel wonderful, but I became more and more conscious of the increased energy I had after doing it. I could feel the blood flowing throughout my body, creating this pure, calm, focused energy, an energy I'd forgotten I had.

This was particularly interesting to me because when I was an athlete, I was regularly chastised by my coach for holding my breath. Instead of breathing naturally *through* my serve or *through* my overhead on the tennis court, I'd gotten in the habit of retaining the air I'd gulped until the last possible moment. I noticed how much tension was released and how much energy emerged in its place when I continued the oxygen flow throughout any physical movement I was doing.

After about a week of this practice, I began to incorporate more and more of this breathing technique into my normal breathing pattern. I was getting in tune with my whole body again and becoming aware of the physical part of myself as a single unit.

I started to think of oxygen as nature's perfect food, because when you breathe, you are actually taking in the very essence of life. You can feel it, and your body reacts almost instantaneously. I realized that the air I was taking in was truly a gift, and that that gift equaled *inspiration.* It's the best meal you will ever consume.

But no one can achieve total fitness by breath alone. Eventually, you have to step up to the plate. In my search for someone who could help me incorporate the principles of *The Warrior Athlete* into some type of specific physical program, I followed up on a tip I'd received concerning a Beverly Hills workout specialist named Mike Abrams. I was a little concerned because I'd heard he was seventy-three years old. But supposedly he could take anyone from wherever they were to optimum fitness for their particular body in a very short period of time. He also designed each program based on the client's individual needs. The final coup de grâce, as far as I was concerned, was that each session lasted only twenty minutes! Although I couldn't have even struggled through a *five*-minute workout program at the time, I figured I could at least learn something.

So, I made an appointment.

The voice on the other end of the telephone was firm and terse. In a "just-the-facts-ma'am" tone, he gave me his address and some instructions.

"Take the elevator to the fifth floor, then up two flights of stairs to the penthouse," he said. "Oh, and one more thing, run up the steps."

Run up the steps? I thought. There was no way I was going to be able to run up two flights of stairs, but I figured he'd never know one way or the other, so I went ahead and confirmed the appointment.

I have to tell you right now that I did not run up the stairs on my first appointment. Nor on the second. I was out of breath just *walking* up one flight. Nevertheless, I made it up to the penthouse and announced my presence by squeezing an old-fashioned horn that hung directly to the left of Mr. Abrams' door. Startled by the loud "Oooga, Oooga" that seemed to ring throughout the entire building, I timidly sat down in the only empty chair next to his "office." His next victim was waiting.

A few minutes later, the door swung open. Ron Meyer—the former Creative Artists Agency co-founder, now the powerful head of MCA/Universal—strolled out with a smile on his face and sweat on his brow.

"Oh, you'll just love him, Cathy Lee, he's great," said Meyer, as he headed for the stairs. Running, of course.

I walked into a moderately large room that had been set up like a gym.

It was, however, like no gym I'd ever seen. There were some workout machines, but also a large stretching area, a padded table, and various other strange-looking training apparatus.

Mr. Abrams looked normal at first glance and possessed an air of absolute confidence. He didn't say a word of greeting, but stood in front of me for at least one full minute, looking me up and down. Suddenly, he turned on his heel, and walked over to one of the biggest machines in the room. He placed the pin at the bottom of the set of weights, sat down, and began lifting the entire stack with only his neck!

I was dumbfounded. If I had any thoughts about his age negatively affecting his athletic prowess, they were completely erased from my mind. That was his plan, of course.

"C'mere, I want to show you something," he barked, walking to his desk.

He handed me some pictures of himself in his bodybuilding days. Before me were photographs of a typical muscle-bound, vein-popping, bronzed behemoth. I couldn't believe that this long, lean, tightly-toned man standing before me was the same man in the pictures.

"Since I learned to exercise in a more natural way, I'm twice as strong as I was back then," he said. "The difference is that now I'm using my full body in sync with my own natural rhythm. Consequently, I'm agile and balanced, as well as being strong as an ox."

Charming. This was obviously not a man for small talk.

I decided to get to the point quickly: "Mr. Abrams, I want you to know that I can't do much in the way of exercise yet," I explained, "because I've had Epstein-Barr and . . ."

"None of that means a hill o' beans to me," he barked. "Just do what I tell you and your body will respond."

I certainly wasn't going to argue with this man, so I figured the best thing to do was to follow his instructions until I could escape. What was twenty little minutes anyway? Boy, would I soon find out!

First, he took me to the doorway. I thought perhaps I'd failed some type of preliminary test and he was sending me on my way. Instead, he showed me how to open my chest cavity by stretching in a doorway. (See page 249). It was a method of expanding the lungs to achieve full breathing capacity.

"Breathe, and every part of you lives," he blustered, "don't breathe and every part of you dies!"

The jury was still out on Mike Abrams, but I was willing to go through the trial and error to find out if there was anything I could learn from him.

After showing me some exercises to help keep my back limber and my hips aligned, he asked me to walk across the room.

Though perplexed by the request, I did as I was told.

"You're walking like a truck driver," he said.

Nothing like a good compliment to raise your self-esteem! Before I could utter a word of complaint, however, he had deftly pulled my shoulders back, tucked my elbows in loosely to my sides, and showed me how to use my feet to "propel" my body forward in a graceful, almost loping fashion.

The result was amazing. I had never really looked at the way I walked, and using his techniques did make a big difference. Not bad.

Next, we progressed to some strength exercises. I tried to ask as many questions as possible during this portion of the session, praying that any conversation would help burn up the allotted twenty minutes, thereby preserving what little energy I had left. Abrams explained that the number of repetitions you do does not directly equal good results. What makes the difference is *how* you do each particular movement. The key is to concentrate only on the muscle(s) being used. If you don't know which muscles are being engaged during a certain exercise, make sure you find out. This way, you can put your mind as well as your body to work.

Precisely at the end of twenty minutes, Mike barked, "That's it. You want another appointment?"

Unfortunately, because of the omnipresent gaping hole in my wallet, I was only able to afford a few more workouts with Mr. Abrams, but the experience proved invaluable. What I learned from the seventy-three-year-old man, with all his gruffness and rough edges, were the basic elements of strength, suppleness, sensitivity, and stamina and their importance in physical fitness. I actually ended up loving the guy, coarseness and all.

I began to get stronger, and as I did, I started increasing the intensity and variety of the movements included in my amalgam of new exercises. In addition to what Mike had given me, I also incorporated some elements of a warm-up I used to do before competing in a tennis match. This time, these movements were backed by specific knowledge.

Within no time, I had developed a definitive routine of my own. Although I could accomplish little more than five minutes of this program at first, every couple of weeks I was able to add another minute or two.

Just to make sure I wouldn't quit until I had achieved my desired results, providence intervened in the form of a telephone call.

"We'd like you to do an exercise video."

It was Jack Gluck of Century Film Studios in New York with an offer I couldn't refuse. Since I'd never heard of Mr. Gluck, coupled with the fact that offers usually came through my agent, I was somewhat hesitant. But I was in no position to hang up the phone. He obviously was a sharp salesman, and began pitching me a mile a minute.

"You can design your own program, anything you want," he said, "with total creative control and a good percentage of the sales."

People had asked me to do exercise videos throughout my career, but I had always turned them down. I just wasn't interested. Being broke, however, tends to expand one's interests a great deal.

"Send me the contract," I said.

So here I was, embarking on a twenty-minute exercise video that consisted of about twelve more minutes of workout than I could presently deliver without collapsing.

"We'll shoot in eight weeks," said Gluck.

"No problem," I lied.

"And we're gonna call it *The Cathy Lee Crosby 20 Minute Beautiful Body Workout,*" he said, signing off.

I hung up the phone and thought to myself, *I must be out of my mind!*

I had eight weeks to get into top shape, not only in terms of stamina and strength, but also in terms of looking absolutely great in a skin-tight leotard before the unforgiving eye of the camera.

Cue the *Rocky* theme!

Cue everything!

I had a job and I had to deliver!

I hastily summoned my friend, Jeff Gunn, who is a personal trainer. In exchange for a part in the video, he agreed to work out with me at my house for free. He not only was going to get me in shape, but was also committed to helping me define my "program."

It was unbelievably excruciating. I'd do five minutes of my twenty-minute workout, then collapse in bed for an hour's nap. Jeff would come back the next day, and we'd start the process all over again. This went on for the entire two months, right up to the day before the video shoot began. Luckily by then, I was finally able to complete the full twenty minute routine. I still had to take a few naps, but they came fewer and further between.

The good news was that when I put on my leotard, which had been specially designed for the video, I looked great! The bad news was that I had forgotten that videos aren't shot in one take. We would be filming from 8 A.M. until 6 P.M. for two days in a row, repeating the exercises in my twenty-minute routine over and over and over again.

My worst nightmare had come true. In the full glare of the cameras, the world was going to witness the demise of a former professional athlete —me. But I was stuck. What else could I do?

When the first day of shooting came, however, and the cameras were turned on, I simply took a deep breath and walked onto the set as if everything was just fine.

Heaven was on my side, and it took the form of four great-looking guys who had been chosen to appear in the exercise video with me. Thank God my libido wasn't dead. Between the guys and the cameras, I found the needed juice to make it through.

The director, Steve Purcell, yelled "Action," and off we went.

"Hi, I'm Cathy Lee Crosby," I said into the camera, as if I'd never left.

We worked four hours straight, and then they called lunch. It couldn't have come at a better time. Everybody else left to have lunch, but I quickly headed outside to my trailer and a pillow. The next thing I knew there was a knock at my door and a voice saying, "we need you in ten minutes, Cathy Lee." The hour had flown by.

I got a quick touch-up on my makeup and stepped onto the set to begin the grind all over again. By the end of the day, after another five hours of constant exercising for the camera, I literally collapsed into the limousine that the production company had provided for my trip home. Once there, I barely took the time to remove my clothes before dragging myself into bed and falling asleep.

The next day was exactly the same.

After we finished filming, I was in bed for two solid days. I don't remember much more than completing the shoot on Friday night and getting out of bed sometime Monday morning. I had "built my back," "firmed my fanny," "crunched my inner thighs," "begone my jiggle," and "toned my tummy," *ad nauseam.* There wasn't one ounce of physical energy left in my body, or one muscle that wasn't screaming obscenities in my mind.

It took me a week before I could even think about exercising again. But when I did, it was because feeling strong, balanced, and supple was more important than giving in to my temporary soreness.

I still use this program today, in one form or another. The great thing about it is that I can do it anywhere, any time—at home, in a hotel room, on an airplane, in an office, on location, wherever. You don't need any special equipment, or even workout clothes. And, no individual movement lasts longer than ninety seconds when done along with my tape. I think the video's tremendous success is attributable to the fact that natural, everyday movements were incorporated into an easily accessible exercise routine that is only twenty minutes in length. (See specifics of video program on pages 249–254).

My re-examination of the world of exercise led to an understanding of the importance of "natural" physical movement. We spend a great deal of our time attempting either to hurry up or to slow down the river of life, rather than simply flowing with it. Trying to "force" our experience in this manner sets up a turbulence that is felt in the body as tension. Though this tension is a subtle pain, I learned it is a signal that something is amiss. It is a red flag telling us we are out of our natural rhythm. If we do not pay attention to the signs and re-balance ourselves, the result is "disease."

Physical training is simply the *process* by which we keep our systems aligned and balanced in the areas of strength, suppleness, stamina, and sensitivity. By resisting our body's natural rhythm, however, and by failing to accommodate the needs of our present physical condition, we are destined to fail at establishing any kind of enjoyable and successful fitness program.

This knowledge was a far cry from the techniques I had utilized as an athlete in the world of competitive tennis. I wondered if I still would have given up the sport at such an early age, had I been aware of these principles?

At any rate, there was no denying that the strength I was feeling as a natural athlete was far superior to the strength I felt back then. Now, I am aware of a balanced, inward stability, and power that is constantly flowing through my entire body. Back then, my strength appeared only as needed, in response to the physical demands that were placed on it in the moment.

When you begin to move as a single, centered unit in all the physical activities you undertake, you begin to see that there is no tension to stop your energy. You are suddenly free to become more and more aware of everything around you. You feel more alive, and that vitality begins to create its own natural momentum. *Momentum* means "of the moment." Boom! You literally explode forth with the inner joy of the activity, yet are always in balance, and always in control.

There was no doubt that I had taken a major step toward finally healing my body. Rebuilding my health, and reconnecting with the natural athlete within me, opened my eyes to a whole new world. I was looking at everything around me in a way I could never have imagined. The storm had momentarily subsided. The seas were eerily calm.

But just when I thought it was safe to come out of the water, I was thrown back into the height of the squall. I was tossed, head first, straight into the eye of the hurricane. And before I knew what was happening, I was plunging blindly into the deepest levels of my soul.

12
The Road to the Gate

When written in Chinese, the word 'crisis' is composed of two characters—One represents danger, and the other represents opportunity.

John F. Kennedy

Not till your thoughts cease all their branching here and there, not until you abandon all thoughts of seeking for something, not till your mind is motionless as wood or stone, will you be on the right road to the Gate.

Huang Po

It's interesting. Women have made tremendous strides in the last fifty years, particularly in America, but we still don't have the same latticework of history and achievement to fall back on that men have. If a little boy has a dream, for instance, he can easily find other men who have scaled similar heights. He can read about any number of great presidents, writers, statesmen, war heroes, titans in business, heads of state, accomplished athletes, and others who have blazed the trail before him. A thousand fingers can point his way to greatness.

Not having this multitude of legacies, women must *search* for their paths. And that search generally comes from within, simply because the answers are not easily visible in the outside world. Fortunately for future generations, we female baby boomers are vastly increasing the richness of our latticework in progress. This groundbreaking effort, is truly a dichotomy in both its positive and negative effects on those of us who are paving the way.

The downside is that, as trailblazers, we must travel a rocky road with no maps to follow except the ones we must draft ourselves.

On a more positive note, we pioneers have no choice but to trust our intuition, and as I would find out later, live out our destinies shooting from the hip. I personally feel that this is one of the greatest gifts a woman has. Not enough credence is placed on this wonderful natural ability to achieve remarkable results without necessarily having a clear, delineated plan as to how to accomplish them. This phenomenon is facilitated by the fact that most women have built in what I like to call a "Know Meter." We just seem to have a strong, undeniable *sense* about certain things. This knowingness, coupled with the ability to trust what we know, and then having the courage to *act* on that knowledge, is the ultimate definition of power, male or female. This power does not rely upon any outside force to work its magic, so by honing this skill, we are empowering ourselves as the "source" of our own lives. This empowerment reinforces our connection *to* The Source at the same time.

Living in California, I, like most everyone else here, had dabbled in the area of self-improvement. I never had any specific goals in mind, and was certainly not looking for any particular answers. I simply checked out some of the mainstream philosophies for information whenever I needed an emotional boost. It was more curiosity than anything else.

New Age was not a term I would ever have used in describing myself. Those two words conjured up visions of white-robed, zombielike diehards, chanting and "ohming" their way to the top of a mountain somewhere. The whole idea of movements and followers made me extremely uncomfortable. It seemed to me that some of these people were using their quest as a crutch, rather than the bridge it really is. They did not realize that the particular philosophy or belief system they had chosen to follow was merely a facilitating factor meant to guide them toward their own personal enlightenment, rather than it being the actual goal in and of itself.

After the hell I had been through over the last four years since my saga had begun, however, I was desperate to change my luck. Even though I had regained the closeness of my family circle and was physically stronger than I had been in years, I was still faced with the seemingly insurmountable challenges of reigniting my career, re-establishing my bank account, and confronting the continuing onslaught of my courtroom dramas.

I had to find something that would light my way and ease the burden of my circumstances. I couldn't wait a minute longer. So, I began by calling a few trusted friends for advice. I was grateful that they were more than willing to help, and had a specific tidbit or two to throw into the pot.

Gary Marshall, director of the film *Pretty Woman* and brother of Penny Marshall, took me to lunch one day in a gesture of sincere concern.

"Trust me," he said over cold poached salmon. "What you need to do is change your patterns—break out of the chains of your old habits. Take some chances! When something like this happened to me about seven years ago," he continued, "you know what I did? I went to a nudist colony. Try it. It's very liberating—just what you need right now. And don't worry about the naked part, you can visit once without taking your clothes off," he added, trying to soothe my obvious trepidation.

What the heck, I thought. *Maybe he's onto something.*

All I can say is, it was a very short trip. I don't know what Gary learned from his nudist colony experience, but I learned that one of the most absurd sights you could ever see is a nude volleyball game, where the participants are wearing only shoes and socks! I never got past the visual, I just couldn't stop laughing. I decided I'd better leave before they got offended and threw me out. Thanks, Gary!

If that wasn't enough, he called me a few months later, offering another pearl of wisdom.

"You know, the real change in my luck came after I altered my handwriting," he confided. "I don't know if that was the specific reason for my change of fortune, but within a year, I was back on track."

All right, I admit it. I was desperate, and jumped right up to door number two. Waiting for me to knock was a woman who specialized in changing your handwriting. During one of her visits to Los Angeles, I went to the hotel where she was staying, and waited outside her room for my scheduled appointment.

As door number two opened, standing before me was my handwriting guru, an extremely large woman, dressed in a brightly colored, ankle-length floral muumuu, with scarf to match. Shocked by the strange sight before me, I couldn't do anything except follow her into the room. After advising me, among other peculiar hints, to open my c's and lengthen my y's, she assured me that if I went home and practiced these changes, everything would turn around for sure. Needless to say, I opened my c's and lengthened my y's, just in case. As a matter of fact, I'm still opening my c's and lengthening my y's.

Of course, everyone in Los Angeles needs a psychic or two. So, I went psychic shopping. I found my first one on the Santa Barbara pier in her own little shop. She predicted, among other gems, that I was going to have terrible trouble with my brother. She charged me twenty dollars. I don't have a brother. Oh, well.

Maybe the answer was in nature. So I went horseback riding with a Native-American guide, who advised me to "open up and trust the horse." That seemed like an easy thing to do. After all, I was a pretty accomplished equestrian, so why not? What I didn't realize was the extent to which this guide would go to show me the depth of his Indian traditions. After leading me to the top of the highest mountain on the horizon, I found my horse and me literally sliding down a loose dirt hillside, in what he called the "ultimate test of trust between man and animal." He also called it enlightenment. I called it quits.

Another friend insisted that I go and hear a famous channeler. She'd always seemed fairly stable and trustworthy, so I figured what would be the harm of spending a couple of hours in a hotel conference room? I actually liked the guy who was the channeler, but when he closed his eyes and allowed the voice of an ancient "being" to come through him, I simply couldn't focus. I kept wondering if all astral entities spoke with a guttural Scottish accent. To make matters worse, I was sitting next to an acting buddy of mine, Sharon Gless, who was constantly oohing and ahhing. "Isn't he fantastic?" she cooed.

He definitely had a lot to say about the mysteries of life. But frankly, I was looking for something I could use in the next twenty minutes.

Even Lionel Richie had a suggestion. We'd known each other since 1980, but I never would have imagined him telling me that the key to *all* my problems was a particular Australian psychic. Just in case this was the answer I'd been looking for, I gladly accepted her number and phoned immediately. My first clue that the results were not going to turn out as I had hoped should have come when I found out that the telephone call was going to cost me more than the half hour reading. Paying no attention, I forged ahead with my long-distance consultation. She proceeded to tell me that I was in the midst of a turbulent astrological cycle (thanks, Lionel), that Mercury was in retrograde, and that Saturn was sitting on the Sun, or some such explanation. She assured me not to worry, because within three and a half years everything was going to be smooth sailing. Three and a half *years*!? *Don't panic,* I thought to myself, *at least the end is in sight.* Reasonably acceptable news, right? Well, not exactly. A few months later, my Aussie psychic, who I barely knew, showed up at my doorstep in Los Angeles, needing a place to say. Evidently, she had recently divorced her husband, her daughter had tried to commit suicide, and she just wanted a place to "hang out" for a while.

Obviously, Mercury was still in retrograde.

In spite of these early expeditions into the bizarre, more and more fruitful avenues of insight began to cross my path.

I met a man named Moshe Zwang, for instance, a former officer in the Israeli Navy. He is considered the Father of Palm Therapy, and has just released his first book on the subject. Moshe works with the lines in your hands to change deeply embedded negative behavior patterns, and thus altering the direction of your life in alignment with your full potential.

"You've been carrying a burden for a long time," he announced at our first session.

How very psychic! I thought.

After that statement, I was prepared for the worst, but he turned out to be both amazingly accurate and very informative. The most striking result after working with him the first few times, was a dramatic shift in my attitude about the challenging circumstances I was still confronting. After working with Moshe, my path seemed easier to define. It was the first time that I could sense I was actually moving *through* the difficulties facing me, and that the light at the end of the tunnel was getting closer.

There were other valuable experiences that followed, each with their own unique lesson. But something was still missing. I couldn't put my finger on it, but I knew I had to continue with my search in earnest to find the missing link.

Certainly, my life had changed and a whole new awareness had begun to color my experience. But, I had no inkling of the extraordinary odyssey that was about to alter my life forever. An encounter with someone at the "center" of things, that would cast a sacred light on the meaning and importance of everything that had happened to me in the preceding five years. My destiny was about to unfold before me, illuminating my first glimpse of the magical essence of life.

13
Searching for Desert Sage

It is only with the heart that one can see rightly; what is essential is invisible to the eye.

Antoine de Saint-Exupery

I was driving south to visit my mother who lived in Palm Desert. It was a two-and-a-half-hour trip from Los Angeles, and about forty-five minutes before I reached her house, I noticed that my gas needle was plunging toward *empty*. I exited the freeway and drove into a tiny, two-pump gas station in what appeared to be a relatively small town—a throwback to a more innocent age. As I stood there filling my tank, I noticed a bookstore across the street.

I'd been intending to pick up a few publications on health and fitness anyway, so with a few minutes to spare, I thought, why not? I paid for the gas, drove across the street, and parked near the store.

As I stepped through the front door, I was awestruck at the sheer volume of books crowding the shelves, tucked away in every conceivable corner of the room. The store was quite large, with natural light, yet retained a certain flavor of old-world simplicity. There were even a few spots where one could sit in overstuffed chairs and read. The inviting scent of freshly brewed coffee filled the air.

I walked up to the counter and found a rather nerdy-looking young man reading what appeared to be a comic book.

"Excuse me, could you tell me where the health and fitness section is?" I asked.

He looked up from his "reading," stared at me oddly, and then hollered across the store seemingly to no one,

"Hey, you got a customer!"

Within seconds, a rather stout, white-haired imp of a man came bouncing out from somewhere in the bookshelves. He was dressed like a cross between a natty college professor and a corn-fed Iowa farmer, but in every other way, he looked like any clerk you'd find in a bookstore in small-town America.

"Could you help me?" I asked. "I'm looking for the section on health and fitness."

He eyed me in such a strange way, that I thought perhaps he didn't understand English. So I began again, only slower this time and gesturing, in an effort to translate for him.

"Excuse me . . . could . . . you . . . show . . . me . . ."

Peering out through the most amazing blue eyes this side of Paul Newman, he cut me off in midsentence.

"Ah, travel," he replied, proceeding to turn on his boot heels in the opposite direction. "Follow me."

Travel? I thought. *Now I know he doesn't understand English!*

Before I could utter a word of protest, he headed off through a long row of bookshelves, insistently motioning me forward, until we stood in a veritable literary canyon. There were multicolored volumes stacked floor to ceiling.

Aware that I had paused to take in the sight before me, he whirled around and addressed me straight on in a commanding voice.

"You see, the important thing is . . . to be ready at any moment to sacrifice what you are, for what you could become," he declared. Then, as an afterthought, he added, "Charles Dubois, 1953."

"Charles Dubois?" I asked. "Who in the world is that?"

But the little man didn't answer. Instead, he dove into the shelves again and this time came up with a purple volume. He held it out so I could just barely read the title: *The Warrior Athlete* by Dan Millman. Then, snapping the book back before I could tell him that I had already read it, he said, **"Before you can arrive at any destination, you must begin a journey.** Am I correct?"

Unbelievable! I thought. *What have I gotten myself into now? The only English this man speaks, he's memorized from these books! Where do employers find people like this, anyway? How can they hire someone who doesn't understand English to work in a bookstore?*

Unaware of my judgment, the bookstore imp kept right on going. "Do you know how many people have stood in the very spot you're standing on right now?" he asked.

"Well . . . actually, I don't," I said. "Listen, I'm really sorry. But I'm awfully late. You see, I was headed down to my mother's house in Palm Desert and she's expecting me in half an hour. So why don't I come back another time and we can talk."

He let out a deep sigh. "People, " he said with a shrug. "They have no idea where they're going, and only the faintest idea where they've been."

He held out his hands, indicating the walls of books.

"This is the station," he bellowed. "The books are the fuel. And their knowledge is the train that can take you to your destination."

"Sir!" I interrupted. "With all due respect, are you paid by the bookstore to do this? I mean, to stand here and quote all these lines from the books in the store?"

"Oh, no," he said.

"So you don't work here?" I queried.

"Well, actually I do . . . In a manner of speaking, of course," he said.

Great, I said to myself. *Here I am, in the middle of nowhere, with a certified nut case. That's it. I've got to get out of here.*

"Sir, you've been most helpful," I said as I turned to the old man mustering up my last available politeness. "Thanks for everything, but I really must be going."

He didn't answer me, of course. I was convinced he never answered anybody. Although it was obvious by now that he did indeed speak and understand perfect English, this was a man who was definitely utilizing a language all his own.

"The journey you are beginning is always sparked by an awareness that something's missing," he intoned. **"Something's missing because life is an illusion. It's an illusion because it's the creation of your own mind. And that creation is colored by our doubts, fears, desires, and life experiences. So, we figure, figure, figure. We desperately try to make sense of things. But nothing fits, does it?"**

"Well, I'm not sure . . ." I stammered. Then, deciding that the only way out of this mess would be to simply agree with him and take my leave, I added, "You know? You're *absolutely* right, I'd never looked at it that way, thanks for filling me in, and now I really do have to . . ."

"You have worn the robes of success," he interrupted. **"But you are still cold.** In and of itself, success has no meaning to you. But now, you've stepped up to the plate. The pitcher is on the mound, so let's begin."

Completely frustrated by his seemingly inexhaustible supply of metaphors, I blurted out, "Listen, the truth of the matter is I have no idea what you're talking about. Besides, I am very, very late, and I have to get back on the road before my mother begins to worry."

He looked at me quizzically, and then threw up his hands apologetically.

"Oh, I'm *so* sorry, I plumb forgot my manners," he said, convincingly earnest. "The name's Samuel Lewis Hastings. But you can call me Sam. Everybody does."

He graciously extended his hand.

"Pleasure to meet you," he said.

Not wanting to hurt the nice ol' man's feelings any further, I perfunctorily replied, returning the gesture. "Thank you, I'm Cathy Lee, and it's nice to meet you, too. But look . . ."

"Sam," he said.

"Okay Sam. Look, I don't want to be rude, but I simply came in to pick up a couple of books on health and fitness. You know, trying to get back in shape and all. But I was supposed to be in Palm Desert an hour ago, so I must be on my way right now because my mother's expecting me."

With that, I started to leave.

Darting in front of my path, Sam turned and looked into my eyes with an intensity that stopped me cold.

"Wherever there is ruin, there is hope for a treasure . . . ," Rumi said, **"The house has to be destroyed so we can find the great treasure hidden underneath."**

"I couldn't believe it! He'd obviously memorized whole portions of these books, not just a few lines. And while I was extremely uncomfortable and unsure of this strange man's behavior, at the same time, I was becoming more and more curious.

Realizing that he had made a definite impact on my naturally inquisitive nature, Sam quickly grabbed another volume, and with a courtly bow, handed me the book with an almost royal presentation. It had a bright orange cover, on which blazed the words *Living in the Light* by Shakti Gawain.

"All of us must go through a place at one time or another—that mystics call piercing of the veil of illusion," he began. **"It's the point where we truly recognize that our physical world is not the ultimate reality and begin to turn inward, to discover the true nature of our existence. At these times, we usually feel emotionally that we are hitting bottom . . . but actually, we are falling through a trapdoor and into a bright, new world. . . . Only by going fully into the darkness can we move through it into the light."**

He shrugged dismissively. "Damn, I used to know that passage by heart," he grinned. "Sorry, but I had to paraphrase a bit. It's not important, the idea's the same."

His feigned naiveté, was not hitting its mark as far as I was concerned. But he certainly had succeeded in piquing my interest.

Scratching his thick head of white hair, he spoke again. "Oh, yes, I remember now! Viktor Frankel said it perfectly: **What is to give light must endure burning.**"

Warily, I looked around the store to see if anyone else was listening. Was I the only one hearing this? But the store was empty. Everyone had gone. Even the young clerk had retreated to his TV dinner, undoubtedly having heard Sam's diatribe many times before.

"Look . . . what I'm trying to find out . . ." I began.

"Sam!" he exclaimed.

"All right . . . Sam. Listen, who are you anyway? And what are you doing here?

There was no answer.

"Why are you telling me all of this?" I insisted.

He grinned and then spoke in a tone that sounded like someone giving directions.

"It's like this. Sometimes a person has to go down just about as far as they think they can go. And then, you see, they gotta keep going. Because before they know it, the bottom's dropped out, the trapdoor's opened, and they've fallen into a whole new world."

That got my attention. *Did he know what had happened to me? And if so, how could he have possibly found out?* It was true, I had gone down as far as I could go. And yes, the bottom *had* dropped out. But the part about the new world? I didn't have a clue what he was talking about.

"What do you mean *new world?*" I implored. "What do you mean *specifically?*"

"Specifically?" he said. "Ah, let me see, *specifically!*"

With a twinkle in his eye, he turned and walked further down the aisle to a table where he had placed the books he had chosen to show me. I knew by now that this was my cue to follow, and for some reason I did. Running his fingers across the jackets, almost as if his fingertips could read, he grabbed the orange book *Living in the Light* once again, and opened it to show me a particular page.

"Specifically," he chuckled, "page twenty-nine. **The ultimate key is aliveness. The more the universe moves through you, the more alive you feel. Conversely, every time you don't follow your inner guidance you feel a loss of energy, a loss of power, a sense of spiritual deadness."**

My mind was reeling. I felt like I was trying to put together a giant jigsaw puzzle, and couldn't even find the first two pieces that fit.

"Are you telling me that we're supposed to do whatever we sense is right, simply because the feeling comes to us?" I asked.

"In a manner of speaking, yes," he said. "To an unenlightened mind, yes."

"But that's impossible," I said. "If you don't know where you're going, how can you achieve anything? There's no structure, no direction, no desire, and therefore, no results. Where do all these things come into play? How can you merely function on "instinct" alone and achieve anything worthwhile?"

"Ah," he said. "That question is not for me to answer. It is part of your journey. **This world was created as a place to learn. It is our playground, our school and our artist's studio. We are here to learn how to consciously channel the creative energy of the spirit and of the Divine into physical form.**"

An earnest expression washed over his face as he parked himself on top of an old worn step stool standing in the aisle.

"Of course, you set goals," he said. "You have to have a destination in mind to be able to figure out where you're goin'. But you can't be ruled by those goals, and you can't be boxed in by them either. That takes all the surprise and the electricity and the fun out of life. It also lessens your power. When you begin to practice tuning in to your intuition and acting on it, no matter what, life literally comes "alive" with possibility. When you let go of the control, and surrender to the natural energy and flow of the universe, you are directly plugged into The Source, and therefore, to all the power within you."

"Wait a minute," I straightened. "You're telling me that I'm supposed to literally *sense* what I need to do, and then just do it without a second thought? Well, that might be fine if you live in a cloistered monastery somewhere. But if you have to live here in the real world, you can't be so footloose and fancy free. You'd never have any control over the results, and you'd never get anything accomplished."

"You can't afford not to," he countered. And then, in a gentle yet extremely pointed manner, he added, "You have been given the gift of life and it is available to you at every moment. What you choose to do with that gift is your business."

Before I could respond, he had turned back to the bookshelf. "It takes courage to stay centered in your heart, living your life shooting from the hip," he said over his shoulder.

I could only stare blankly at the figure before me. I was almost numb from the experience of my encounter with him. But as for Sam, he seemed totally energized. He was practically dancing in the aisles, darting from book to book, as if merely touching their jackets as they stood erect on the shelves was allowing him to reconnect with their magic. He continued to recite multiple passages in rapid succession, each time choosing the exact words that struck a deep chord within me.

For some unknown reason, I was no longer afraid of this country wordsmith, and in fact, was becoming strangely entranced by him. I felt like I was watching a master performance artist at work, an aged Robin Williams in bookstore-clerk drag.

With neither preamble nor pause, he forged straight ahead.

"Ever heard of Fernando Botero, the Colombian artist?" he asked, breaking through my thoughts like a hot knife through butter. Turning my attention to a hand-carved wooden plaque hanging on the wall, he quoted Botero's words without so much as a glance in their direction. **"When you start a painting, it's somewhat *outside* of you. At the conclusion, you seem to move *inside* the painting."**

"And of course . . . Eugene, I've been forgetting all about you, haven't I?!" he continued, reaching across me to touch the spine of a thick art book. "Eugene Delacroix! Now, there's an artiste! **What moves men of genius, or rather what inspires their work, is not *new* ideas, but their obsession with the idea that what has already been said, is still not enough."**

Fully enjoying his own creativity, he jumped to another section of the shelves. "Or you might prefer Degas," he quipped. "Yes, of course! Rich with understanding, movement, and passion! He's perfect for you! **Only when he no longer knows what he is doing, does the painter do good things."**

He laughed again as if relishing this private joke, then bolted to the end of the entire section. **"Life shrinks or expands in proportion to one's courage**—Anaïs Nin," he continued.

"Paul Gauguin: **I shut my eyes in order to see."**

Then wildly pointing to yet another book he recited eloquently: "Amos Ferguson: **I paint not by sight but by faith. Faith gives you sight."**

He was totally consumed, and I was dizzy from just watching the spectacle exploding before me. This venerable enchanter was filled with a passion I hadn't experienced in a long, long time. Not only did he know the passages, but he seemed to know the entire books as well. I got the feeling that he almost lived amongst their pages, as if they were a part of his soul. The mere thrill of touching them seemed to electrify him.

"Hold on to your hat!" he practically shouted. "We're just gettin' started."

I looked at my watch. I was extremely late and wondered if I should call my mother. But I knew Mom would understand and would want me to stay and listen.

"I don't suppose you're Jewish," he cackled. "The Talmud is a pretty amazing piece of work. **Every blade of grass has its Angel that bends over it and whispers, 'Grow, grow.' "**

He smiled at me warmly.

"You're in luck, my dear," he said, once again picking up on my thoughts perfectly. "I've got plenty of time to *whisper* this afternoon."

In that instant, I became aware of Sam, the person, for the first time. I no longer focused so much on his strange manner, or his rather odd-looking clothes. Instead, I began to see his warm, joyous nature shining so brilliantly that it overshadowed any of my remaining judgments or doubts.

"Never mind the title of this one," he said, interrupting my musings. This, of course, brought my attention immediately to the words printed

on the front of the book he was holding in his hands: *The Pathwork of Self-Transformation* by Eva Pierrakos.

He began to shuffle the pages like a card dealer. "Oh, yes, here it is," he said. **"For those feeling uncertain, here is the key."** Finding the page he was looking for, he handed me the book and asked if I would read it aloud.

Through the gateway of feeling your weakness lies your strength.
Through the gateway of feeling your pain lies your pleasure and joy.
Through the gateway of feeling your fear lies your security and safety.
Through the gateway of feeling your loneliness lies your capacity to have fulfillment, love and companionship.
Through the gateway of feeling your hopelessness lies true and justified hope.
Through the gateway of accepting the lacks in your childhood lies your fulfillment now.

"About as good as apple pie, isn't it?" he said.

After a long pause, I turned to Sam and connected in a way I could not have anticipated. "Do you think a person's journey through fear and pain is truly the doorway to happiness?" I asked.

"I'm saying nothing," he replied with a knowing smile, as if acknowledging a secret just between the two of us. "I'm just a bookstore clerk. All I know is what I read."

He began to laugh the freest, most genuinely funny laugh I'd ever heard. It was contagious. We both began to howl. He was obviously orchestrating a game that he realized I had no idea how to play, and he was having a ball. I felt he was throwing only the basic "rules" at me, just to see how long it would take me to figure out how to play. He must have known that I was athletically inclined, because he had woven his web in the form of a game. What better way to focus my normally wandering attention.

"Sam, can I ask you another question? Am I the only one who can see you? I mean, are you *real?*"

"Well, I sure hope so!" he chuckled. "'Cause my car's going to look pretty strange driving down the road with nobody in it. I'm as real as you are. A good, solid hunk of muscle and bone. Only difference is, I know how to pan for gold."

Just when I thought I was getting the hang of this, he had lost me completely.

"Pan for gold?" I asked.

"Yep," he nodded. "You know, alchemy. You've heard of alchemy, haven't you?"

"Well," I stammered. "I've heard the word but . . ."

Without a pause, he chimed in, "A medievel chemical science aimed at achieving the transformation of base metals into gold. Or, the transformation of something common into something special."

He grinned a prospector's grin. "Some people call it magic, I suppose."

He quickly flashed a purple book cover.

"The Alchemist, by Paulo Cohelo, an insightful fable about the quest to fulfill one's destiny," he continued, weaving his own thread of unique luminosity. **"No heart has ever suffered when it goes in search of its dreams, because every second of the search is a second encounter with God and with eternity."**

That's it! That's the final straw! I thought to myself.

How could he possibly have known the perfect arrow to pierce my heavy armor? After a few moments of stunned silence, I suddenly felt the urge to tell him everything—every single little detail about what had been happening to me over the last five years . . . the losses, the illness, the bankruptcy, the lawsuits. But before I could get a word out of my mouth, he aimed his crystal-clear blue eyes directly into mine in a way that let me know he already knew. Again, it stopped me cold.

"What you need to understand is this: **Before a dream is realized, the Soul of the World tests everything that was learned along the way. . . . That's the point at which most people give up. It's the point at**

which, as we say in the language of the desert, one 'dies of thirst' just when the palm trees have appeared on the horizon."

The absolute truth of his words echoed in the deepest part of my heart. I felt weak. I looked for something to lean on, but there were no posts or pillars nearby. Taking a couple of steps backward, I literally fell into one of the upholstered chairs I'd seen on my way in. For the first time since I had stepped inside the bookstore, maybe even for the first time in my life, I was absolutely filled with an overwhelming sense of the meaning of our life on this earth. The particulars weren't totally evident, or even important. But at last I could see the whole picture, once and for all. I finally realized what the jigsaw puzzle would look like as a finished picture.

Good old Sam, however, this eccentric, yet compelling bookstore sage, kept right on rolling. He had me on the ropes and wasn't about to let me get away.

"You see, as the old woman in *The Alchemist* said, **'You came so that you could learn about your dreams, and dreams are the language of God.' "**

My head was spinning with the profoundness of it all. But Sam didn't stop for rest.

"When you want something," he continued, **"all the universe conspires in helping you to achieve it."**

I was trying desperately to understand the complexities of this newly felt sense of awe and wonder.

"But Sam!" I exclaimed. "I don't know what I want! I used to think I knew what I wanted. But somehow, I've forgotten."

"Not a problem. Not a problem!" he repeated. "Just decide to go forward and seek your treasure. Know that every hour you spend is part of your dream. **And that,** as the alchemist told the little boy, **will allow you to discover things along the way you never would have seen, had you not had the courage to try things that seemed impossible for a shepherd to achieve. The closer one gets to realizing his destiny, the more that destiny becomes his true reason for being."**

"Sam, I feel so stupid," I said. "I feel like I've missed so much! It seems like I've wasted all this time."

"No, no, no," he said. "Each, in his own time. You see, you did exactly what you had to do. You've been on the journey all along, you just didn't realize it. The only difference is, now you have reawakened your destination. It's all so simple, really. Life is simple. Like the alchemist who learned that the world had a soul. He realized that, **whoever understands that Soul can also understand the language of things. . . . Many alchemists have realized their destiny and discovered the Soul of the World, the Philosopher's Stone, and the Elixir of Life. . . . But these things are all so simple that they could be written on the surface of an emerald."**

"Well, that's easy to say, Sam," I said. "If you understand the Soul of the World. But how do you *do* that? How do you actually go about understanding it?"

"First of all, realize that you are an alchemist. We all are," he explained. "And the answer's right in that book you're holding. **How do I immerse myself in the desert? Listen to your heart. It knows all things, because it came from the Soul of the World."**

I had to laugh, out of pure frustration more than anything else. I felt I had lost my connection with him for sure. What he was saying was coming across to me like a foreign language. I needed some specifics! I needed direction! I needed a clear explanation!

As if anticipating my every thought, Sam was answering my questions before I had even asked them. **"You now see everything through a veil of associations about things. . . . You've 'seen it all before.' . . . You see only memories of things, so you become bored. Boredom, you see, is fundamental nonawareness of life; boredom is awareness, trapped in the mind. You'll have to lose your mind before you can come to your senses."**

Well, if that was all it was going to take, I was off to a grand start! Bring on the straightjacket! Enlightenment comes upon hospital discharge, I thought.

Sensing my difficulty in grasping his point, Sam didn't miss a beat. He placed *The Way of the Peaceful Warrior* beside me onto the increasingly formidable stack of books. After giving me some much-needed time to digest all that was running through my brain, he quietly sat down cross-legged on the floor in the center of the aisle and motioned me to sit beside him, which I did. He carefully unwedged a thin volume from the bottom shelf with the toe of his boot, slipped it out of the stack, and placed it on his lap. I could see the title, *The Urban Shaman,* by Serge King. Sam waited a long time before speaking, uncharacteristically choosing his words carefully.

"Why is your world so full of darkness, when you want to attract the light?" he asked finally.

He hit me right in the gut. A real sucker punch, and I never even saw it coming. I couldn't breathe. I had no answer, because it was a question I had asked myself so many times within the safety of my own thoughts.

He began to speak slowly and deliberately.

"Extending into the metaphysical realm, we come across the idea that thoughts will telepathically attract their equivalent. In other words, to put it very simply, positive thoughts will attract positive people and events, and negative thoughts will attract negative people and events."

I wasn't sure if he was paraphrasing, because the way he spoke and the words from the books had become indistinguishable. I couldn't really tell where the text ended and Sam's words began. He checked my face for a reaction. He could see that I was taking it all in, but wasn't ready to comment. Sensing this, he continued driving his point home.

"Nothing ever happens to you without your participation. For every event that you experienced, you creatively attract it through your beliefs, desires, fears, and expectations, and then react to it habitually or respond to it consciously. Cathy Lee, you are connected to the Universe. It's a part of you and you are a part of it. And you always have been."

It was the first time that he had used my name. It was almost as if his infinite wisdom had been brought into a narrow focus, a perfect beam of light aimed directly at me. I'd heard and felt every single word. And sitting there on the floor next to Sam, I realized that he had instinctively known about the hole in my heart all along. He also knew that in order for it to disappear forever, I had to fill that hole for myself.

Without saying a word, he rose and walked stiffly to a back room. He soon returned carrying his jacket and a well-worn paperback book which he proceeded to place reverently in my hands.

"This is one of my favorites: Millman's *The Sacred Journey of the Peaceful Warrior,*" he said. "It's my own personal copy. I carry it with me, as you can see. It's a little torn and tattered, but I want you to have it. **The main thing I want to emphasize now, is that the world mirrors your new level of awareness.**"

Something seemed to have changed in Sam. There was a depth of understanding that was becoming more and more evident. When he spoke, it was as if all the knowledge of the world was speaking. When the afternoon's incredible odyssey had begun, he seemed like nothing more than a happy-go-lucky, slightly off-center character, who just happened to possess a great command of the written word. What I was beginning to realize, however, was that the "lines" he had been reciting were simply vehicles through which he was driving home the "truth" in any way he could. And he was delivering his message in a manner that I could both comprehend and experience at the same time.

"**Like attracts like,**" he said. "**And people whose home base is the first floor are attracted to first floor kinds of music, books, drink, food, sports, and so forth. The same is true of the second and third floors. Until your awareness rests securely on the fourth floor, in the heart, your motives are ultimately self-serving.**"

He gently took both of my hands in his, helped me to my feet, and stared deeply into my eyes. "It's time for you to climb to the higher floors, my dear," he said simply. "That's where your true destiny lies."

I couldn't utter a word; I needed to sponge up every drop of this moment between us. He was right, and it did seem simple! I had been playing on the *lower* floors, while my heart had been longing to take the elevator to the top.

"You have opened the door to the alchemist within you, harnessing the power of the gold in your soul," Sam smiled, surrounding me with a blanket of comfort I had never known in my life. "In other words, just embrace your true self. **For when a woman has owned her passionate nature . . . her thoughts will grow wild and fierce and beautiful. Her juices flow. Her heart expands. She has glimpsed the enchanted kingdom, and the vast and magical realms of the Goddess within her. . . . When a woman conceives her true self, a miracle occurs and life around her begins again."**

After what seemed like an eternity, during which he gave me the full amount of time I needed to absorb the meaning of these compelling words, Sam used his humor, as always, to dissipate the intensity of the moment, and to guide me back to reality.

"I never get that one right anymore!" he apologized. "My memory must be going. I used to have all of these memorized word for word. But I guess when you've lived the books long enough, your experience and the words get all mixed up."

"But Marianne won't mind," he said. "She understands what I'm saying."

I guess he didn't feel like speaking for a while, because he took the book, *A Woman's Worth,* turned to page thirty-two, and handed it to me, pointing out the following passage:

"When we break free and see the game for what it is, we will let out a howl. . . . We will hear the holy choir of angels, our eyes will brighten, and our smiles will burst forth. We will see the angels and know the angels, and do lunch with them, and speak their case. We will be intimate with the stars and ride rainbows to ancient lands. We will light up like lamps, and the world will never be the same again."

I slowly closed the volume, and stared silently at the floor. Tears began to drip down my cheeks. Although Sam and I had been together for a mere five hours, it had seemed like a lifetime. The sheer joy that was swirling within me, was more than I could handle. I loved this man! He had taken the void in my heart and helped me fill it with a light that was impossible to describe. I felt totally complete, and yet alive with an infinite connection to everything. Slowly, Sam reached out and rested his hand on my arm.

As I looked up, I said only two words, but I knew Sam would understand the enormity and depth encompassed in both of them.

"Thank you," I said in a whisper.

"Guess it's time to close," he said softly, knowing that the connection had been made, the gift had been delivered, and the bond between us had been cast in gold.

He grabbed his coat. I grabbed my purse. Silently, we walked together toward the front door. Just before we stepped outside, I took one last look at the room to record every minute detail indelibly in my mind. When he knew I had finished satiating my memory, he reached out and shut off the lights. We stepped out into the crisp night air, and he locked the door. It was dark out, but the sky was lit with a full moon and a veritable carpet of twinkling stars. The last thing I remember before Sam disappeared down the sidewalk was him standing a few feet in front of me with his hands in his pockets, reminding me to listen to my heart because "it knows all things."

I watched him amble down the street, and then turned and walked to my car. As I climbed in, the books he had given me spilled from my arms onto the floor. As I was stacking them back on the seat beside me, I noticed that *The Alchemist* had flipped open to a page into which Sam had placed a well-worn leather bookmark. Had it been intentional? Of course it had. There wasn't any doubt in my mind. He'd known all along what my destiny was to be.

Holding the book carefully in my hands, I began to read the explicitly marked passage: **"There was a moment of silence so profound that it seemed the city was asleep. No sound from the bazaars, no arguments among the merchants, no men climbing to the towers to chant. No hope, no adventure, no old kings or destinies, no treasure, and no pyramids. It was as if the world had fallen silent because the boy's soul had."**

So this was the "Soul of the World." I finally understood what Sam had been talking about. And indeed, it was so simple that it could have been written on the surface of an emerald.

Slowly, I closed the book and sat for a long moment, taking in the penetrating sound of a world fallen silent. I had heard something like it before, but this time, it was a pure, unbridled silence in which all things seemed possible. I had joined with the Soul of the World, and the exalted pulse of its beating heart within me, was the most beautiful feeling I had ever known.

14
Bankrupt in Bel Air

Act without doing; work without effort.
Lao Tzu

When the heart weeps for what it's lost, the soul rejoices for what it's found.

A Sufi verse

After my experience with Sam, I watched in awe as my world began to change in the most fascinating manner. I remember him telling me about the experience most people go through at one time or another in their lives, where they pierce "the veil of illusion." He was right. My "reality" had shifted in a way I could never have dreamed possible. I had indeed emerged into a bright new world. Not only were the actual events of my life dramatically changing, but so was my experience of them. Sam insisted that I understand that this world was created as a place to learn. It is our playground, our school, and our artist's studio. We are here not only to master the actual *process* of creation, but also to learn how to consciously channel this creative energy of the spirit, and of the Divine, into physical form. At the time I heard his words, however, I didn't fully realize the depth of the wisdom behind them. It was simply enough to have a sense that a mystery was beginning to unfold before me, a sense that the "magic" was about to begin.

The first sign of this magic came in the form of a very unusual coincidence. I was attending a Sunday brunch with my girlfriend, Sonia Cole, her husband Chris, and their son Christopher, in Malibu. I hadn't really felt up to going, but Sonia insisted.

As we were eating lunch, someone at our table who was aware of all the legal proceedings against me, asked how things were going. As I started to mumble a reply, the man interjected, "Listen, if you're not happy with who's representing you, I have this great lawyer you should call. He's really tough in the trenches and loves defending people who are being unfairly taken advantage of."

My normal reaction would have been, "Another lawyer? Forget it. That's the last thing I need." But for some reason, I didn't protest. I just wrote down his name and address and put it in my purse.

On a whim, I called that lawyer. His name was Brian Oxman, and believe it or not, he turned out to be a godsend. For the first time, I had strength and legal brilliance on my side, coupled with a large dose of chutzpah. His confidence gave me confidence, and I no longer was afraid to stand my ground. The tables began to turn on the legal front, and in a very short time, in every other aspect of my life as well.

"Don't worry about a thing," Brian reassured me. "I know just how to remedy the situation. But first, since the desire to take your house away from you is such a major issue in the legal proceedings, for your own safety and peace of mind, I want you to move out of your house by Monday."

Move out of my house? By Monday? He had to be kidding. It was Thursday! That would give me a little over three days to pack up my entire household, find a new place to live, and move in! But he meant it, and I trusted that he knew what he was doing.

The packing was easy. My first call was to Paula Charlton, my trusted friend and cohort who had been running my household for the past fifteen years. Her response was predictable: "I'll be right there." This wasn't the first time that she or I had needed each other's help, and it probably wouldn't be the last. I could count on her beyond a shadow of a doubt, and that's all I needed to know. Her caring nature, her strength, and her sense of humor have made a tremendous impact on my life. Some friendships exist beyond words or explanation.

Next, I enlisted the help of some other good-hearted friends: Madeline Cummings, Ed Viramontes, Lynn Thoma and Troy Garrison, the last of whom, to my surprise, brought with him six former gang members who had taken part in my Foundation's program. It was an interesting visual, to say the least, but the price was definitely right: all the pizza, fries, and Coca-Cola they could consume. This "motley crew" and I proceeded to pack everything, lock, stock and barrel, finishing around three o'clock in the morning. Great, I was all packed with no place to go!

Two days and counting. The race was on. I enlisted a couple more friends to help me search for living quarters. We found four or five possibilities, but kept running into a roadblock. As soon as I checked the "yes" box on the obligatory financial application that read, *Have you ever declared bankruptcy?* I was out the door and out of luck.

Then another coincidence occurred. My friend Larry Otting called and said he'd found the perfect house. What he failed to mention was that this "perfect" house was in a privately owned, gated community in Bel Air, one of the ritziest suburbs in Los Angeles. I don't know what made me agree to meet him there in the first place, but I did.

I followed him up the hill and pulled up to a set of imposing wrought-iron gates protecting the community. After the security guard carefully checked both of our credentials, he opened the electronic gates and let us in. I remember thinking to myself, *Larry, you're out of your mind, there's no way I can afford this.* But I kept going. After all, I figured, *I'm already here, what harm could it do?*

Not only was the house to die for, but the owners offered me a special deal on the rent in return for the right to use my name in their advertising materials to promote future sales. Unreal. How could I lose? Even more unbelievable, in the excitement of having me there, they didn't even ask for a financial statement or credit report, as had all the other places I'd looked at. Obviously, they assumed Cathy Lee Crosby was flush with cash, and I, of course, didn't correct them. I borrowed the first and last month's rent from my mother, and moved in.

I was bankrupt in Bel Air.

Month number two? Don't even ask. I had no idea where I was going to get the money, as I was not even close to being out of the woods financially. I also had a steady date with the bankruptcy trustee, as well as with Joe's lawyers. But, physically, spiritually, and emotionally, the energy had shifted. I felt strong and invigorated, and I was filled with anticipation, as if anxiously waiting for the next magical surprise to cross my path.

Now that I had come up with the initial rent payment, so hey, no problem, I had thirty whole days to breathe.

The first order of business was to get some money coming in! So, I decided to call a few people in the entertainment business who had always been my champions. Perhaps one of them was producing a project that I could begin working on immediately. An absence of five years is an ice age for an actor, but David Wolper, bless him, happened to be filming the next sequel in the miniseries *North and South,* entitled "Heaven and Hell." How ironic!

Once he found out that I could do a proper southern accent, I was cast as the southern belle who warns the black townsfolk of her own husband's impending plan to destroy them, eventually incurring her husband's physical abuse for going behind his back to try to save the slaves. After all that I'd been through, it was a piece of cake for me to pull off as an actress. Although I worked incredibly long hours for three solid weeks in one hundred degree heat, dressed in the full costume of the period, it seemed like a vacation to me. I was thrilled to be back on the set doing what I loved best.

The icing on the cake was that I had the second month's rent, as well as some living expenses to boot. Needless to say, my salary "quote" had taken a nose dive. But it was a start, and I was grateful.

In the entertainment business, a career hits many peaks and valleys. And when you're starting in a valley and heading toward a peak, it takes awhile to gain momentum. This certainly was true in my case. During this time, thank God for great friends and a manila file I had labeled *Freebies.* As for my friends, I had a whole new appreciation of each and every one of my friends who had stood by me. As for my dust-gathering *Freebie* file, which included offers of free clothes, airline tickets, hotels, and so on given to me as perks over the years, I had never used it. Basically, I'd never needed to. But believe me, I worked it for all it was worth during this period.

As I had learned from Sam, I was fast becoming an expert at the skill of alchemy on many levels. I realized that these freebies were "gifts," plain and simple. The specific items themselves weren't important, but rather, the fact that I had closed the door on receiving them. For some reason, I had regarded them as unimportant and, in doing so, was not allowing the Universe to provide for and assist me.

One of the more valuable gifts that came from my freebie folder was frequent-flyer miles. Because of my work and peripatetic lifestyle, I had accrued dozens and dozens of coupons toward free flights. Rather than continuing to accumulate them in my manila treasure trove, I began to use those coupons whenever I needed to fly somewhere. I was learning to flow with the natural rhythm of the Universe, remaining open to the gifts that were coming my way. Not only that, I was beginning to open the door to this momentum in every area of my life.

Before long, I began making use of other gifts as well. I gratefully accepted the L'Auberge Hotel's offer to join them in Del Mar for an all-expense-paid weekend at their beautiful hotel. I welcomed L.A. Gear's offer of free sporting goods. Before, I guess I was too embarrassed to make use of these offers. I was working, so why shouldn't I pay for them? I didn't realize or acknowledge that this was something they *wanted* to do. Again, I was stopping the flow of magic from finding its way to me. I was hindering the natural process of life that is available to all of us.

Now that I partake of each and every gift that comes my way, the floodgates have opened and the surprises flow freely into my life.

For instance, on one occasion, I met John Paul Dijoria and his wife, Eloise, owners of John Paul Mitchell hair products, on an airplane, and we spent the entire flight simply having a wonderful conversation. For

Christmas, they sent me a two-foot by three-foot box filled with multiples of every hair and cosmetic product they make: shampoos, hairbrushes, conditioners, hairsprays, and so on. I was overwhelmed! Little did they know how much that gift meant to me.

In another instance, I happened to walk into the Sports Club L.A. to meet a friend after his workout. I had desperately wanted to join a gym, but obviously couldn't afford it. Amazingly, just as I reached the front desk, the owner happened to walk by and came over to say hello.

"Hey, Cathy Lee, it's great to see you!" he exclaimed.

"Oh, great to see you too!" I replied, not having a clue who he was.

"Are you here to work out?"

I hemmed and hawed. Stammered and stuttered.

"By the way, did I ever give you your honorary membership card?" he asked.

"Well, no," I replied.

"Come on," he said, leading me into his office where he handed me a gold card.

"I wanted to thank you for that appearance you made for us when I was trying to get the club off the ground," he said. "This is the least I can do."

Damn, I thought. The good old Universe was coming through again.

I was also asked to be an honorary member of the board of directors of a new restaurant, for which the owners gave me $500 a month in free food. What a godsend. Now I was able to return the favor to all the people who had been treating me when I needed it.

Some gifts were significant, and others were relatively minor. But they were gifts just the same, and therefore, worthy of my acknowledgment.

Yes, a number of these gifts were a direct result of my being famous. But the phenomenon is true for anyone. If you become aware of and receptive to the bounty everywhere around you, you'll be amazed at what comes your way!

If I needed to travel to pursue a career opportunity, another gift popped up, in addition to my free airline miles. Avjet, a private airline charter company in Burbank, offered to "dead-head" me on any flights that weren't full. For example, if I were in Los Angeles and they were sched-uled to pick up Tom Cruise in New York, they would let me ride on the plane from Los Angeles to New York for free, since the plane was going there anyway. All I had to do was talk up their business, which I gladly did.

Unbelievable!

What a way to live, I thought. I was beginning to open myself up to the bountiful gifts that were coming my way, and having an absolute ball doing it.

Talk about fun—I was in an art gallery in Santa Monica with Ivan Menchell, an incredible writer as well as one of my closest friends for the last ten years. We were looking at some absolutely beautiful, yet prohibitively expensive paintings by Joan Chen's brother, Chase Chen.

The owner kept saying, "Buy it! You should have it!"

"I'd love to own it," I responded honestly, "but I can't afford it right now."

Ivan and I went back two or three times just to enjoy the artist and his display. On the last occasion, the owner said out of nowhere, "Ms. Crosby, Mr. Chen would very much like to give you the original signed lithograph that you loved so much."

I was blown away. *Why,* I wondered in spite of myself.

Well, the truth of the matter is, there is no why. It was a beautiful gift and a sincere gesture, and my job was simply to receive it and be thankful.

An interesting lesson I learned about coincidences is that sometimes we do not characterize the actual circumstances that bring them to us as being "good." In other words, I realized that gifts can also come out of what we might term "bad" circumstances.

On one such seemingly "bad" occasion, my car caught on fire while I was driving up Sepulveda Boulevard in Los Angeles. It couldn't have happened at a worse time. When I had it towed to the nearest dealership, they informed me that it would cost about $5,000 to fix. I certainly didn't have sufficient funds to repair the damage, nor to buy a new car. Having become more and more aware, however, of just how the energy of the Universe worked, I asked the salesman what he'd give me for my old car, in exchange for a newer model. I couldn't believe it when he told me that not only would he give a new car at a great price, with reasonable monthly payments, but also some cash back as well. He was willing to do this simply in exchange for an autographed picture for his office!

The key is to be open to the magic awaiting you regardless of whether your judgment of an experience is "good" or "bad."

I continued to put one foot in front of the other, and sure enough, coincidence by coincidence, more and more opportunities presented themselves. But something was different. The experiences in my life were becoming a part of a larger picture, as Sam had said they would. They were becoming the canvas, the paint, and the tools in my artist's studio, and I could literally feel the creative energy flowing through me as a result of my accepting its presence in my life. I was drawing, writing, and painting my own *playground.* There was a true sense of excitement as I began to see the joy of living life in this manner. I felt alive with my reconnection to that wondrous energy I had known as a little girl. Again, the sky was the limit.

On one hand, it was frightening because I didn't have a clue where I was going. On the other hand, it was exhilarating for exactly the same reason.

I was still bankrupt, and I was still fighting to survive financially, but my relationship to the situation had changed dramatically.

Bankruptcy, Bel Air, and the *Bliss Zone.* In some inexplicable way, I knew that my life was moving forward exactly as it was supposed to. Orchestrating my ride was the echo of the last words I had read just before Sam and I left the bookstore. He'd known all along where I was headed, and had made sure that I was well on my way to getting there . . .

When we break free and see the game for what it is, we will let out a howl. . . . We will be intimate with the stars and ride rainbows to ancient lands. We will light up like lamps and the world will never be the same again.

Marianne Williamson

15

Drafting the Playing Field of a Game Called "Future"

You see things; and say "Why?"
But I dream things that never were;
and I say "Why not?"
George Bernard Shaw

He who asks questions, cannot avoid the answers.
Camaroon Proverb

An interesting phenomenon occurred as I was beginning to enjoy living in the natural rhythm of the Universe. Questions arose that I had no answers for. Would I live the rest of my life like this, just shooting from the hip? Would living in the *Bliss Zone* negate my desire and/or need to have specific goals and achieve those goals? Could I create a viable future without losing my connection to this wonderful world of exhilaration and surprise? Was it possible to marry my heart and my head? Was it conceivable to merge my new inner reality with the outside world?

In the middle of this mental deliberation, came another prophetic coincidence which provided the answers to these questions. True to my recent experience of such uncanny events, this one came out of nowhere, when I least expected it.

I was having a creative meeting with a virtual reality company in Los Angeles called Emanate. One of the partners, Michael Glock, was explaining how he had entered the CD-ROM business in the first place.

"Two years ago, believe it or not," he laughed, "I was computer illiterate. And then, almost out of necessity, I taught myself everything there was to know about computers. Eventually, I became so fascinated by the possibilities of this new medium, that I decided to start my own company."

"You were computer illiterate two years ago and now you're running an entire CD-ROM company?" I queried. "How did you do that so fast?"

In telling me his story, he mentioned, among the many steps he took to get his new venture off the ground, working with a man named Jim Channon. In passing, Michael explained that Jim was a business consultant who worked with companies and organizations ranging from DuPont to the U.S. Army. On rare occasions, he also worked with individuals like Ted Turner, helping them to visually and experientially map out the potential playing field of their future.

"People refer to him as an *imagineer,* Michael concluded, and then went back to the business at hand.

But the name Jim Channon kept repeating itself over and over in my mind. *Imagine! Someone bold enough to be professionally referred to as an "imagineer!"* As the meeting was coming to a close, I couldn't resist the impulse any longer.

"Michael, do you have a way to contact Mr. Channon?" I inquired.

"Sure, he lives on the big island of Hawaii," he said, and gave me his office phone number at the Arcturus Virtual Studios in Hawaii. It was as simple as that.

Coincidentally, of course, I happened to be going to Hawaii for a job, in two weeks. As soon as I got back from the meeting, I picked up the phone and called Mr. Channon.

"I understand people call you an imagineer and, quite frankly, I'm curious about what you actually do."

We spoke for a long time about many things, but nothing specifically regarding his work. He carefully side-stepped in-depth discussion of it. At the same time, he was open, funny, smart, insightful, and very encouraging.

I asked him if he would send me some information on himself and his services, and told him that I would do the same. I sent my standard PR package that afternoon: a resume, career credits, as well as a short biography.

The next morning, I received Jim Channon's biographical information by fax. The word BALIAN (Balinese for *shaman,* as I found out later) was written atop the cover sheet. Underneath this logo, were the words *Strategic Design Studios.*

His resume was even more iconoclastic than his title:

"Moved fifty times . . . commanded sixty-five men in combat . . . have preserved one hundred nine acres of forest . . . created master strategies for ten of the largest one hundred companies on the planet . . . am intensely spiritual . . . pray in seven spiritual systems . . . am building a social architecture for the planet . . . have hung with indigenous tribes . . . live in paradise with a great spiritual partner . . . own enterprise center/ restaurant called *Bamboo* with twenty-three employees who depend on my income to do their art . . . have thirty protégés I work with as an elder . . . I love dragonflies . . . Jimmy Buffett . . . Dave Barry . . . Gilda Radner is my guru . . . Charles Lindbergh is a role model . . . And, I can do the hula."

With that kind of a description, and in light of everything I'd been told about Jim Channon, I wanted to meet him. I called his office again the next afternoon, and told him just that. I also explained that at the present time, money was particularly tight.

"Don't worry, we'll figure out an appropriate exchange," he replied without hesitation. "I'll come to Maui while you're there, and we'll begin."

Two days later, I received another fax from Mr. Channon, on which seven questions were typed with instructions to write out complete answers to them before our meeting in Maui.

The questions were as unique as Channon's biography:

What are you at your essence?
What is it that you radiate?
What is your gift?
What is your relationship with yourself like?
What is your higher purpose?
When are you most alive?
What is your bliss?

I couldn't believe it! I was about to tackle the essence of all the questions that had been rummaging around in my brain over the last year. Not only that, as I studied them further, I suddenly realized that they were merely variations of the two long-buried childhood questions I'd never been able to answer either: *Who am I* and *why am I on this Earth?*

On another page of the fax was a rendering of a bearded, bespectacled man seated before an easel, drawing a cresting wave. Under the drawing was written, "He draws while you think out loud."

Interesting, I thought.

I decided to sit down right there and then and write out the answers to his questions. How bad could it be? Certainly, they were no different than those posed to the major corporations and titans of industry he'd helped in the past. I picked up a pen and began.

Let's see, question number one: **Who am I at my essence?** Aaaaahh, my essence . . . obviously, I had one. I could certainly feel it. But I couldn't seem to find the words to express it. It was driving me crazy. Maybe Webster would help. Essence: "the properties of a thing that make it what it is; the fundamental nature of something," advised the dictionary. Great, how much more ambiguous could you possibly get? Now, I was even more confused.

I struggled for another two hours with this question without writing a single word. I couldn't believe how difficult it was to verbalize a clear answer to such a simple little question. It was not only difficult to find the right words to express my feelings, but in addition, every time I wrote a few lines down on paper, they seemed grossly inadequate.

Each of Jim Channon's remaining questions proved equally as difficult.

I guess my impressions about myself had always been geared toward specifics: my achievements, who I was in relationship to my family, physical statistics, and accomplishments. But this process involved redefining the "who," without relying on the "what." Why was it almost impossible to value myself simply on my essence? I would soon find out.

After more than four hours, I had finished my homework as best I could and packed it away in my suitcase for the trip. Our work session was to take place at my hotel in Maui the morning after my arrival.

I was apprehensive about meeting a total stranger in my hotel room. I was also somewhat embarrassed to discuss something as personal as my dreams about the future with someone I barely knew. In spite of my trepidation, I decided to go through with it, knowing I could always figure out a way to bow out gracefully.

At nine the morning after my arrival, I opened my door and there stood Jim Channon: a tall, attractive, bearded, bright-eyed free spirit, dressed head to toe in what looked like a cross between native Hawaiian and jungle garb. Old heavy silver bracelets covered his wrists, Birkenstock sandals were on his feet, and a wraparound piece of brightly colored native fabric, vaguely resembling a skirt, was tied around his waist. Had he dressed like this just for me? I certainly hoped so, because I couldn't imagine him going before the leaders of DuPont in such a get-up. If it was his intention to scramble my circuitry, he had certainly succeeded.

"Jim Channon here," he bellowed. "And you must be Cathy Lee."

It was one of those moments when you think to yourself: *Okay, that's it. Now, I've really gone too far. This "going with the flow" thing, this "following your intuition thing," is obviously getting way out of hand.*

But something about his presence—a cross between corporate professionalism and eccentric creativity—allowed me to at least invite him in to sit down.

For the next half-hour or so, it was a minute-by-minute decision on my part, whether or not to continue with Mr. Channon. I was judging and evaluating his every word and action, trying desperately to fit him into my mental computer's definition of acceptability.

Before I knew it, however, I had become fully engaged in an animated and energetic conversation with my guest. My self-imposed half-hour search and discovery had turned into a two-hour stretch before I could blink an eye. My mind's probing evaluation system must have broken down, because all I was aware of was pure creative energy flowing between us—student and teacher.

We worked for about ten hours two days in a row, stopping only once or twice for a short break to grab a bite to eat or visit the restroom. The results were extraordinary and it wasn't long before I fully realized the true brilliance of Mr. Channon's work. He had perfected the process of "reinventing" a corporation, or in this case, myself.

He began by saying, "What I try to accomplish is to awaken, ennoble, and activate the dreams of a corporation or an individual. Everyone has dreams, you see, but they park them somewhere along the way. My job is to get the cars out of the parking lot and back on the open road again."

Receiving much of his early training in the Army, he told me that he basically works on two "fronts." First, the *strategic planning side,* or "getting your dreams on paper and then mapping them out on a visual playing field"; and second, the *spiritual/soul side,* "pulling you out of your ordinary thinking in such a way that your dreams and you actually become one and the same."

Although Mr. Channon deals partly with dreams and the spiritual side of a corporation or individual, he is not just some airy-fairy New Age philosopher. He is an extremely intelligent, well-organized master strategist, who has devoted a lifetime to his technique.

During his early military career, he was commissioned to undertake an in-depth study of human performance, and then write an entire manual on the subject for the army leadership. They had deduced that if a global war were to ensue, Russia and the United States would be matched evenly in terms of war machinery and manpower. It was felt that if push came to shove, the deciding factor in another world war would be the *human* one. Therefore, they wanted to draw from every possible source, in order to find the key to optimum human performance.

His inquiries took him to the far corners of the Earth, living with and learning from many tribal cultures: the Masai in Africa, the Australian

Aborigines, the Tibetan horseback culture in the Campas of Southwestern China, the Pacific voyaging canoe societies, and the Montagnard Hill tribes of northwest Vietnam, to name a few.

In an effort to present the material he had collected for the final manual in the best possible light, he created a "futuristic mythical unit," called **The First Earth Battalion**™. It was a Robin Hood like band of courageous men and women, who were committed to protecting life on this planet in the twenty-first century by the use of a new concept called eco-tactics.

He explained that the tactical maneuvers and strategies developed for *The First Earth Battalion,* on both the human side as well as on the battlefield, are still being used by the Army today.

How could he apply military strategies to the life of a civilian like me? I wondered. I would soon find out.

He began by asking questions, curious about the way I answered them, even more than the answers themselves. Our conversations soon grew into an electric dialogue in which he became a mirror for me and my experience. The more I participated at this intense level of communication, the more creative and detailed the process became. In addition, while I was answering a particular question, he would sketch out certain ideas on a large tablet without breaking stride in taking his notes. I would learn the purpose of this later.

After the initial seven questions of "homework" he had faxed me had been fully analyzed and discussed, Mr. Channon introduced the next step of his work with **Question Number 8: What do you feel are your three most unfulfilled or suppressed dreams? Tell them as if they had already been attained.**

"Give me a full picture of how this dream would look if it were currently playing itself out in your life," he said. "The purpose of this is to develop a new *language,* or image, or frame of reference for yourself. As you do this, you will begin to formulate a mental image as rich in detail as you could possibly want. And then, after I have mapped that image out on paper, your brain will automatically begin to use it as a 'magnet.' Anything you look at from that point on, will be bounced against this new frame of reference. It would be like a father asking his son what he wants to be when he grows up. And the son says, 'Oh, I'm going to be a fireman.' The next day, if that little boy happens to walk by a toy store, he will subconsciously look for fire trucks. It's as simple as that. Believing begets seeing."

I quickly discovered that while the result might be very simple, getting there was certainly not. I guess that's why he called them "suppressed dreams." Once you get in touch with them, however, you begin to see that they are colored by all sorts of conditions, old decisions, self-imposed rules, and the like. Consequently, you are reluctant to bring these dreams to the forefront because you think they are impossible to achieve. Try to answer this question yourself and you'll see what I mean. Immediately, you begin to censor yourself, omitting anything that seems unattainable, too grandiose, or that you've tried unsuccessfully before.

As Jim Channon and I communicated a surprising thing began to happen. I started getting a clearer and clearer sense of what *really* made me happy. The "critic" inside me became ill with laryngitis, and specific ideas began to spring forth with increasing ease. Indeed, the actual process of trying to clarify and express my three suppressed dreams had proved to be the key. Once I could state them succinctly, they seemed very real.

With a playful grin, my bearded professor added, "If you're not a writer and you need something more tangible to solidify a certain concept, then we can even model your suppressed dreams in clay."

I assured him that that would not be necessary. In light of my total lack of talent in the clay department, the ensuing embarrassment would only add insult to injury, making the suppressed dreams retreat even further. But he had made his point: We spend our lives not really knowing, understanding, or utilizing something as basic as the essence of who we are.

"Let me give you an example," he said. "Suppose you're riding through Africa right now in a Jeep, and I say to you, 'See all the animals?' The truth is, until you know their exact silhouettes, locations, and patterns, you won't be able to see them. You can't actually visualize anything in the world that you don't know about. So the idea is to build a special language just for you, so that you can recognize the pieces of your dreams as they appear out in the world before you. Soon, a natural integration of these pieces takes place, and you begin to live your destiny."

As soon as I heard his words, the concept made total sense and I began to understand the value of allowing coincidences to play themselves out in our lives.

What Jim Channon had done for me was to clarify what Deepak Chopra calls "stepping into the dance of the Universe." It is about utilizing all the possibilities available to us in every moment, and allowing the energy inherent in each one of them to carry us forward. This concept was the very core of Mr. Channon's work, and it was becoming more and more evident with each sketch he tacked to the wall. At this point, I asked how he intended to use them.

"The way the world is set up right now, our attention is directed more toward the *drama* of life, instead of toward the *possibilities* of life," he said. "It takes a rather special kind of intervention to get a person or a company to recognize, and then refocus on those possibilities."

"An intervention?" I asked.

"Exactly," he nodded. "When trying to uncover dreams, it has to be more than just a discussion. All the senses have to be activated as well. That's the reason I use art and storytelling, in addition to direct, focused communication, to achieve the desired results."

The next piece of the puzzle was **Question Number Nine: Describe a moment in your life when you remember being filled with warmth and love.** "This will become a very important clue to finding the playing field of your ideal work in the future," he explained.

I tried to answer as truthfully as I could, but again, the words didn't come easily.

"Mr. Channon, it's really tough to come out with an inspired answer to this question," I said.

"Just keep going, you're right where you should be at this point," he replied. "And please, call me Jim."

Again, it wasn't my specific answer to this question that was nearly as revealing as the process of my getting to it. I also noticed that the more I searched, the clearer the question itself became.

In answer to the question, I began to recall incidents where I had felt a particular sense of love and warmth. The more I concentrated on recalling those feelings, the deeper I felt them. And the deeper I felt them, the more I realized that answering the question had ceased to be my prime focus. Instead, I began to bask in the joy of the wonderful moments I was recalling. I related my progress to Jim, while he continued to take notes and sketch away.

Once again, the process had been its own reward, and we moved onto the next question.

"What is your ideal work?" he asked. **"This is Question Number Ten."**

Searching for the answer was painful, yet particularly insightful. I realized that the entertainment business, or how I had been spending the majority of my time, included only a few things that I loved doing. This fact made me more than uncomfortable, and all my censors became immediately activated. Suddenly, thoughts about my *ideal* work became "too broad," "too grandiose," and "impossible to delineate." Realizing my dilemma, Jim suggested that I start by telling him what I liked to do most, no matter how trivial it seemed.

Believe me, I was shocked at what I wrote down. Some of the activities that appeared on my list were: "holding puppies, ice skating, singing, dancing, playing Solitaire on my computer, reading, listening to the Gipsy Kings, eating Mexican food, lying in my hammock, deep sea diving, and driving fast cars." These were included with more traditional person-focused and work-focused joys.

While discussing my list with Jim, I had an amazing revelation. Not even one quarter of the activities on my list were actually included in my everyday life or work! It was obvious how much more fulfilling my life would be if only I incorporated *half* of those things that I loved to do! Another piece of the puzzle had become crystal clear.

The eleventh question seemed absolutely ludicrous. I had no idea where Jim was headed, but I had learned to just roll with the punches and go for it.

"Your house is on fire, and you have thirty seconds to get out," he began **"If you only had time to choose three items, excluding people and animals, what would be the first three you'd grab?"**

Jim put down his pen. "What I'm after here is sentiment," he said. "Because people usually reveal their particular sentimental associations by what items they grab. This gives me a direct line into their heart. I certainly wouldn't want someone to expand their life path if it didn't trigger their heart. The whole idea is to find a way that you can feel fully alive at every moment of the day. That's the ultimate goal."

My answer to the question made me laugh. What I had chosen sounded so silly, but I guess feeling that way was part of the process as well. I chose to grab my purse, my appointment book, and all my family photos. The idea that I would take these three items, while allowing everything I'd worked for my entire life to go up in flames seemed absurd. But, there was a method to Jim's madness, as I would find out later.

Question Number Twelve: seemed even sillier than the previous one: **"When was the last time you did something with your hands that excited you, and what was it?** By this question," Jim explained, "I can find out what you might have been missing in your life that relates to your physical sense of well-being."

My first thought, which I couldn't believe, was a bit sexual in content, and I certainly wasn't going to communicate it to Jim. So, upon necessary further analysis, I came up with, "building things out of wood . . . furniture, bookshelves, fences . . . " Wow! I'd forgotten. I love to build, and I love to create something from scratch. It made perfect sense that the making of a piece of furniture very closely resembled why I so enjoyed being a part of the entertainment industry in all of its creative facets. What is creating a character, a script, or an entire film, but *building* something piece by piece from a single spark of imagination and a few tools? Interesting.

Question Number Thirteen: "What experiences in your life have really touched your emotions?" Jim asked.

As I sat back in my chair and gazed out the sliding-glass doors at the far end of my hotel room, I took a moment to relish the incredible sight of the Maui surf below.

It made me realize how much passion I have when it comes to my feelings. Whether the experience was one of joy, sadness, frustration, or exhilaration, my thoughts and reactions tended to be equally passionate. Taking a closer look, I became aware of those things that fueled my fire on a daily basis in a positive way, and also those that affected me in a negative way. It was obvious that I was stuck in certain behavioral patterns that were not conducive to forward movement, much less the achievement of my dreams.

Again, Jim scribbled away on his board, talking all the while.

"Now, when I combine all these answers, all of a sudden this really interesting picture begins to surface," he said. "It's composed of many different pieces, which I call *elements*. Any of these elements alone would not be that amazing in and of itself. But when all of the elements are illustrated together, it produces an exciting picture of someone's actual possibilities.

"When I do this with corporations, I usually write and draw on the wall if possible. First of all, they get a sense of really being listened to. And second, they realize that their ideas are a helluva lot more tangible and important than they ever thought possible.

"Next, I take all the drawings and weave them together in such a way as to create an actual visual 'map.' Finally, I translate that map into a story, which I then repeat back to them, with music if possible. All of a sudden, these concepts, which hours before had seemed nothing more than elusive dreams, now appear to be very much attainable. What I'm sketching here is the basis for what will become your *Visual Action Map™.*"

"Oh, you mean like a to-do list, with specific dates by which certain things have to be accomplished?" I asked.

"Actually, no. I don't believe that's the most powerful way to get any job done," he said. "I think the key is to keep your Visual Action Map *alive,* constantly burning inside you. You can do this by going back and reviewing it as often as you like. Eventually, however, this 'pictorial destiny' will become so much a part of who you are, you won't even need to refer to it anymore. Then, as you go out into the world on a day-to-day basis, tangible signs will become evident that will keep you moving in the right direction toward your destiny. Likewise the world will deliver to you the exact things you need to live out that destiny."

Ah, the mystery of coincidence was becoming more and more tangible, I thought.

For two days, Jim Channon had been interviewing me, sketching, taking notes, asking questions, and leading discussions. We worked as we ate, as we walked, while sitting, and while standing. At first, it had been a struggle. Perhaps it was not knowing how far I could go, or should go, in describing my dreams, having never done the process before. There was a feeling of vulnerability and trepidation that the words pouring out of me were simply words and nothing more. Jim was aware of this, and therefore had created an atmosphere of trust that allowed me to press forward in spite of my reservations. I cannot ever recall feeling as open, as connected, or as alive in any kind of learning situation.

After two solid days, all the questions had been answered and all the pieces of the puzzle had been assembled. Jim was finally ready to sketch out a rough draft of my map. Accordingly, we decided to take the only real break we'd had in two days, so he could return to his room and assemble the pieces. After about thirty minutes, Jim returned with three or four sheets of large drawing paper under his arm.

"Well, are you ready?" he asked.

I came in from the porch and sat in my designated chair. I watched with fascination as Jim took the pages and tacked them up on the wall in a row. It's impossible for me to describe how I felt as I saw everything I'd related, or thought, or dreamed, or examined for two solid days, presented before me in a beautiful, full-color, organized *playing field.* He had taken all my random thoughts, ideas, and imaginings, and had turned them into an incredible *playground of possibility.* Before me was the imagineer with his artistic rendition of the full potential of my destiny. (See page 262.)

At the top of the map of my playing field was a group of hand-drawn, lifelike *characters* that represented the essence of my being in relationship to everything on my map. Capturing the totality of my destiny, the words ANGEL WARRIOR were printed in bold script. Overwhelmed by the sight before me, I was speechless.

Realizing that I needed time to digest the magical vision on the wall, Jim sat quietly and waited. And then, at just the right moment, he said,

"Cathy Lee, you had already begun the process of reinventing yourself when you called me. I'm just here to blow a little wind on the flames.

"In your case, as you can see from the sketches, I was looking for an *archetype* to build your whole playing field around," he continued. "I was looking for a group of pictorial characters that I felt you could 'step into' and 'add on to' as a basis for your visual language. Doing this allows the subconscious to get into the game. It's the same for everybody, but in your case, I felt that ANGEL WARRIOR would be the perfect name to spur you on. And every time you fully experience that you *are* that ANGEL WARRIOR, every ounce of your being will follow along and deliver to you whatever you need to fulfill your destiny."

As I focused on my *playground of possibility,* I had the most exhilarating experience. What once had been merely a grandiose assemblage of comments, dreams, and thoughts had suddenly become a totally ingrained Universal truth. The chart not only represented who I subconsciously had the potential to be, but who I was now. All I had to do was look at the picture, and I could ignite the experience all over again. There were no longer any limits on my life, imposed by me or anybody else. Jim's creation was an indelible confirmation that I was indeed on track.

"After hitting bottom, one has to ignite their own pilot light before anything else can happen," Jim explained, "and you did. In a sense, you had a near-death experience. You are not the same person. Now you're open to all possibilities, and nothing is holding you back."

A smile came to my face with the realization that somewhere, out in the desert, a certain white-haired imp of a man was laughing. I could see his face as clearly as if he were standing next to me. Perhaps he was.

"Just think of the future as a game," Jim smiled, "and that this is your playing field. Be ever mindful that *playing* is the key word here, because, believe me, levity works a helluva lot better than gravity."

He knew that I needed time to fully digest all that I had taken in, so he began to pack his supplies.

As he made his way to the door, I found myself searching for just the right words to fully express how thankful and appreciative I was. But it was one of those moments when I knew that no matter what I said, it wouldn't be enough. So, I thanked him with everything I could muster at the moment, and then each of us went our separate way.

Several weeks had passed after my *imagineering* session with Jim Channon, when I decided to take his renderings and put them up on the wall in my office. Looking at them once again in all their vivid detail, I remembered my feelings about women not having the same rich choices of role models that men have. But right here before me, on these very pieces of paper, I had created my own visual *latticework of possibility.* It had come from within, it was securely attached to my heart, and it was set up to reflect my future participation in life, exactly as I had always dreamed. My destiny and I had become one.

As if what I had experienced wasn't enough, a short time later I received a video from Jim that he requested I watch when I was in a particularly receptive frame of mind. I immediately sat down in front of the television, popped in the video, and pushed *play.*

At the beginning of the tape, the screen was completely covered with a close-up of long grass, moving in waves with the wind. Then the camera slowly panned to a beautiful seascape with waves crashing over black-lava rocks, and finally it settled on the futurist/imagineer himself, sitting on the stones of a wall surrounding an ancient Hawaiian village.

He began to tell a story about me as if it were the year 2040, and I had died. He began recalling what he remembered about my life and who I was. He spoke of all the successes I had had in the intervening years. He spoke of fictitious movies that I had starred in and produced, all intercut with illustrated characters representing those various movies. He also talked about the contributions that I had made to the world, followed by other illustrated characters representing those contributions.

It was utterly fascinating to see all the possibilities that had sprung from his initial concept of the *ANGEL WARRIOR*. The characters were alike only in that they represented what he felt were the optimum aspects of my being: tactician, full-on Olympian, champion of the human spirit, playful imp, loving companion, and following in his shoes, an imagineer-in-training. To top it off, the entire story was set to an inspiring native soundtrack, underscored by a slow, Gabriel Roth-type tribal drum beat. The emotional effect of his scripted eulogy was unlike anything I had ever experienced.

When I called to thank him for the gift, he insisted I watch it once a week, while doing some kind of improvisational, physical movement. Since I was an athlete, he explained that my deepest learning would be best anchored through my physical body. Thus, the tape would become a sort of "moving meditation." He stressed that when people reinvent themselves, especially in respect to a performer, it's not enough to just use words and simple affirmations to lock in a newly realized set of qualities. Physical movement is a mandatory addition to instilling them deep within.

I now had a clear vision of a whole new playground of possibility available to me in this game called "future." It was well within my sight, and I was ready to accept it for all it was worth.

As good old Sam had predicted, I had finally "taken the elevator up to the fourth floor."

16
The Magic of the Fourth Floor

The great man is he that does not lose his child's-heart.
Mencius

Flow with whatever may happen and let your mind be free: Stay centered by accepting whatever you are doing. This is the ultimate.
Chang tzu

I was certainly ready and open to live my life on a day-to-day basis in this new realm of pure potential. I was eager to let the *magic* begin. Having the desire to play the game is one thing, however, and knowing *how* to play it is quite another.

So much had changed in the way I experienced my life that to rely on my past methods of accomplishing tasks seemed ludicrous. All of my behavioral patterns in regards to "doing" had been erased, yet nothing had taken their place. Somehow, I had to figure out a way to marry my new perception of life with the day-to-day reality of living. I also had to learn how to utilize the energy of the Universe as it flowed through my heart in dealing with my everyday existence.

It was obvious that both the stagnant state of my career, and the financial and legal turbulence still facing me needed immediate attention. But how was I supposed to take action, and not *do* anything at the same time? I knew I had to try to stay centered in my heart, trusting that the Universe would provide me with the next step. But knowing what to do intellectually, and actually putting that knowledge to practice, is a whole different ballgame.

After "piercing the veil of illusion" and "falling through the trapdoor," I knew I had no choice but to move forward. So, as Sam had instructed, I stepped up to the plate and waited for the pitch. The ballgame was about to begin.

It was 1994, and the first pitch came in the form of a telephone message from Judy Girrard, president of Lifetime Television Network.

I returned the call immediately. Yes, I was *doing* something, but the difference was that now I was acting in response to a coincidence. I was following the natural "flow" of life.

"I didn't think we could pull it off," Judy informed me, "but your movie is a go, and we want to start filming immediately."

"What?" I practically shouted. "Are you kidding?"

For eleven years, I had been doing everything I possibly could to get the book, *One Child,* produced as a movie.

The story had affected me deeply. It centered around the true story of a violent six-year-old little girl, who had been physically abused by her father, sexually abused by her uncle, and abandoned by her mother, who had literally pushed her out of a moving car onto the freeway. The trauma of the child's early life culminated at the age of five when she tied a two-year-old boy to a tree and set him on fire. The child becomes a ward of the state and is temporarily thrust into a class of emotionally challenged children while awaiting placement in an institution for life. During this time she comes into contact with a very special teacher who, because of a hole in her own heart, becomes determined to reach her. She believes that all children are worthy of love, and through the resulting rage, violent confrontations, and ensuing trust that develops between them, both the child and the teacher are able to heal their emotional wounds.

It had taken nine of those eleven years and many hours of trial and error before I could even secure the "rights" to the book, generally the first step in getting a film made.

Acquiring the rights at all was the first miracle, and it came at the hands of a man named Leslie Moonves. He is currently president of CBS Entertainment, but at the time, he was president of Warner Bros. Television. I was introduced to Mr. Moonves by Michael Solomon who was at the time the head of foreign sales at Warner Bros. Studio. The meeting went extremely well, and the company decided to develop a comedy series for me.

During this development period, Mr. Moonves asked if there were any movies I was passionate about as a first step to helping me develop some much needed career heat. I told him about the book, *One Child,* as well as the trouble I was having optioning the rights.

He read the book, loved it, and decided to help me take one more stab at acquiring them. It was a pretty gutsy thing to do in view of the near freezing temperature of my status as an actress at that time, but he did it nonetheless. When he called to tell me that Warner Bros. Television had been successful in securing the rights and wanted me to executive produce and star in the movie, I couldn't believe it! Not only had the embers of my once-blazing career begun to glow again, but I also had the opportunity, as a first-time producer, to actively tend them. I hung up the phone and screamed. All that was left was getting a green light from a network, so we could begin production, which we did almost two years after the phone call from Judy Girrard. All I can say is thank you, Leslie, from the bottom of my heart.

Looking back, I realized that for almost eleven years, I had marshaled all of my willpower to try to *force* this project through. It had been push, push, push with absolutely no results. In fact, just six months prior to Leslie's phone call, I had actually given up on the project altogether. I decided that I would fight the battle no more, and I threw in the towel. I figured this project wasn't meant to be, and that was that.

But when the *One Child* project became a reality, I could no longer deny that something truly extraordinary was at work in my life, something that had nothing to do with me and my little desires or my little plans. I had let go of a project that I desperately wanted, and in letting go, the Universe had delivered it back to me at exactly the perfect moment. As a matter of fact, though I didn't know it at the time, I also received a gift far bigger than a movie. During the preproduction and filming, I would, coincidentally, find the answer to one of the childhood questions that had eluded me my entire life. Soon, I would experience the true essence of my being.

In preparing for my role as the teacher, I began my normal process of character research. The first step was to interview teachers who actually taught emotionally challenged children. I was familiar with the child's point of view. Like her, I had no understanding of how to constructively express the incredible anger and pain of trying to cope with the trauma of my father's unwarranted wrath. But what I couldn't connect with as an actress, however, was the teacher's perspective. How could anyone love a child who had tied a two-year-old boy to a tree and set him on fire! Who was this teacher whose limitless compassion drove her to risk everything —her job, her relationship, and even her life?

The question started me thinking about a nun named Mother Mary Concepta (now Sister Jane Roach), who had taught me in grammar and high school. She was extraordinarily loving and supportive during my difficult years with Dad, and I wondered if, perhaps, she could help me understand my character. I was curious what she had seen in me that allowed her to express her love so effusively. Perhaps she could give me a clue to defining my interaction with the little girl in the story.

Finding her wasn't easy, however. It took two weeks of diligent phone calls all over the country to locate her, but when I finally did, she was shocked and thrilled.

The conversation blew me away.

She remembered being aware that I was having trouble at home, but at the time, had no idea how unbearable it actually had been. She said she was drawn to me because I always had a smile on my face and was totally immersed in my absolute love of life. She said my "sense of play" was unequaled. As evidence, she reminded me of the time that I had somehow managed to convince four friends of mine from two neighboring all-boys high schools to help me attach a fire chain around the upper and lower gates of my school. When the bell rang at three o'clock, no one was able to leave. For three hours, the entire student body, as well as the faculty, had to wait inside until the fire department had torched through the chains. It was obvious why I had forgotten this incident.

She also reminded me of the time when two girlfriends and I were caught in the nuns' living quarters, going through closets to find out the secrets of convent life.

She felt that my ability to enthusiastically embrace any challenge that presented itself, left a particularly strong impression on her. But at the same time, she felt it was my purity and lightness of spirit, that made her want to help and protect me. It was wonderful to reconnect with her and to re-establish our friendship. I am most grateful that we have continued to stay in touch.

After our telephone call, I wondered if perhaps the teacher in the story had seen beneath the gnarled behavior of the little girl, and sensed her precious inner spirit. It was certainly more than enough of a spark for me to begin creating my role, and, for that, I was more than thankful.

After I'd finished putting all of the pieces of my character together, the next step was to "personalize" the little girl in the story. I needed to make her "real" to me, so that when acting with her, my performance would become more centered, defined, and emotionally grabbing for the audience. Although watching the children in the special-education classes I was observing proved helpful, it still wasn't precise enough. So I began to look at pictures of my godchildren, my friends' children, and my niece. Still, they weren't personal enough. They didn't draw me any closer to the script emotionally.

Then one day, after putting some books away in my bookshelf, I happened to notice one picture in particular. It was an 8-by-10, black-and-white photo of me around age five. (See page 256.) I must've seen it a hundred times before, but for some reason, on this occasion, it struck me deeply. I picked up the picture frame and stared at the photograph. I saw a little girl, dressed in a white-collared sundress with matching Mary-Jane shoes. She was sitting outdoors on a redwood chaise lounge, holding a little boxer puppy. Her eyes were shut tight in absolute ecstasy, with her arms wrapped tightly around the little dog whose ears had been cut and wrapped in bandages to make them stand erect. She was hugging this puppy with all her might, and, with a look of absolute joy on her face seemed to be thinking, "I can make him better. I'll just hold him until he's all well."

While staring at myself in the photo and connecting with this innocent child who was pouring out all of the love she could muster, a strange thing happened. I consciously experienced who I was at the core of my being, who I had been all along.

I truly connected on every level with that little girl in the photo. A wave of emotion deeper than any I had ever experienced washed over my entire body. That blissful little girl was *me*. The distance between us had been erased. Our hearts had joined, and we had become "one." In that moment, I experienced all of the things that were once part and parcel of my heart.

How much I had forgotten. I'd somehow lost the joy of what it meant to be that child. All my life, I had worked to make other children feel better: through my charity work, my efforts with inner-city kids, and my relationship with my young godchildren, niece, and the children of my close friends. But I didn't understand until that moment, that only one thing had been missing. It was my awareness that all of my interactions with children had simply been a reflection of the core of my heart. Beyond a shadow of a doubt, I knew exactly who I was and one of my burning childhood questions had finally been answered for good. Coincidentally, of course, the name of the movie I was about to begin shooting was *One Child*.

The definition of a Buddhist is said to be someone who has reawakened his or her joyous sense of awe and wonder. When I looked into that faded photograph, I reconnected with that very same joy in me. The pure innocent wondrous little girl had suddenly become *available* to me once again. She had always been with me, of course, but she had been buried under the unbending focus of my will, my success, and my dogged pursuit of fame and fortune. All my life, I had simply wanted to be someone special. We all do. Isn't it funny that we spend so much time and effort trying to be something we already are?

One Child began production one day before the rights to film the book were to revert back to the author. Again, coincidence, of course.

During the first few scenes with Ashley Lauren, who played the little girl, I had the distinct sense I was actually talking to myself, speaking directly to the little girl inside me. It was a phenomenal experience. Within the parameters of filming the movie, as the teacher was healing the little girl, I was actually healing myself as well.

As each day passed, that precious child within me became stronger and more visible; and by the end of the shoot, the scars of her heart had been mended forever.

After the movie aired in the fall of 1994, I returned to the books that Sam had given me and began to read even more voraciously. But now, I was assimilating what I was reading in a totally different manner. I realized that I was beginning to rebuild myself, piece by piece, as an adult whose heart was fully connected to her inner child.

Energized by this success, I was willing to leap to the next step. What that step was exactly, I didn't know. No scripts or jobs miraculously appeared at my door. Furthermore, I didn't have an agent. As a performer, this is tantamount to death. Ah, the beauty of nothingness . . . who said that?

When I had set out to become an actress, I had very specific goals in mind about how I wanted to achieve my success. I envisioned working steadily toward them, carefully planning each step along the way. There was no room for peripheral vision in my plan.

Having goals certainly isn't wrong; conversely, it's an absolute necessity. But unfortunately, particularly during the success of *That's Incredible,* I was so centered on my plan, that I could only see one way of achieving it. I realized that this had closed many of the doors that were available to me at any given moment. In my single-minded pursuit of my objectives, I didn't fully enjoy each step of the journey toward achieving them, and I also lost sight of the entire realm of possibility around me.

In addition, my goals always seemed *out there* somewhere, separate from me. So when I took a job, my decision to take it or not was always a conscious step *toward* my goal, instead of being a distinct part *of* it. Consequently, I was always living in the future and never in the present.

Now it was different. My experience of life had changed emphatically, and I certainly knew that I had to remain open to the magic of the Universe and trust that the answer on how to proceed would come. So I waited . . . and I waited . . . and I waited. After three weeks of waiting, however, I began to get a little anxious. I had to work, that was clear. But nothing was happening, and I began to lose my nerve. I began to worry, to question everything I had learned. How was I going to get a job without "doing" something? Was I on the wrong track? Was there something else, I was supposed to learn, and just wasn't getting it? Was I supposed to change careers completely? Was it fate that I was to live the rest of my life in poverty?

Thank God for the telephone again, which rang just in the nick of time.

It was one of my long-time friends and associates, Janie Cummings, who had been the entertainment and program director of my foundation, Get High on Yourself. She had called to invite me to a birthday party for her mother, Madeline, also my long-time friend and the former executive director of my foundation.

It was a lively affair, but needless to say, I was preoccupied. And then, I saw it. On the table in front of Madeline were all the presents she had just opened, including a book entitled *The Celestine Prophecy*. This was prior to the novel becoming a best-seller. In fact, nobody at the party had ever even heard of it.

But I couldn't take my eyes off this book.

I picked it up and glanced through it. I was mesmerized! I had to read this book, and I had to read it immediately. I excused myself from the gathering a little early and rushed to the nearest bookstore to buy a copy that very night. As I began reading, I became totally swept up in the main character's epiphanous journey as he searches for an ancient manuscript in the back country of Peru. I *became* that character and took the journey with him.

According to the story, the ancient manuscript contains nine insights that the human race is in the process of grasping as it enters a new millennium of spiritual awareness.

As each insight unfolded, the story confirmed more and more of the path I'd been on and what I had come to understand. Through the words of this book, I was actually "seeing" and reexperiencing my own journey first hand!

Triumph and tragedy, joy and pain, each step had been an essential evolution toward this moment. I finally understood that the collective experience of all the losses and pain of the past six years, had actually turned out to be one of the greatest gifts I'd ever received.

Where there is a ruin, there is hope for a treasure.

Sam's wisdom, once again, had hit its mark.

It was true. Though I had achieved a remarkable degree of "success," only after I had lost everything and had been *forced* to let go of the controlling aspects of my will, was I finally able to get out of my own way. Only then was I able to receive the gifts and coincidences that the Universe was ready to give me, and had always been ready to give me.

The Celestine Prophecy simply presented a new twist on the subject. The main character not only learns about the phenomenon of synchronistic forces, but also learns how to actively attract those forces. His training begins with a heightened sensitivity to beauty—in people, plants, animals, and all living things. The more he becomes aware of this beauty, the more he feels connected to the energetic pulse or *dance* of the Universe. And, as he continues along his path, in tune with the music of this flow, he becomes more and more aware of the coincidences that propel him forward toward the answers he is searching for. Therefore, the answer to his dilemma is no further away than the next coincidence, and the next coincidence is possibly no further away than the next second.

Following the main character through his discovery of the nine insights in succession, I understood the importance of every step he had taken from awakening to synchronicity, through dealing with energy, the struggle for power, the message of the mystics, the clearing of the past, and engaging the flow.

I saw that *each step* of my journey had been important. It was almost as if I was seeing my life as a movie and watching in amazement as it unfolded in my mind. There I was, the two-year-old at the bottom of the swimming pool; the teenage tennis champion smiling in the winner's circle yet crying at home; the daughter; the sister; the niece; the friend; the healing wife; the premed graduate; the striving drama student; the successful actress; the star; the soul mate; the defendant; the debtor; the Epstein-Barr survivor; the seeker; and, finally, the child of the Universe. I saw myself happy and sad, rich and poor, healthy and sick, blind and visionary. And I became thankful for it all.

I could see that when you live life from your heart, which is the conduit for the pulse and power of the entire Universe, *nothing* in this world can really harm you.

I also saw that everything I had done or achieved or experienced in my life to this point, had been missing one important aspect: the essence of my being. I had known the momentary thrill of victory and the exhilaration of success, but I was forced to suppress the awe, wonder, and surprise abundant in each and every moment it had taken me to get there.

Concurrent with the main character's Peruvian journey, I had *consciously* stepped back into the *Bliss Zone*. No longer were happiness, adventure, and excitement merely a function of *doing,* but rather, a function of *being.* At this moment, I truly experienced what being *alive* really means.

There were lots of new skills to learn, but now I knew what it felt like to be *home.*

The struggle was over. I had reconnected with the *Bliss Zone* and stepped back into the *dance* of the Universe, not just for the moment, but for life.

A mighty flame follows a tiny spark.
                                    Dante

17
Learning the Way of the Peaceful Warrior

*In Buddhist teachings, the term **skillful means** is used to describe an approach to making decisions and dealing with problems in a way that is appropriate to the situation and causes no harm. **Skillful means** always arise out of compassion, and when a problem emerges, the idea is to address the offense without denying the humanity of the offender.*

> Phil Jackson
> Head Coach, Chicago Bulls

The weak have one weapon: The errors of those who think they are strong.

> Georges Bidault

How would someone who has re-established their foothold in the *Bliss Zone* fare in the cold, cruel world of the courtroom? I was about to experience a baptism by fire when a discovery by my lawyer inadvertently brought my legal battles to a head.

It would be my first opportunity to test what Sam had taught me about living as a peaceful warrior. I had learned that a peaceful warrior only fights back as an absolute last resort; but, if he has to fight, *how* he fights is the key.

After four-and-a-half years of being aggressively pursued and beleaguered by all the legal proceedings against me, my lawyer, Brian Oxman, advised me that it was now time to fight back.

His argument was sound, but I was still apprehensive about moving forward, as his words made me uncomfortable. With the exception of competitive tennis, "fighting back" was not a natural pattern of behavior for me. The words conjured up too many memories of the combative experience I had known as a child, when I had been reluctant to take a stand for fear of the repercussions. I assumed that if I did, the "opposition" would mount an even stronger offensive.

In addition, though I understood the concept intellectually, based on everything I had learned, I certainly didn't know how to use the energy of the confrontation itself, to precipitate its own destruction. I questioned whether it was possible to stand up to an inequity and respond with strength, without losing my connection to the *Bliss Zone.* Could I "fight back" without separating myself from that magical place I had so gratefully reconnected with?

Before I could decide whether or not to allow Brian to address the issue, I had to face my childhood fear that standing tall in the face of aggression would automatically trigger negative consequences. My next step would have to be a giant leap of faith. I would have to trust myself to act based on what I knew, and what was right in my heart, regardless of any remaining doubts in my head.

In the final moments before making my decision, I remembered Sam telling me that "life shrinks or expands in proportion to one's courage." Hearing his words over and over in my head was the final gust of wind that lifted me into flight.

I gave Brian permission to take the appropriate action, and he filed complaints on my behalf against both the U.S. bankruptcy trustee, David Haberbush, and Joe Theismann.

The essence of the charges against the trustee included gross negligence, violation of ethical duties, conflict of interest, and violation of fiduciary duties. Appropriate damages were asked for, and that Mr. Haberbush be removed from the case. As far as Brian was able to discover, no one had ever sued a bankruptcy trustee in the state of California on this basis. The trustee's attorneys responded with a denial of the charges, as expected, but within a short period of time, the bankruptcy was brought to a speedy and final resolution.

The essence of the complaint filed against Joe Theismann included breach of contract, abuse of process, and infliction of emotional distress. His attorneys responded with a denial of the charges, as expected, but within a short period of time our case was brought to a speedy and final resolution, as well.

My lengthy legal saga had, at long last, come to an end.

Finally, I was free.

I had spent four-and-a-half years of anguish, almost one million dollars in legal fees, plus an extraordinary amount of additional money to free myself, once and for all, from every courtroom entanglement.

And now, it was over. Though I still had to deal with some residual effects of this fourth and final traumatic event, the everyday assault on my life and my livelihood was gone for good.

Not only that, the experience strengthened my understanding of how to live my life as a peaceful warrior. It served as a reminder that true strength is not about the exterior symbols of money, power, or fame; but rather, about staying connected to your heart no matter what the circumstances.

I also learned that the intention of a warrior living in the *Bliss Zone* is not about being aggressive just for the sake of winning. It is not about doing anything to anyone at any cost, just to win. It is, however, about standing up for what is right and fair, and then "responding," using only the amount of force that is absolutely necessary to achieve a just resolution. There is a "right" and a "wrong" at the very core of things, and most of us instinctively know which is which. Rest assured, your heart alone holds the answer.

We signed all of the necessary papers, and then my lawyer, his staff, and some of my closest friends and family went out for a veritable feast in celebration.

I chose the particular restaurant for a very good reason, of course. I hadn't used any of the current month's five hundred dollars worth of free food and beverage, and was thrilled to be able to spend it all treating those who had been so supportive.

The *Bliss Zone* was getting interesting . . . really interesting.

18
The Choreography of a Coincidence

The choreography of a coincidence . . .
At the turning point, there was eternity
Behind a moment's glance.
David Wilcox

Above all that you hold dear,
watch over your heart,
for from it comes life.
Proverbs 4:23

There was no turning back. I had plunged into the maelstrom of my life and successfully navigated its turbulent waters. In the process, I had regained my health, vanquished my legal demons, steadied the sails of my career, re-established my family bonds, and awakened to a whole new world of possibility. It didn't matter anymore that I didn't know exactly what I was supposed to "do." I had learned the importance of going with the flow, and wherever it led me, I was willing and eager to go there.

It sounds easy, but in reality, it's particularly difficult to finally let go and put the theory into practice on a daily basis. The amount of trust involved is unbelievable. Yet, along with this learning process came an intense excitement, simply because I didn't know what to expect. There was an electricity within me that was so powerful, it began to serve as a magnet, bringing in more and more coincidences at an ever-accelerating pace. I could feel the energy in the air, and I was enjoying the dance of the Universe in earnest.

One of my first poignant glides to the music came in the form of a thank-you note. Shortly after reading his book, *The Celestine Prophecy,* I wrote James Redfield a simple expression of my appreciation for what he had written. The note itself was effortless; finding him, on the other hand, was a bit more of a chore. On a hunch, I ended up calling a prominent hotel in Birmingham, Alabama near his hometown and found a bellman who was able to locate the author's address.

About three days later, I sent him my letter. It felt great! Just knowing that Mr. Redfield would read it was enough.

The following Sunday, however, I happened to pick up a telephone call forwarded from my office, which I almost never do.

"Hello," came a distinctive Southern drawl over the line. "This is James."

"James?" I inquired. "James who?"

"James Redfield."

I couldn't believe it. I was completely flustered. I remember stuttering and stammering for a few minutes before I could regain my composure.

Before long, however, my nervousness had disappeared, and I became totally engrossed in a terrific conversation with the author. Then, out of nowhere, I heard myself say nine words that seemed to echo in my ears as if I were standing in a canyon: "I want to produce a movie of your book."

Talk about an example of zero premeditation! I had no money, no feature-film production experience, no game plan, no nothing . . .

"Okay," Redfield replied, "why don't you send me an offer?"

I hung up the phone, stunned. Talk about going with the flow and following the Universe! I felt like I was in the middle of the rapids! It took me a full day just to recover, much less muster the nerve to drive over to see my entertainment lawyer, Steve Breimer. His firm, Bloom,

Hergott, Cook, Diemer & Klein in Beverly Hills, is regarded as one of the top law firms in Hollywood and a major "player" in the entertainment industry.

I wasn't exactly sure where to begin, so I got right to the point.

"Steve," I began, "I want to make an offer to secure the film rights for a book."

"Great, which book?" he asked.

"Well . . . actually . . . you've probably never heard of it . . . *The Celestine Prophecy,*" I choked.

His face went white.

He stared at me as if perhaps he had misunderstood.

"Let me get this straight, you want to option *The Celestine Prophecy,* the book that just hit the best-seller list?"

"Well, yes . . . yes, I do," I whispered.

"Cathy Lee, with all due respect, do you realize how many well-financed, successful movie producers will be after this book?"

"Well, I know you're right, but it's just something I feel I must take a shot at. Either it's supposed to happen or it's not," I said, going for broke. "The author asked me to send him an offer, and that's what I'd like to do."

Knowing my present financial situation and being the diplomat he is, Steve couched his next remark in the kindest possible manner. "Okay, let's see then. The option price you're considering would be . . . ?"

"Right . . . the option price," I stalled. "Well . . . I'm not exactly sure how much it should be, so just offer him whatever's fair for an author in his position."

Taking a slightly more direct route, Steve looked straight at me and said, "Cathy Lee, how are you going to come up with the money to do this?"

Ah, my first test of doing business in the *Bliss Zone*. Here it was, right in front of me. *All right,* I said to myself, *just tell the truth, come from your heart, and go with the flow.*

"Steve, I don't know where I'm going to get the money," I answered hesitantly, "I just know that if I'm supposed to acquire the rights, then the financing will come, and I will find the right partners to help me do it."

There was a long silence. I had only been a client of Steve's for a few months and had certainly not come to him at a "peak" in my career. I knew this was a moment of decision for him. Because he was working with me on a percentage basis, as many industry attorneys do, he had to weigh whether or not his time was going to be well spent representing someone who was embarking on a way of doing business in Hollywood that was completely opposite the norm. I'm sure he considered the fact that his firm represented such high profile stars as Arnold Schwarzenegger, Sylvester Stallone, and Bruce Willis, and therefore, didn't have to take chances if he didn't want to. Would he be able to rationalize to the other members of the partnership his going out on a limb like this? As he turned to look at me I knew he'd made his decision.

"All right, why don't I do a rough draft of a fair offer for a best-selling book and get it to you for review?"

I thanked him for taking the chance, and left his office feeling eerily calm and peaceful. The mere fact of making an offer of this magnitude, regardless of the results, had validated my new understanding that living in the *Bliss Zone* indeed opened the door to pure potential.

A week later, Steve's offer arrived. With a few minute changes, it was ready to go. After several conversations with Mr. Redfield, we decided that I would fly down to Birmingham, to personally present it to him and his wife, Salle.

Talk about riding the energy of coincidences and accepting the ensuing magic, this was the antithesis of any Hollywood meeting I'd ever had. And yet, I felt totally comfortable that this was exactly what I was supposed to be doing and how I was supposed to be doing it.

I will never forget the plane flight either. Here I was, using a ticket obtained with my free mileage once again, without a penny in my pocket, flying down to make an offer to buy the rights to a best-selling book. James had told me in one of our phone conversations that twenty-two people, some of whom were among the biggest producers in Hollywood, had placed substantial offers on the table over the last six months. He also informed me that he had not personally met with any of them. It was clear to me that our paths were meant to cross, even if it had nothing to do with the possibility of my producing a movie of his book. I had to make the journey regardless.

James, Salle, and I met for lunch and spent three hours talking about everything under the sun: my six year saga, his career prior to writing, our thoughts and beliefs about life in general, as well as specific ideas about how his book could be turned into a film. I felt very much akin to these people. They were simple, gracious, open, caring individuals. It had been a most interesting afternoon, capped by my handing him the paperwork he was expecting. We finally said good-bye, and he reassured me that he would call as soon as he had a chance to study the proposal.

James responded immediately with interest; and after coming to an agreement on some of his specific issues concerning the contract, I told him my plan to bring in a partner on the financial end. I assured him that whoever I chose would first have to be acceptable to him. Once I had assembled the necessary financial backing, as well as the team of producers, I would get back to him.

Instead of continuing in the same vein that I had been and waiting for a clear sign as to how I should go about finding a financial partner, unfortunately, I reverted back to an old habit. It would prove to be *Big Mistake Number One.*

I started "making a list" of everyone in the entertainment business who was thought of as a "power player," as well as independently wealthy entrepreneurs that might be candidates. I remember thinking at the time, *big book, needs big money, needs big important names.*

Shortly thereafter, I began to "reach out" and talk to these people, hoping to "convince" them of the project's tremendous merit. I carefully "planned" everything I was going to say prior to saying it. I didn't seriously take into consideration "who" they were but only that they were successful and powerful in their fields.

Because the book was receiving tremendous publicity by this time, I got responses immediately, two of which I thought would be a perfect match. One possible partner was a dynamic independent entrepreneur; the other a very successful, high-profile Hollywood producer.

Everything seemed right on track. And then, lo and behold, right before my eyes, I got to experience firsthand, *coincidentally,* of course, a chapter right out of James' book, "The Struggle for Power."

I sat back and watched dumbfounded at what was taking place. Just as we were trying to finalize the business points of our partnership, before I presented anything to James, tempers flared. It was obvious that both of the new players wanted control at any cost, and a battle began in earnest. The main issue at hand was: which one of them was going to be the boss.

Soon, the battle itself became the primary focus, and there was no longer any concern for the good of the property, or the good of James Redfield, or the good of the partnership. In the ensuing chaos, I was caught in the crossfire.

It didn't take long for me to realize my mistake. It hit me square in the face. How could I have fallen back into my old pattern? Once again, I had gotten caught up in "doing" rather than simply listening to my heart and staying with the flow. It was obvious that I was going to need a bit more practice getting the hang of living in the *Bliss Zone,* with respect to the entertainment business.

I decided right there and then to rectify the situation as best I could. I would simply sit back and wait until I absolutely knew the right way to handle it. Even though it seemed on the outside that I couldn't have picked two more perfect people for this project, I had made a serious error in judgment.

Unfortunately, the struggle for power had gotten too far out of hand, and all my efforts at appeasement proved fruitless. It was evident that the best thing to do was to simply withdraw, so I notified each person of my decision. My business representatives thought I was crazy, but I knew what had to be done.

I also called James to tell him about the error I had made and exactly why I was bowing out. Because I had been keeping him abreast of the situation by sending him copies of every piece of communication I had received, he understood. He had seen firsthand what was happening, so it was no surprise to him at all. We were both disappointed, but I remember him saying to me at the time to "Just keep doing what you're doing. It'll all work out." I knew I had made the right decision, because as soon as I withdrew from the situation, the energy began to move again in every area of my life.

As far as I was concerned, that was the end of my efforts to secure the rights to *The Celestine Prophecy*. In addition, I told each of my erstwhile partners that they were perfectly welcome to pursue the book on their own, either separately or together. And while attempts were made by both of them, in partnership, as well as individually, to secure the rights, all of these efforts failed. It was a good lesson for me to remember: If you engage in a struggle for power, everyone ends up losing, even if it looks like, in the short term, one person has won.

Coincidentally, some five or six months after withdrawing, I began to get telephone calls from various producers and other money sources, who said they were extremely interested in producing a movie of the book with me. They had "heard" through the entertainment grapevine that I was the one who was going to end up with the rights. I assured them that this was not the case, and in fact, I had withdrawn my efforts in that direction completely. But the calls kept coming anyway.

Quite by chance, during a meeting I was having with Tim Bogart of Wolfcrest Entertainment regarding a completely different film project, I happened to use *The Celestine Prophecy* as an example of the feeling I wanted to achieve in the script we were working on. He had no idea what I was talking about. I suggested that he read the book over the weekend, before we reconvened on Monday to forge ahead. Par for the course, I had no idea that our Monday meeting would open the door to a whole new adventure.

It started as soon as Tim walked into the room. He was pacing with excitement, going on and on about what the book had to say about life, and what an important movie it could be. He was hooked, and asked me point blank if he could be my partner and produce it with me. I explained to him that I had withdrawn from pursuing the project. He asked again. I proceeded to tell him the history of why I had withdrawn in the first place.

He asked again. I informed him of all the people who had been contacting me, who I likewise had told that I was not pursuing the project. He asked again. This time I didn't reply. There was nothing left to say.

Instead, I took a real long look at the person sitting across the table from me. Yes, he was a twenty-six-year-old. Yes, he was the son of a beloved record-company entrepreneur who had died when Tim was twelve. Yes, he certainly was a brilliant writer and capable producer. And yes, he was funny, sensitive, and open. There was also no denying that we worked extremely well together. But, even if I was willing to consider pursuing the rights again, was this the right time? And if it was, by chance, the right time, was this the right partner?

I wasn't completely sold until Tim began to tell me the particular reasons why he wanted to be involved with this particular book. He'd been on a journey of his own and had traveled a long, long way. And though our paths had taken different routes, coincidentally, we had arrived at a very similar place.

My course of action was no longer in doubt. I knew that our partnership on *The Celestine Prophecy* was meant to be and agreed to step up to the plate once again. And thus, just like that, the incredible odyssey continued . . .

Normally, you get the rights to a book and then you secure the money for the budget to film it. But life in the *Bliss Zone* has its own unique set of business practices, as I was rapidly learning.

Having gone through the motions once before on this project, I was well aware of what had to happen before I could even consider taking a complete and final offer to James. The first element I needed was a reliable, caring financier who was emotionally attached to the book. Nothing less would do. I also knew that a majority of the approximate forty-five-million-dollar budget would have to be guaranteed up front in order to allay any fears the author had that the movie would sit on a shelf and not go into production. I also had to be sure that James would be given a good measure of creative control over the choice of director and/or screen writer, as well as active participation in the production itself. The final requirement was that any deal had to include a percentage of the profits on the back end for all of the major creative people involved in the film, including James. Additionally, this percentage had to be based upon a true definition of the *gross* profits from dollar one.

Hollywood had become notorious for their net definitions of profit. Simply stated, the *net* is what's left over after every conceivable expense from any film a studio has released in the recent past that has not been successful, has been deducted. Obviously, most people with net definitions never see a dime.

If I was going to produce this film, even though it would be my first for the big screen, I simply refused to be part of a deal that was based on a lie from the word go.

Tim was happy to let me call the shots on this one. He knew that my practice round had prepared me in terms of what would have to happen in order to close the deal.

Coincidentally, our first meeting with a financier would turn out to be the only one we needed. We hit a home run our first time at bat. Not only that, the meeting occurred as a result of a casual conversation that Tim Bogart had with the financier during the course of a meeting the two of them were having on another project. Again, the Universe had provided our next step.

Mark Damon of MDP Worldwide (Mark Damon Productions) was an unusual choice. Generally producers go to the studios, secure the money, make the film, and then go to the company like Mark Damon's to handle the release of the picture in foreign countries.

Because of the phenomenal success of *The Celestine Prophecy* in overseas markets, Tim got the idea of reversing the process. We would first secure the foreign financing by preselling the book as a film in foreign territories through MDP Worldwide, and then use that money to make the movie. A top studio would be brought in at a later date to ensure a major release of the film. This would provide us with maximum control over the film itself, as well as the profits on the back end. This procedure is not widely utilized, but one of the few notable exceptions is the great film *Dances with Wolves.*

Because Mark Damon loved the book, the negotiation process moved smoothly in terms of finalizing Tim's and my partnership agreement with him. All the points that we were concerned about were covered, and when the final contracts were signed a very short time later, it was clear the three of us were in synch.

What a wonderful experience it was for me to call James Redfield and tell him the good news. Finally, I had been able to assemble a team that I was proud of, one that I could assure him was dedicated to delivering the type of film that was worthy of his book. He asked me to fax him the offer.

The message that I received from the author four days later was one I had been dreaming about for over a year and a half! "The offer is extremely interesting, and I've asked my attorney, John Diamond, to call you and open formal negotiations."

Unbelievable! What a feeling! I had listened to my heart, followed its direction, and trusted that the Universe would take care of the rest. I had no attachment to the outcome, and I truly felt that whatever happened was exactly the way it was supposed to be.

John Diamond called a short time later and the discussions began in earnest.

I like to call this particular phase of the negotiation process *the courtship dance*. No stone is left unturned. Calls, meetings, faxes, ad nauseam! It's extremely difficult for all involved to remain patient and allow the process to unfold at its own pace. Needless to say, there is a great deal of difference between the tempo in Hollywood and the tempo in the South. It's like five cups of coffee meeting up with a sloe gin fizz. Not exactly an ideal coupling.

The dance continues, and though I have no idea when, or even if, a final contract will be signed, as is often the case with many entertainment endeavors, for the first time in my life, I am truly enjoying the process itself. My eyes are wide open and I'm allowing my well-centered intuition to rule my behavior. It's remarkably satisfying to know that you are doing your best, and that doing your best, in and of itself, is fulfilling enough. I am enjoying the adventure, and I'm delighted to be along for the ride, regardless of the outcome.

This experience was my first test of marrying the entertainment business with living in the *Bliss Zone,* and I had passed with flying colors.

The amazing thing about participating in the dance, is that as you join in with the energy flowing around you, the more new doors keep opening along the way.

For instance, my initial encounter with producing the film *One Child,* had opened the door to *The Celestine Prophecy.* And likewise, *The Celestine Prophecy* opened other doors exponentially. Within no time at all, my production company (CLC Productions) was ablaze with projects, all of which had come to me by equally fortuitous circumstances. And, no two were alike. Some I would produce and act in, some I would just produce; some were feature films, and some were movies for television. The point is, there was no particular "method" to the madness, so to speak, and yet, the results were definitely leading me in a specific direction on a much more dynamic scale.

All systems were *go* in my professional life once again. Everything was running smoothly until one day when I happened to receive my invitation to the Academy Awards.

Simple enough, get a dress, get a date, and go. Though finding a dress proved to be no problem at all, as I had a closet full of formal attire that hadn't been seen publicly for a while, finding a date was quite another story. The entire subject conjured up images remarkably similar to a torture chamber.

Obviously, there was one area of my life that I had neglected to address during my journey back into the *Bliss Zone.* There were no two ways about it, the invitation had arrived, and it was clearly addressed to me.

19
Looking for Love in All the Wrong Places

I was lookin' for love in all the wrong places; Lookin' for love in too many faces; Searchin' their eyes, lookin' for traces; Of what I'm dreamin' of.

Mallette, Ryan, & Morrison

If we do not change our direction, we are likely to end up where we are headed.

Chinese Proverb

Not only did I detest the idea of looking for a date, but I had absolutely no desire to date either. I couldn't even consider the *thought*. The possibility of entering into another relationship was tantamount to standing naked on the Golden Gate Bridge for the six o'clock news. It just wasn't going to happen.

In addition, my recent experience with trying to arbitrate the overpowering egos of my initial partners, during my efforts to secure the rights to *The Celestine Prophecy,* had brought up a sore issue. It was obvious that from my early childhood, up to and including the present, I still had not overcome my inability to deal with this type of overbearing individual. There seemed to be a common theme in all of these situations that I had not previously been aware of. Even Joe fit this mold as well. I guess the sum total of these experiences had finally hit its mark, and I closed down emotionally, rather than dealing with the issue head on. Besides, I had so many other necessities of a much more practical nature to attend to that even thinking about the subject of relationships was more than I could handle.

In every area of my life, the challenges and changes had been profound: family, nutrition, exercise, friendships, and my career. There was a new feeling of joy and fulfillment, and life had become so much more vibrant and alive. However, there was one more door yet to be opened, the final passageway to the "center" of things. As Sam had shown me in the book *Journey of the Heart,* this step was "the doorway to the ultimate human experience, the ability to bond with someone else in an absolute being-to-being connection . . . which taps each of us into the divine." Not only had I never been there, I didn't even know that such an experience existed.

Rest assured, however, when you're traveling in the *Bliss Zone,* allowing the universe to carry you naturally in the direction you should be going, you'd better be ready for whatever new threshold comes your way.

Again, Sam had woven another piece of my magic carpet. Because of the book's title, I initially thought it was merely a further explanation of the path I was on. I assumed it was referring to one's connection to the inner core of one's being. Had I bothered to read the subtitle when I happened to pick it up again, *Intimate Relationships and the Path of Love,* I might have been a bit more prepared for what was about to happen. I might have been able to foresee that I was on the verge of grasping the very heart of intimate man/woman relationships.

The book takes intimate partnerships out of the boy-meets-girl scenario, and throws them into a whole new realm. Romantic unions are presented as an opportunity for one of the most powerful sources of growth and aliveness possible. In other words, an intimate relationship between two people can be the most direct path into the core of who we really are as individuals.

Intimate relationships force us to face all the core issues of human experience—our family history, our personality dynamics, questions about who we are, how to communicate, how to handle our feelings, how to let love flow through us, how to be committed, as well as how to let go and surrender.

I had always looked at a relationship as something that just happened. You see a person, you get a sense of them, and either chemistry occurs or it doesn't. If it does, the "dating game" begins. Everything is blissful in the early stages, but then, invariably, difficulties arise. You choose to stay or choose to leave. In my case, I guess you might say that I looked at a relationship as a "product."

But the book described a relationship as a "path." It said that "when problems arise, they should become an integral part of the path itself, forcing us to develop our inner resources—patience, generosity, kindness, bravery. . . ." In other words, using the intimate connection as a direct line to the "center" of things.

I'd never looked at a relationship as being part and parcel of my own inner growth. I think we all are caught up in the "dream" of love, rather than the real, conscious "path" of love. In my case, I was always trying to match whoever it was I had chosen, to the "inner vision" of who I "thought" I wanted to be with. The result was that I ended up *unconsciously* choosing my relationships for all the wrong reasons: physical attraction, my own imagined psychological deficiencies, a subconscious playing out of my familial dramas, and, frankly, for the heart-pounding thrill of a red-hot, full-tilt romance.

And so, with each new experience, I would begin the cycle again: the quest, the adventure, the playing of the game, and then the ultimate resolution. Perhaps these partnerships were reflections of a particular piece of unfinished business within myself. But whatever the reasons, as I look back, I realize that each relationship also brought with it a gift, offering me the chance to examine a part of myself and to play that part out to its healthy resolution.

Of course, this profundity is seen from the clarity of hindsight. At the time, I was simply swept up in the moment. As had been true in every area of my life, my love relationships, from my husband up to and including Joe, had been marked by a single omission: the essence of my being. Because I didn't know that the key to having a genuine connection with someone on an intimate level rested *inside* myself, I was always searching *outside* for the answer.

"There is a difference between *getting* a partner and *attracting* a partner," writes Marianne Williamson. "Getting implies that our hooks work; attracting means that our light is bright and appears like a beacon to the one who is meant to see it. When we *try* to get a partner, we increase our chances of getting the wrong one. Yes, we can hook one, but a hook in him is a hook in us . . . when we attract love by an intensified connection to the spirit inside . . . we take responsibility for the energy around us, harmonizing with it in such a way that those who come forward—who we sense are meant to be with us—connect with us out of similarly pure intent."

If relationships are a mirror of the self, then all I can say is mine have reflected every conceivable part of my personality. They run the gamut from A to Z in terms of how totally different each one was from the other. Seeking to make some sense of this tangled arena in my life, in light of all the new information I was learning, I pulled out a pad of paper once more and began to write. Perhaps I could trace the roots of this most unusual collection of adult relationships. It wasn't long before I began to see a very interesting pattern. Each of them seemed to reflect some subconscious, unacknowledged longing within me.

At the top of my list of prime examples was a scenario that certainly has played itself out in all of our minds, if not in our actual lives.

The Ozzie and Harriet Rerun—All of us long for the security of hearth and home, a lifetime commitment from the altar to the grave. We imagine perfection, stability, a mate for life. Girls, especially, are brought up to believe the standard litany of childhood, education, marriage, children, and then living happily ever after. I realized that I had married my husband, Alec, based on this litany. And why not, he encompassed all of the attributes of what I had grown up to believe was the ideal spouse: reliable, family oriented, decent, kind, and a provider. I'm not saying these weren't wonderful qualities, it's just that I wasn't able to identify and acknowledge them in myself, so I couldn't value them in someone else. Accordingly, I couldn't fully appreciate the value of our marriage either. As I looked back, I could see that the marriage served as a haven from what I had been through at home. It was a safe place where I could "rest," in a manner of speaking. Unfortunately, at the time, all I remember was the underlying feeling of emptiness that kept gnawing at me. I didn't know where to turn to find the salve to heal the hole in my heart. Not knowing how to look within myself, I felt my only option was to sever my ties to the marriage and venture out to see if I could find the remedy. Again, as I had done in so many other areas of my life, I looked for a solution to the problem "out there."

I'm Comin' Out!—When you are the daughter of a strict Southern Baptist disciplinarian, who did everything he could to make sure that his daughters lived properly, according to his rules and regulations, sooner or later the dam bursts. After my divorce from Alec, a powerful need awoke in me to break free, breathe, test my wings, and again, to see what was "out there." The first man I started dating was carefree, light-hearted, fun-loving, and someone with whom I could share what I loved doing best—acting. He was a struggling performer himself, so we formed a bond, you might say. He was a real friend and a buddy, almost like a brother to me. We even looked alike. I remember how much I enjoyed his tremendous energy and love of life. The relationship remained strong until my career began to seriously take off. It was difficult for him to deal with my success in light of his continuing struggle. Though the relationship ended, we are still friends today. I could see that friendship, by itself, is not an answer unto itself.

Rebel With a Cause—There seems to come a time in everyone's formative years when they decide to tell the world, "It's my life and I'll live it as I damn well please." A woman in this frame of mind tends to forsake everything for a man who mirrors her desire to live her life on her own terms. I embraced my rebellious side during a movie I was filming. He was a major action star who was handsome, doe-eyed, sensuous, romantic, and famous. He literally swept me off my feet. I felt the fact that he was black was destined to become a major issue in my family. My father had disowned my sister, Linda Lou, for many years simply because she married a man who was Jewish, and now, "Guess who's coming to dinner?" But, my father had moved to Australia by then and, much to my surprise, the rest of my family adored and accepted my boyfriend totally. Looking back, he mirrored the wild, rebellious, devil-may-care part of me, and I desperately needed to experience that rebellion for reasons that had nothing to do with him. Rebellion, however, is not any kind of a basis for a lasting relationship.

Harlequin Romance—Why is it girls in particular dream of being swept off their feet? We fantasize about a tall, dark stranger, stepping out of the shadows, and taking us firmly but gently by the hand, into a world where love reigns supreme. . . . Well, I couldn't have written the script better myself. In fact, it must have been particularly appealing to me, because I fell for it hook, line, and sinker, *twice!* The second chapter was obviously my whirlwind romance with Joe. The first chapter, however, was the infamous hairdresser-turned-studio-mogul-turned-producer.

Two girlfriends of mine had talked me into going to his Beverly Hills salon for a haircut. Sitting in the waiting room, I saw him staring at me from the doorway.

"Cancel everybody," he suddenly said to his receptionist. "I'm taking this client next."

My girlfriends were astounded; I was totally embarrassed. But when I tried to beg off, he wouldn't hear of it, and ushered me straight to his chair. After what was probably the best haircut I'd every had, he informed me that we were going shopping.

"Are you out of your mind?" I exclaimed. "You can't just take off work like that."

"Watch me," he laughed. Grabbing his jacket, he told my girlfriends he would see to it that I got home safe and sound. Then, he practically dragged me out onto Rodeo Drive.

My new beau didn't return to work for the next two weeks. Our relationship took off fast and furious. I hardly had a chance to breathe. I was attracted to his exuberance, his dynamic energy, and his absolute confidence in who he was. He knew what he wanted, and didn't take "no" for an answer. I'm almost embarrassed to say that his sweeping me off my feet was immensely appealing, but everything he did was intense, including how he dealt with me. In a short while, however, it became evident that our relationship was actually being produced, rather than being lived.

For instance, he threw a party one Saturday night to introduce me to about fifty of his closest friends.

"Wear white," he said. "I want everybody dressed in white."

I arrived to discover one of the most amazing visual scenarios I'd ever witnessed, and it was all in my honor: The entire house was decorated with white flowers, white candles, and tiny white lights, all added for the evening's special occasion. It was surreal. Yes, it was romantic, but it also served as a visual metaphor of our union: a fairy tale with absolutely no basis in reality. It was fun, fast, and furious, but not exactly fodder for a homebase.

I Love Paris in the Springtime—Being a hopeless romantic, I've always loved dreaming of exotic, foreign lands, shrouded in mystery and intrigue. My leading man in those dreams was quite often a character that seemed to be straight out of the pages of a good novel: a glamorous type, celebrating until long past midnight in some chic Parisian nightclub without a care in the world. I literally entered this fantasy at the hands of a devil-may-care, French-speaking Swiss. He was gregarious and extremely social, as well as being an expert on fine wines, good food, and international society. After *That's Incredible* soared to the top of the ratings and being social became more of a necessity, he and I were a natural. We were constantly jetting off to Europe for work and play, sampling all the "best" that our particular destination had to offer along the way. It was a whole new world for me, and it was a great hors d'oeuvre for awhile. The problem was, we never got to the main course because our relationship lacked any kind of sincere heart-felt connection. Living in a Jackie Collins' novel is tantamount to the depth of one of its pages.

Desperado—There's something about the strong, silent type that has always appealed to me. Someone who lives life on his own terms, without a thought to the consequences. If he radiates raw unbridled talent, so much the better. If he seemingly lives on the fringe of law and order, so much the better. The very thought of a man like this unleashes something wild within us, something long cloaked by our strongly ingrained sense of decorum. He makes us want to do things most people only fantasize about doing.

I was working in New York one week, when I got a call from the new man in my life, the lead singer/songwriter of a hugely popular rock and roll band. Since the weekend was approaching, he told me to expect a surprise and to just "trust him and go along with it."

At about 3:30 P.M. the next afternoon, I answered the phone in my hotel room and heard a limousine driver saying he was there to pick me up and take me to the airport. Forgetting the conversation I had had the previous day, I assured him that there was some mistake, as I hadn't ordered a limousine. Completely disregarding what I had just said, he announced that the bellman was on his way up to my room to deliver a note that would explain everything. Indeed, the doorbell rang and the bellman handed me an envelope.

"Don't ask any questions, you're in for the time of your life," the note inside read. "All my love . . ."

The entire setup was indicative of everything I adored about his personality: reckless, impromptu, and totally irresistible. I hurriedly packed my bags, imagining some private rendezvous at a hotel in upstate New York.

I made my way down to the limo where I found two dozen roses, a bottle of chilled champagne, and a single crystal glass waiting for me. He certainly had my attention.

After a forty-five-minute drive, we pulled into a private airport and up to a Lear jet that was waiting there. The pilot took my bags from the driver, and helped me up into the plane where I fully expected to see my boyfriend awaiting me. Instead, the jet was filled with more roses, more chilled champagne, and another note which read, "See you soon. All my love . . ."

"Where are we going?" I asked the pilot as we took off into the dusk of night.

"I'm sorry, but I'm not allowed to tell," he said.

"That figures," I mumbled to myself.

It was impossible for me to discern which direction we were flying in, so I decided to just sit back, sip my champagne, and enjoy the ride.

After an uneventful three hours in the air, the jet landed at another private airport in what seemed to be the middle of a deserted field. Another limousine was waiting with more roses, another bottle of champagne, a crystal glass and of course, another note.

This one read: "Never say never. All my love . . ."

I couldn't figure out what was happening, but the adventure was turning out to be exciting.

I still had no idea where I was. Not even a clue. And the windows were tinted so dark, that I couldn't actually see anything outside.

About twenty minutes later, I began hearing a faint noise. It was getting louder and louder with every mile we drove. Around the next bend, we entered a parking lot and started driving toward this huge tunnel. As we entered it, the noise became deafening, and I could see through the front windshield the faces of thousands and thousands of people that were seated in this gigantic stadium.

Oh, my God, I thought. *No way.*

This was going to be my introduction to seeing him and his band perform live. The fact that I had never attended one of his concerts had been a standing joke between us.

Security escorted me down to the first row where I took my seat, flanked by bodyguards. Being so close to the speakers, my hearing was shot in about fifteen minutes, but my eyes soon focused on the set the band was performing on. Pasted at various strategic locations were small, humorous pictures or clippings of me during different phases of my career. It was hysterical, romantic, and inventive, and I was enjoying every minute.

A short time later, however, it became clear that the intensity of his restless nature would be too overwhelming on a full-time basis. I'm sure this was partly because it too closely resembled my own.

Lean on Me—A part of all of us longs for protection, to feel that there is someone out there who we can really count on. When we haven't tapped into our own inner sense of security and strength, we tend to seek it outside ourselves. We inadvertently look for the strong, the self-reliant, and the powerful. My search for these seemingly missing elements in myself led me to someone who filled the bill to a tee. He was a studio mogul who was a significant number of years older than I, and he was smart, tough, blunt, caring, and very successful. His voice alone could shake a soundstage.

It seems that a lot of children who are abused by their fathers in their young life seek to resolve the trauma through their male/female relationships. Looking back on it, this person came into my life to provide the strength and presence I needed to deal with my father face to face. He flew with me to Australia for what would turn out to be the last time I would see Dad alive. My father died of pneumonia not six months later, in Sydney, where he had lived for the last eleven years of his life. Not only had I not seen my father since he had left the U.S., but I had no idea how I would handle being with him again after everything that had happened between us. I wanted to try one last time to reach him and repair the damage. Although that would not turn out to be the case, at the end of the trip, unbeknownst to me, he took my dad aside at the airport.

"I don't think you understand who your daughter is," he began. "She's kind, loving, smart, and tremendously talented. She's even started her own charitable foundation. I'd have to say that Cathy Lee is one of the most unique and exceptional people I have ever met."

My father's answer? "Well, of course she is. She's my daughter, isn't she?"

Our relationship allowed me the opportunity to try to deal with my traumatic experience with Dad firsthand. But a relationship unconsciously built on one party's need to handle a family trauma, is not only detrimental to building a healthy bond between the two people, it is also not basis for any kind of lasting commitment either.

Looking back on all of my varied unions, I could see why the deepest part of me was not available to any of them. I still had one remaining piece of the hole in my heart and was looking to fill that void through my relationships. In addition, as far as the nuts and bolts of having a successful relationship were concerned, I was a carpenter without tools. I had no idea how to build a partnership and keep it strong. So I plunged into one after another, seeking the answer. It was certainly an adventurous time in my life, but when each partnership ended, I was still left with a deep sense of longing. For what, I didn't know.

My dating life was like a virtual reality game. With each new partner, I would put on the glasses and play out a different aspect of myself with full intensity. The only problem was, when I took the glasses off, my reality had not changed and the longing continued.

With Joe, however, I was positive that our relationship was going to be different. I thought I'd found the answer. Not only did we have a common love of athletics, travel, and adventure, but there seemed to be a real loving, passionate connection. Because the relationship filled so many of our individual needs, and because of its sheer intensity, it *seemed* to have all the depth I was searching for. For a period of time, even my awareness of the void dissipated, and I therefore assumed it had left for good. Unfortunately, it hadn't. My relationship with Joe so consumed every ounce of my energy that when I ended it, my awareness of the void not only returned, but this time, it was overwhelming. I had to close down emotionally to protect myself. It was the only way I could handle the realization that the hole in my heart was still there.

Returning to the wisdom I was uncovering in *Journey of the Heart,* what I had been missing was increasingly apparent.

The ground of a strong and lasting commitment is the passionate connection between two people whose beings say yes to each other. When two people connect being-to-being, they experience a deep "soul resonance" that goes beyond mere romance or desire. Something powerful and real inside them starts waking up and coming alive in each other's presence. . . . Out of this passionate resonance grows a devotion to each other's unfolding—which can allow them to persevere through difficult times and overcome any obstacles that threaten to come between them.

How could Sam possibly have known? How could he have been able to anticipate so far in advance, exactly what I would need to read?

My new understanding of love was allowing me to awaken a whole new realm of possibility. I could see that a love relationship was about *being* together, instead of merely *staying* together. The former is a *path,* the latter, a *product.* I was realizing that an intimate partnership was a continuously unfolding process through which both parties could truly realize their ultimate potential and growth. Until I was able to enter such a relationship with the true essence of who I was, living in a *being-to-being* partnership would not be possible. It was all too evident that I was still unable to give or receive unconditional love. I also lacked the spiritual maturity to connect with another person at that level.

My past relationships had indeed fueled my personality and emotions, but they hadn't fueled my heart nor connected with my soul. Passion is extremely important in any union, but the key is to ride that passion, rather than to get swept up in it. The first experience allows you to utilize and enjoy the energy, while the latter experience puts you at its disabling effect. Passion with no basis in the heart is merely an emotional roller-coaster ride. Therefore, when the car periodically descends, as it naturally does in the course of any relationship, the connection suffers and the passion cannot refuel itself. That is why so many relationships eventually fail. This was certainly true in my case.

Although this new insight into the area of intimate relationships was profound, I simply chose to file the material away. As far as I was concerned, I was intellectually satisfied. I had cleaned up the area, and that was sufficient.

The only trouble is, when you begin dancing to the rhythm of the

Universe, connecting solidly with your heart, the mirror of who you have become has a funny way of finding you, always of course, when you least expect it.

Only after circumstances had forced me to let go of everything in every other area of my life—all the plans, pretenses, expectations, material possessions, desires, preconceptions, and judgments—could any light enter this one, unexplored cavern in my heart. And when it did, in order for me to see it, I would literally have to be dragged toward it, kicking and screaming all the way, like a mule being pulled up a mountain.

20
Prelude to a Waltz

Imagination is the Eye of the Soul.
Joseph Joubert

For one human being to love another . . . that is perhaps the most difficult task of all . . . It is a high inducement to the individual to ripen . . . something that chooses us out and calls us to vast things.
Rainer Maria Rilke

In my new adventures of going with the flow and remaining fully aware in each and every moment, I consistently began to put into practice everything I had learned. It wasn't necessarily easy at first, but it was always exciting.

Time seemed to move more slowly, thus allowing me the opportunity to fully enjoy each minute of the day as if it stood alone. I had never understood how to be *in the moment* before. But, as I began to immerse myself in the richness of each and every moment, my experience of life was becoming eminently more fulfilling in every respect.

Not only that, living your life in this manner allows you the opportunity to come as close as possible to reaching the full potential of your vast creativity. You can literally "create" your experience consciously, moment by moment, utilizing the magnitude of the energy present within each and every one of those moments.

As you begin to do this on a consistent basis, you become aware of a natural rhythm, a momentum that literally propels you forward, without disconnecting you from the flow. Connecting with this natural rhythm provides you with a constant source of natural energy, and this phenomenon applies even if your experience of a particular moment is what you might call a *bad* one. In the overall scheme of things, that *bad* moment is only a minute part of the continuum. The dance continues, *good* steps and *bad*, propelling you effortlessly toward the full potential of your destiny.

The coincidence that was about to occur, could surely have been defined as a "bad" one, had my dance consisted solely of one step. Instead, this fateful incident proved to be merely the opening four bars of what would eventually crescendo into a fully orchestrated, melodious waltz— a composition of which even Johann Strauss would have been proud.

These opening four bars would prove to be the final step of my breaking the only remaining familial chain of my past and allowing the last spark of fire to fully light the beacon I'd been searching for, the glow that had always resided in my heart.

The overture began when I happened to be in Hawaii again, only this time for a photo shoot. When I checked into the Grand Wailea Hotel, I was given a certificate for a free massage. As soon as I had unpacked my bags and gotten settled, I decided to head straight for the spa. As I lay on the table, Daniel Fowler, a specialist in the Hawaiian technique of Lomi Lomi, said out of nowhere,

"You know, you ought to read a book called *The Urban Shaman.* I think you'd really like it. As a matter of fact, I have a copy downstairs in my car. After we finish, I'll leave it at the front desk and you can pick it up any time you like."

The name of the book rang a bell, but I couldn't quite remember where I'd heard it. Later that night, I took a look in the envelope Daniel had left for me. Seeing the cover of the book instantly brought my memory into focus. It was one of those Sam had given me during our bookstore journey, but one I had so far neglected to read. As I looked through it, one chapter in particular piqued my interest: "Changing Your World with Dreaming."

Interesting . . .

Since I had already discovered that what we experience as "reality," is just the reflection of our own inner reality, I was taken with the chapter's premise. Supposedly, it was possible to change one's perception of the events of his or her past, in such a way as to change his or her present experience of life. The book purports that one of the most effective ways to achieve such a change is through dreams, because they are "real" experiences as far as our mind is concerned. Therefore, if our memories of the past can be altered, this can also have a positive effect on our beliefs, habits, and behavior in the present. Dreams are, in effect, a language unto themselves, a language that is at work both consciously and unconsciously in our everyday lives.

I was curious. Could I actually change my perception of a past negative experience in my own life? The step-by-step procedure provided in *The Urban Shaman* seemed relatively easy to accomplish: When you're in the middle of a dream and begin to wake up just enough that you're conscious of what's happening in it, begin to manipulate the events that are occurring, so that the situation turns out just the way you want it to. The idea is to keep going over and over the scenario in your mind until everyone does just what you want them to do. Supposedly, by this process, you are altering your past experience for good, and thereby your present memory of the situation forever. In other words, you would actually be able to break the hold of a past incident that had been unconsciously affecting your life. It was a little hard to believe, but I was intrigued enough to want to try it.

Coincidentally, of course, three days later at about four in the morning, I woke up consciously aware that I was right in the middle of a dream, interestingly enough, involving my father. If I had not written down everything I'm about to tell you immediately after it occurred, I wouldn't have believed it myself. But this is what happened.

In my semi-dream state, my father and I were in a room. He was furious, staring at me with the same angry, crazed expression that I remembered from my childhood. I decided to go for broke and try out the procedure. Consciously, but with my eyes loosely closed and within the scenario of the dream itself, I turned to him, and for the first time in my life, one to one, let him have it. I had to keep repeating this action several times in order to keep myself in the dream, without the whole "picture" fading out.

"Now, stop it," I yelled. "Just stop it! You can't hurt me! I'm not a child anymore. Furthermore, you and I have to have a talk, because there are a lot of things I need to tell you."

Several times my father started to fade out of the dream, but I wouldn't let him. I consciously drew him back in immediately.

"No, you come back here," I said, and sure enough, he would return to face me. If he tried to veer away for even a moment or started to get that angry look again, I would stand my ground and demand his attention immediately, and sure enough he would return.

A short time later, I began to notice that his face had changed. It had become a little softer. His demeanor had mellowed and I remember being aware that I was beginning to allow him to stand physically closer to me.

Within this dream state, I consciously watched and participated in our conversation for what turned out to be a good two and a half hours. During this time, I vented every conceivable emotion and resentment that I had withheld from the earliest moments of my life. I wouldn't let up. I told him how his drinking, his beatings, and his overbearing need to be in control had made an important part of the entire family's life a living hell. Valid or not, I ranted and raved about everything I felt he had stolen from me as a child—my innocence, trust, and above all, my ability to play in the magic of the world I had so loved. I told him that all I had ever wanted from him was his love, and to simply be listened to, protected, and hugged.

No sooner had those last words fallen from my lips than I noticed my father had begun to cry. I was frozen in the purity of the moment. A tunnel had suddenly been formed between two caverns. Two hearts had finally reconnected.

And then, as if magic and the Heavens had conspired, I "watched" as he did something that I had prayed he'd do my entire life. He apologized with complete honesty, for all of his anger and abuse. He left no stone unturned in dealing with everything that I was throwing at him. Then, he proceeded to tell me about his own life . . . his fears, his parents, why he drank, and how his own dreams had eluded him. He told me, not as an excuse, but simply because he wanted me to know.

He was deeply ashamed at what he had done, and told me that his being sorry would never be enough.

By this point in my "dream," my father was behaving exactly as I wanted him to without needing any further prodding on my part. It was as if the entire nature of my relationship with Dad had shifted, and I no longer needed to actively manipulate his behavior. His actions and my new perception of those actions were now able to play themselves out on their own.

The truth of his words began to affect me deeply. In my "dream," I suddenly became five again and started calling him Daddy. I asked him if he would ever hit me again and he said, "No, never." And I knew he meant it.

I couldn't believe this was happening! I was *consciously* aware of everything that was occurring, and at the same time, realized that the scenario had changed forever with the help of my imagination.

"Daddy, is this really you?" I asked.

"Yes, Cassman, it is," he said, using a name I hadn't heard since I was twelve years old. As far as I was concerned, the experience was as real as it had to be, and that was all that was important.

"I'll be right here whenever you need me, Cassman," he said, and I knew he would.

Before it ended, the dream expanded to include my mother. Now, however, I began speaking to my father in the calm secure voice of an adult. "Why did you beat Mom?" I asked him.

He began to stutter. I could feel his pain. Gathering his courage, he raised his head and sincerely and truthfully told his ex-wife, my mother, how sorry he was. Almost immediately I saw her face relax for the first time in years. There was a long moment between them, and then she faded away.

After I had said everything I'd ever wanted to say, and had said it over and over, the strangest thing occurred. The impact of our past traumatic relationship had magically disappeared, and for some reason, the entire scenario became humorous. Within my dream state, he and I started laughing, a full-bellied raucous laugh that was long overdue. As the laughter subsided, both Dad and my dream began to fade away. There was no sadness, however, because our relationship had been healed as far as I was concerned, and I felt complete. I experienced what it felt like for a daughter to be truly loved by her father for the first time in my adult life.

I jolted up in bed and looked at the clock on the nightstand. I couldn't believe that two-and-a-half hours had actually passed. Without a moment's hesitation, I grabbed a pen and paper and wrote down every detail of my "dream" that I could remember. I was amazed. Word for word, it was almost the exact same experience I'd had in my dream.

I am well aware that something like this can be very hard to believe. I certainly can't explain it, but I can tell you that it happened, and it worked. I felt like an incredible weight had been lifted off my shoulders. I was finally free from the last familial chain that had been unconsciously holding me back from experiencing life with an entirely clean slate.

I'm sure it was one of the strangest telephone calls she'd ever received, but I just had to tell Mother. She took it all in, asked me how I felt about it, and then told me how glad she was that I'd finally resolved everything with Dad.

A rather amazing morning, and it was only 7:30!

The rest of the day flew by.

I gobbled up life with a new gusto. I couldn't get enough. I was living life to the fullest and wasn't about to quit.

Let's celebrate! Sure, why not!? Lunch? Bring it on. Let's eat everything! I'd been the picture of health for a year, so what the heck, let's splurge for a day.

Dinner? Of course. A rich French meal sounds scrumptious. Life was a banquet, and today, I had appointed myself "guest of honor."

Let's celebrate! Why not?!

21
Waltzing to the "Center" of Things

The love between a man and a woman also presents a sacred challenge: to go beyond the single-minded pursuit of purely personal gratification and to tap into the larger energies of life as a whole.

John Welwood

What now seems to you opaque, you will make transparent with your blazing heart . . .

Rainer Maria Rilke

Why not? I'll tell you why not!

It's called "welcome to the morning-after celebration of Montezuma's revenge." I was more than just under the weather. I was down for the count, stricken with the worst case of gastrointestinal upset that I could ever remember. Was it something I ate? Gee, what was my first clue?

At any rate, I desperately needed medical attention. Much to my horror, the hotel doctor wasn't on call because it was Sunday. In addition, no one at the front desk could reach another physician. The last telephone call I had the energy to make was to the masseur, Daniel, to plead my case.

"Well I do know someone," he said, "but I'll have to see if he's willing to make a house call. By the way, he's a rather unusual man."

"I don't care if he's King Tut," I said. "Please give him a call."

I was so sick I didn't remember much about the man they call Dr. Joel, except that he had long hair and was accompanied by his seven-year-old daughter. He obviously knew what he was doing, because within forty-eight hours I was well on the road to recovery.

A few days later, however, he returned to check on me, concerned that I might have a parasite. He suggested a blood test and a stool sample. Charming. Sensing my uneasiness, he suggested taking the blood now, which he did, and then promised to send a stool kit to me at my office in Los Angeles.

On my return, I received my little package and did as I was instructed.

Three weeks later, Dr. Joel called with the results. Indeed, I had a parasite. He called in a prescription to take care of it, and said he'd check back with me in a few weeks.

As promised, he telephoned a short time later to find out how I was doing.

"Great," I said.

"All right, discontinue the medicine, and I'll send you another stool kit to ensure that the parasite is gone for good."

Is nothing sacred? I thought to myself.

You may wonder at this point why I'm telling you this particular story. I decided to include it, simply because it's another perfect example that life is a dance, and you never know where the next step is going to lead you.

He sent the second kit, and again, reluctantly, I did as I was told.

About five weeks later, he called with the results and sure enough, the parasite was gone. He asked me, however, how long it had been since I had had a general blood test. Because it had been a couple of years, he suggested I get a complete chemistry profile.

Sure, why not? I thought. *A little blood here, a little stool there, what the heck?*

"I'll be happy to mail you the results of your test as soon as I get them."

"Actually," I said, "I'll be back in Maui in a few weeks attending a seminar."

"Perfect. I'll make sure the results are dropped off at your hotel."

"Thank you," I said, and hung up

After my arrival back at the Grand Wailea, Dr. Joel called to tell me that he was in the area and would be happy to drop my results by the hotel.

"Fine, I'm on a break and I'll be in my room for the next hour," I said.

Suddenly, I realized I had no idea who was going to arrive at my hotel room door. Unfortunately, in the haze of my illness, not too much had registered, and I couldn't remember anything about the doctor's looks except for his long dark hair. Not only that, I felt uncomfortable inviting a strange man up to my room, physician or no physician. But even more curious, I was nervous. What in heaven's name was going on? By the time I heard the knock on the door, I had worked myself up into a frenzy. *Oh for heaven's sake, let him in,* I thought.

When I opened the door, the person facing me looked nothing like what I remembered. He was tall, tanned, with long black hair pulled back in a ponytail, and had the deepest blue eyes I'd ever seen. We sat on the couch and talked about my blood—every girl's dream of the ideal afternoon.

Why am I so nervous?

I was finding it extremely difficult to communicate with him. Then I noticed the clock. Mercifully, I realized that I had to be back at the seminar in ten minutes.

Thinking it would be rude to just take my leave abruptly, I asked if he'd like to tag along for the rest of the day's program. There was a rather long pause, after which he replied simply, "Sure, that would be fine." So off we went.

Much to my horror, there was a new category up for discussion in the seminar.

"We're going to tackle the area of relationships," the leader boomed.

I couldn't believe it! When I'd left, we were talking about money!

"Pick a partner," instructed the voice over the sound system, "and then each of you write out what the description of your ideal mate is. Be very specific about what you really want, and when you're finished, turn toward each other and share what you've written."

Here I was sitting next to a relative stranger who already knew more about me than I'd cared to think about.

And now I'm supposed to tell him what I want in my love life?

This was not my idea of a good time. I knew one thing for sure, after having shared my stools and my innermost desires for the perfect mate with this person, it was going to be *adios* as soon as the seminar was over.

But for the time being, I was stuck. To heck with it, I decided. I'll consider the experience a gift, and I'll write down everything I've ever wanted to the nines!

With vigor, I dove into the project at hand and proceeded to write forty-seven attributes on my list almost without taking a breath. I wanted honest, kind, funny, spiritual, tall, athletic, supportive, a good dancer, loyal, and so on. I couldn't write fast enough. It was as if I was on automatic pilot, and I was enjoying every minute of it. As I got near the end of my lengthy laundry list, I casually glanced over at his paper.

That's impossible! I thought.

He had only written down five qualities: honest, genuine, funny, loving, and intelligent. I couldn't believe it.

He would be happy with someone who had only these five qualities? No way, I thought. I didn't buy it for a minute.

We proceeded to face the dreaded task of telling each other what we'd written. He went first.

"Is that all?" I laughed. "That's all you want? That's all it would take to make you happy?"

"That's it," he replied.

Okay, so I'm picky. Hey, I deserve to be picky! In fact, under the circumstances, I'm going to be unbelievably picky, and I'm going to savor each and every minute of picking.

I proceeded to read him my entire list, relishing each and every quality

I'd put on the paper, including the last item which read "a legendary relationship."

"You want a *legendary* relationship?" he said. "What in heaven's name is that?"

"Never mind," I replied, having no idea myself. "It's not important."

Not long after this exercise, he had to leave. I guess that's as close as the good doctor wanted to get to my "legendary" laundry list. As far as I was concerned, that was that.

But a curious thing began to happen over the next two days. My laundry-list partner kept popping up in my mind at the most unusual times. I had this strange desire to call him. It was as if there was some unfinished business to sort out. This confused me. I definitely didn't want any part of a relationship, but I still kept thinking about him. I wasn't sure what to do. Questions began to see-saw in my brain.

If I call him, he'll assume . . . blah blah blah . . ? If I don't call him, he'll think . . . blah, blah . . . ? Maybe I should just wait and see if he calls me. Why do I even care!?

I began to laugh. *All right, I know a coincidence when I see one. I'll make the call but I'll be very clear and very up front about my intentions.* I picked up the telephone and dialed.

"I was wondering if we could have lunch or something while I'm here in Maui," I said, "but, I don't want to mislead you in any way, because I'm not interested in having a relationship of any kind. I had a very bad experience the last time around, four-and-a-half years of absolute hell, actually, so I'd simply like to get to know you as a friend."

He was quiet. "Well, let me give that some thought," he said simply.

I stuttered. "Oh, sure, sure," and hung up as quickly as I possibly could.

I was mortified! *Let me think about it?!* Nobody had ever said that to me before. I couldn't believe I thought calling him was a good idea. It was a terrible idea, how could I have done it!? If I could have crawled under a rock at that moment I would have. I did everything I could to erase the memory as quickly as possible.

When I arrived back to the hotel that night, however, a message was waiting.

"I accept your offer," it said. "I'll pick you up Sunday morning at 7 A.M."

Seven o'clock?! Friend or no friend, seven o'clock was not exactly what I considered a social hour. What in the world could we possibly do at seven in the morning?

Dressed for the great outdoors, he picked me up in a van, and told me that he was taking me to the Haleakala Crater for a hike.

Oh, what a great idea, I thought, *a nice walk in the fresh air.* I instantly relaxed. *Big mistake number two!*

In the back seat of his van was a knapsack filled with water, a small flashlight, some food, and a few other items. I explained that I had never been on a serious hike before, much less in a crater, but he assured me that it wouldn't be a problem.

Actually, I was kind of excited. I pictured a peaceful walk through lush greenery, topped off by a sumptuous picnic lunch. Right.

We parked the car, gathered our gear, and started out.

As soon as we began our descent into the crater, I noticed that not only wasn't it green, it in fact looked very much like a desert—almost a moonscape. Furthermore, the only way to descend was a spindly little path that wound back and forth down the almost three-thousand-foot decline. We walked. And walked. And walked. An hour passed. Two hours passed. The heat was beginning to get to me, and my legs began to ache.

Interestingly, without my saying a word, Joel intuitively picked up on my fatigue.

"Walk in my footprints, and stay in my shadow," he instructed, "match my rhythm as you move, and you'll get a real burst of energy."

Never one to argue when I'm hot, tired, and sweaty, I fell in behind him. To my amazement, it actually worked.

The next hour passed with ease, and before long, we came to a plateau. Joel took off his backpack, sat down, and motioned for me to join him. He took out two books, some fresh fruit, and a gorgeous long-stemmed, handmade Indian pipe with a bowl in the shape of an eagle's head.

"This pipe has great significance because it was given to me by a medicine man named Mad Bear," he said. "It's one of a kind, and whenever I use it, it reminds me of him and a very special time in my life."

A medicine man named Mad Bear? Surely he must be kidding.

"Smoking the pipe shifts your reality so you become perfectly centered and filled with a sense of peace. It is a way to connect with the elemental forces of nature and to remember your connection to all living things."

Oh, no, I'm thinking. *I'm stuck in the largest dormant crater in the world with a pothead!*

"Gee, that sounds great," I stammered, "but . . . uh . . . actually, I don't do drugs of any kind."

"Neither do I," he laughed. "The pipe is filled with crushed cedar leaves, and smoking it is not about what you put in it, but rather the frame of mind that you create while smoking it."

He lit the pipe, ceremoniously smoking it toward the north, south, east, and west. After a few moments he handed it to me.

This is one for the books, I thought to myself, as I took a puff.

We shared the pipe in silence for about ten or fifteen minutes, taking in all the beauty around us. When the fire had gone out, he laid it down and picked up one of the books he'd brought along. It was a biography written in the thirties about a Lakota Sioux named Black Elk. He began by reading a quote at the beginning of the book which described the Native American tradition we had just shared:

I fill this sacred pipe with the bark of the red willow; but before we smoke it, you must see how it is made and what it means. These four ribbons hanging here on the stem are the four quarters of the universe. The black one is for the west where the thunder beings live to send us rain; the white one is for the north, whence comes the great white cleansing wind; the red one for the east, whence springs the light and where the morning star lives to give men wisdom; the yellow for the south, whence come the summer and the power to grow.

But these four spirits are only one Spirit after all, and this eagle feather here is for that One, and also it is for the thoughts of men that should rise as high as eagles do. Is not the sky a father and the earth a mother, and are not all living things with feet or wings or roots their children? And this hide upon the mouthpiece here, is for the earth, from whence we came and at whose breast we suck as babies all our lives, along with all the animals and birds and trees and grasses. And because it means all this, and more than any man can understand, the pipe is holy.

Who is this man sitting next to me? I thought. *This is either one of the most extraordinary people I have ever met, or one of the craziest.* I wasn't as yet sure which.

Just as I was reveling in the wonder of it all, Joel took out another book, *No Way* by Ram Tzu and proceeded to read it aloud:

> *First . . .*
>
> *You use your mind as*
> *The ultimate jigsaw.*
> *You take Totality*
> *And cut it up*
> *Into a million tiny pieces*
>
> *Then . . .*
>
> *Having tired of that game,*
> *You sit down and try to*
> *Reassemble this jumble of pieces*
> *Into something comprehensible.*
>
> *Ram Tzu knows . . .*
>
> *God invented time*
> *Just so you could do this.*

That's it! Now my circuitry was completely fried. Sitting beside me was a long haired, homespun medical doctor who smokes Indian pipes, loves rigorous hikes in the outdoors, and quotes everything from ancient Indian wisdom, to a Rodney Dangerfield version of enlightenment. This was a coincidence beyond all definition, and I could hardly wait to see what would happen next.

We finished our break and continued hiking for another two hours. We were three quarters of the way down the crater when Joel sat down beside a large bush, again motioning for me to join him.

"No way," I exclaimed.

The bush was alive with the buzzing of hundreds of bees! Next to tarantulas and snakes, being around bees is about neck and neck on my scale of enjoyment with having a root canal. Not only that, I'm allergic to them. One sting and I swell up like a watermelon.

"I don't do bees," I said.

He began eating, unfazed.

"They won't harm you," he said. "They're very special creatures. Just sit down calmly, and I promise they won't sting you."

His voice was so even keeled and reassuring that, against my better judgment, I decided to take a chance. I gathered my courage, timidly sat down next to him, and within minutes . . . just as I had feared . . . ten to twenty bees were crawling all over my arms.

"Don't worry, they're just thirsty," he explained. "The bees are look-ing for salt. They'll walk on your arm, lick a bit of the salt off and then fly away. Bees don't sting unless they get agitated."

What he had to say seemed logical enough, so I decided I would try to stick it out. I followed his instructions to a tee. I seriously attempted to be in harmony with the bees. I gave it my very best effort to remain calm, cool, and collected—and it worked—for about three minutes. Then, not being able to stand it one second longer, I jumped up and ran a good thirty feet to safety.

"That's not bad for your first try," Joel said smiling. "Next time, you'll be able to last a lot longer."

Right.

Whatever it is that bees have to offer was going to take a long time for me to get in touch with.

On we went. Across valleys. Up and down dunes. Climbing through rock formations and stopping, every so often, for a main course of *Black Elk Speaks* and a dessert of *Ram Tzu.*

Suddenly, we came upon what appeared to be a cave.

"It's called a lava tube," Joel informed me.

Actually, it was a long, cavernlike tunnel accessible only after descending into a large hole. Peeking inside this lava tube, I became aware of two extremely important facts: one, that no matter what he called it, it was looking more and more like a cave. And two, it was so dark inside that I literally couldn't see a thing!

My decision was immediate. It was definitely in my best interest to continue hiking, and leave this darkened wonder behind.

"It's really awesome," I said. "But you know, the weather's so beautiful out, why don't we just enjoy the rest of the day hiking out in the valley?"

"What's wrong?" he asked. "Are you afraid?"

Afraid? I thought, trying to hide any visible sign of trepidation. *First of all, I don't like the dark. All right, I* hate *the dark. Second of all, it's a cave for crying out loud. Caves have scorpions, bats, spiders, and God knows what else in them.*

"Afraid?" I answered nonchalantly, "Of course not, why would I be afraid?"

"Well good, since you're not afraid . . . let's explore it," Joel bantered.

"Fine. No problem," I replied, desperately trying to figure out a way to abandon this proposed tour.

He took out a flashlight the size of a ballpoint pen and handed it to me saying, "Here, you lead the way."

"What?" I asked. "Oh, no, no, no, don't be silly, you should lead," I said, stalling for time, "besides, I wouldn't know where I'm going."

"Well, I guess you'd have to just feel your way through then," he said, "unless of course you're afraid."

This guy was beginning to annoy me. He was pushing just the right buttons to awaken my competitive nature.

"I am not afraid," I snapped. "Give me the flashlight and let's go."

Taking a deep breath, I hesitantly took my first few steps into the pitch-black lava tube. Just as I was about ready to swallow my pride, and turn around to come back out, I heard Joel's voice behind me.

"Just tune into the energy of the cave. It will tell you where you're supposed to go."

Great ... I'm in the middle of a volcanic cavern, surrounded by such darkness that it doesn't even matter if my eyes are open or closed, I muttered to myself ... *There are probably bats, scorpions, and spiders everywhere, and I'm supposed to tune into the energy? ... Well, fine. If this was going to be the game, then two could play it as easily as one.*

His tactic had worked. He'd gotten me just aggravated enough to forge ahead in spite of my fears.

For the next twenty-five minutes, I climbed and crawled my way through the lava tube, over and around boulders and heaven knows what else, following what I prayed was the "energy of the cave."

I was managing quite well, carefully inching my way along the cavern, when suddenly, I realized I had come to a "Y." I had no idea which way to go. Again, I heard Joel's voice. He instructed me to make a sound in each direction, and then to proceed along the path where the sound was the clearest. Sure enough it worked; I made the right choice.

We continued our trek, and after what seemed like an incredibly long period of silence, Joel suggested I find a comfortable spot and sit down.

"What?" I shrieked, my voice echoing off the walls of the cave. "Sit down? Where?"

I didn't even want to think about what I would end up sitting next to, or worse, sitting *on.*

Gingerly, I felt around for a spot that had the fewest rocks and sat down in the darkness for what I prayed would be only a few minutes.

It was strange, but I began to relax. It didn't seem so frightening after all. I even began to notice how refreshingly cool it felt.

"Listen to the sound of the silence," Joel whispered.

And I did. The silence was so loud that it was actually deafening. Only two times in my life had I ever heard anything like it before. Once, on that prophetic morning when I woke up after my first hellish day in bankruptcy court; and then again, sitting in my car outside the bookstore where Sam and I had met. But in those two instances, it had been within a particular experience. There were sights and objects that accompanied that silence, so although it was profound, it was still defined by the context of the experience.

This, on the other hand, was something different. I'd been here before. Where was it? This was pure, absolute silence in all its glory. The memory was coming back, this was the same purity of silence that I had felt traversing the bottom of the pool at the age of two. How similar this realm of silence was to the realm of magic that I so loved as a child. The magnificence of it was so loud, I had to sporadically put my hands over my ears to muffle the thunderous ringing in my head.

There was nothing to do but sit and enjoy the energy and innocence of the moment. It was the sound of a four thousand piece orchestra with no music. It was full. It was boundless. It was blissful. It was a return to "nothingness," and at the same time, a magical connection to everything. I could even hear my own heart beating, keeping time with the rhythm of this profound simplicity. It was absolutely peaceful, yet totally invigorating. It was bizarre, and yet so beautiful. It encompassed everything, yet it contained nothing.

We sat for a long time, but as far as I was concerned, eternity wouldn't have been long enough.

Finally, the splendor was broken by Joel's voice, once again.

"Just tell me when you're ready to leave," he said.

I had the strangest urge not to answer, but I knew it was time.

"I'm ready," I said quietly.

"Okay," he said, "wait here. I'll go ahead and check the exit and then come back and get you."

After about ten minutes, I heard him cry out, "Oh, my God!"

"What? What's the matter," I shrieked.

"The exit has caved in!"

I bolted upright, spun around and immediately began trying to retrace our steps back to the entrance. *Stay calm,* I said to myself, feeling my heart racing.

"Which way? Which way?!" I yelled back in Joel's direction.

Then, just as I began to really panic, I heard a strange sound.

It seemed like laughter. I couldn't believe it! It *was* laughter.

"What are you laughing at?" I implored.

"I'm sorry, the exit's clear, I just couldn't help myself," he howled. "It was such a perfect set-up."

"I can't believe you did that! What a rotten thing to do!" I exclaimed. "Just remember, paybacks are my specialty," I said, as I made my way clumsily in his direction.

I was experiencing the world according to Dr. Joel: with every good dose of *Black Elk Speaks, Ram Tzu* was never far behind.

After another fifteen-minute crawl, we came out the other side of the lava tube and headed across one of the most beautiful valleys I'd ever seen. It was almost dusk, and the perfect time to take in all the shadows and sights of the setting sun. We walked along in silence for quite a long time, until we stood almost face-to-face with what appeared to be a three-thousand-foot, rocky incline. The only way up was a narrow path that snaked all the way back up to the top of the crater.

"It's almost dark," Joel said. "We'd better start up."

"Up what? . . . Up that?!" I moaned, pointing to the tiny ribbon of a path winding up the mountain. "You're kidding?"

Silence.

He's not kidding! We have been hiking ten-and-a-half hours over some of the most rugged terrain I have ever seen, most of it in ninety-degree heat, and now he expects me to climb three thousand feet all the way back up to the top?

Before I could scream, Joel took off up the narrow path. Too tired to stand my ground, and too afraid to stay below, I indignantly took off after him.

About a third of the way up, I *had* to stop. It was getting more and more difficult to breathe because of the dramatic change in altitude, and my legs were beginning to shake. In addition, the sun had gone down behind the mountains, and because of the cloud cover, there were no stars or even a sliver of a moon. It was getting darker and darker by the minute.

"C'mon, we have to *move,*" Joel instructed. "You can do it."

In spite of my loud protest, again he headed up the path, knowing that I was not about to stay there alone in the dark. I was angry that he wasn't taking my complaints seriously, but the adrenaline gave me energy, and I made use of it. I darted after him.

Without breaking stride, Joel yelled back, "Did you hear the one about . . ."

I wasn't exactly in the mood for jokes, but it was obvious I was going to get them anyway. Pretty soon, I even found myself telling some. It seemed to help pass the time as we crawled, step by step, over the treacherous terrain.

Then came the songs. He actually started singing! Stupid songs. Crazy songs. Silly songs. Even country songs he'd written. When I finally gave up and joined in, I discovered that singing was actually giving me more energy.

Soon, however, the going got even rougher, and I had reached my physical limit. I was ready to collapse, jokes and songs not withstanding. I could not remember ever being so exhausted. Every inch of my body ached. I grabbed hold of his sleeve and said, "Listen, you don't understand. I can't go another foot. I feel like Jell-O."

"I know you're tired, but we only have forty-five minutes to go from what I figure," he said. "Time is of the essence, and the last thing we want is to have to spend the night on this mountain."

Forty-five minutes! I prayed he was wrong. I didn't think I could last another forty-five seconds. It was almost as dark as it had been in the cave. So dark, that in order to continue, Joel had to shine his small flashlight in front of him, proceed ten feet, then turn around and flash the beam toward me so I could climb up to where he was standing. We stumbled along like this for a good thirty more minutes until suddenly he stopped dead in his tracks.

"No moon and no stars," he said thoughtfully, looking back and forth. And then he added, for my benefit, "Makes it pretty hard to tell which direction we should go in."

"What?" I exclaimed, missing his point once again. "We've been hiking twelve hours! You've been here before! You know the area! And now you're telling me that you don't know how to get back?"

He'd gotten the reaction he needed to help me make the final push home. I took off up the hill with absolute resolve, not caring if it was the right path or not. I was going straight up that mountain, and sooner or later, I would arrive at the top of something.

Sure enough, after another fifteen minute struggle, we arrived at the summit. I was so stiff and exhausted that I could barely even climb into the car. But I was safe. I'd made it.

Sitting in the front seat, I turned my head and took a good, long look at the man sitting next to me, perhaps the first real look I'd taken since we'd met.

So this is who you are, I thought to myself. But I was too tired to think any further.

I laid my head back and closed my eyes for a much-needed rest during the ride back to my hotel. When I awoke, however, we were pulling up to a simple house in the middle of what appeared to be a rural neighborhood.

"I thought you might feel like a shower," he said.

I was too numb to refuse, so I got out of the car. Besides, I would've killed for a hot bath. But as I walked toward the front door, I suddenly came to my senses.

Wait a minute, I thought. *I can't believe it! This guy's making a move! If he thinks I'm gonna have sex with him after what I've been through, he's got another "think" coming.*

Just then, the door opened.

"Oh, there you are," he said. "Here's your towel, and the bathroom is the first door on your left."

Cautiously, I entered the house and did as I was instructed. After a long, hot shower, I was greeted by the smell of food coming from the kitchen. Stepping out of the hallway, I stood in amazement at the sight before me. A complete home-cooked dinner had been placed on the table. Fresh vegetables, fresh fish. Fresh bread. Fresh everything. I thought I'd died and gone to heaven. What the heck, I could stay for a few more minutes. Whether I was merely following Joel's lead, or just too exhausted to speak, we ate in silence.

As we were finishing dinner he said casually, "Look, it's very late and it's an hour drive back to your hotel. I'd be happy to take you, but you're welcome to spend the night here if you'd rather."

I knew it! Typical. Sooner or later, they all go straight for the same old line. Doesn't this guy understand that I'm completely drained? I have no interest in doing anything except going to sleep and . . .

"You can sleep in my daughter's room," he continued. "Isaac and Eileen are with their mother for two weeks."

"Oh, well, sure, thanks," I stuttered.

He stood up, went to the back of the house and returned with an extra large T-shirt.

"There are clean sheets on the bed, and I hope this'll do for night-clothes."

Before I knew it, I was standing in a bedroom surrounded by toys, drawings, stuffed animals, and dolls, typical of a little girl's room, changing into my nightshirt. But for some strange reason it was perfect. It was as if I was "home" again, surrounded by the comfort and magic of my own bedroom as a child. I collapsed into bed and had just pulled up the covers, when Joel knocked on the door.

"Would you like me to read you a bedtime story?"

A bedtime story? I thought to myself, *Now that's a new one.*

"It's a beautiful story about loss, change, and greatness. It's called "Jumping Mouse" from the book *Seven Arrows,*" he said, showing me the book.

He was serious. I couldn't believe it, I was so touched. I hadn't been read to since I was seven or eight years old, when my grandmother used to lull me to sleep with stories of her youth. There was something so comforting and familiar about the gesture that I must've said yes, because he started to read. The last thing I remember was looking up at the ceiling of this child's room, where iridescent stars and moons had been applied by loving little hands to make it look like heaven. And it was. The magical clouds that I had once created as a childhood haven, were now painted before me as a living masterpiece.

With that thought, I fell asleep.

I don't remember even moving until sometime the next morning, when I awoke to the smell of waffles, not packaged ones, but fresh waffles made from an assortment of freshly ground grains. This wouldn't be the last time that I would see Dr. Joel. Unbeknownst to both of us, a journey to the "center" of things had begun. All of my senses had been touched in a very simple, yet deeply moving way. I had no idea what this could lead to, or would lead to, and it didn't matter. The waltz had begun, the music filled the air, and we had joyously stepped into the swirling circles of its rhythm.

I tell this story because it reflects so well the experience I had been looking for and what I had been trying so hard to find outside myself. Joel was simply a mirror of who I had become.

It is such a joy to be able to look at someone and see those parts that you love about yourself shining radiantly in them. At the time, I had no conscious desire to have an intimate relationship with this person. Likewise, I didn't know and still don't know what the future will hold. But, I did know what it felt like to have my soul acknowledged, to have made a deep connection without any effort at all, and to feel totally supported and cared for, simply because this person and I naturally reflected those things in each other.

My experience of my previous relationships was like watching a movie. Each one had a beginning, a middle, and an end. Some were comedies, some were dramas, some were documentaries, and yes, some were even farces. But they all began, intensified, and then culminated in the need for a decision to continue, or not. Although the leading men changed, watching myself in the relationship did not. I always felt as if I was merely a spectator, constantly judging the movie's merits or deficiencies. Consequently, I always lost my sense of self. And therefore, of course, the relationship was doomed to fail.

Obviously, I had changed. Instead of thinking of the other person as merely a player in the movie I was watching, constantly editing and improving upon, I was now envisioning the movie taking place *around* me. It was still a moving picture, but this time I was allowing life and our connection to each other to unfold naturally.

Is my connection to Joel magical? In many ways, yes. First, it is a relationship born by coincidence, out of a pure being-to-being connection. Second, it is a love that is a reflection of who we both are. When you are in touch with your heart and you're creating your life and your relationships from that place, that is magical, in and of itself. But when you consciously choose to step into the dance of the Universe with another being, it is a dance to the "center" of things, and a willingness at the very core of your heart to *let the magic begin.*

> *In your presence, I fell in love with the best of myself.*
> William Cummings

22
Let the Magic Begin

You need chaos in your soul
To give birth to a dancing star.
Nietzsche

Only the heart knows the correct answer . . . It taps into the cosmic
computer and takes everything into account . . . The heart has a com-
puting ability that is far more accurate and far more precise than
anything within the limits of rational thought.

Deepak Chopra

As I come full circle and look back on my six-year saga, what amazes me
most of all is the wondrous gift I received from such an incredibly difficult
time in my life. I lost everything that I'd worked my entire life to achieve,
everything I thought mattered; and yet, I *consciously* regained my connection with the essence of who I am. It's almost as if the "wounding" was
sacred in its ability to reconnect me with the Divine purpose of my life.

These words seem profound, yet what else can they be? To regain your
sense of awe and wonder, to regain your ability to create life from the
core of your heart, and to re-enter the realm of pure possibility by living
moment to moment in the *Bliss Zone,* is just that—profound. And the

truth of this profundity *is* so simple, that it could be written on the surface of an emerald, just as Sam had said.

Perhaps, it is merely looking at the world through new eyes, but I feel it's a very exciting time in the evolution of us human beings. Dissatisfaction, alienation, frustration, aggression, and battling to survive are no longer acceptable definitions of life to us. We know that there is a better way to live, but ofttimes we keep this thought to ourselves, because we are not quite sure what to do about it. We also know that we have gone *outside* of ourselves about as far as we can possibly go, searching for the answers to living a successful, yet meaningful, creative, and connected life. Now, we have come to the conclusion that there is no other direction to go but *in*.

Having taken the journey myself, I have come to understand that life is, indeed, a circle in which we all play a distinct and unique part—emotionally, spiritually, and psychologically. We belong to, and are a part of, it all. We are part and parcel of everything that can be seen, heard, or known about.

Furthermore, I've learned firsthand that this circle consists of the Divine or the Whole energizing each one of us, and each one of us, in return, utilizing this dynamic, creative force to glorify, re-ignite and reconnect with the Whole. Without this circle, chaos reigns. Life becomes out of balance, and therefore, so do we. Our lives become a struggle to survive in a game of dog-eat-dog, might makes right, and I win—you lose.

Unintentionally and unconsciously, I did just that; and in reality, what it cost me, financially, emotionally, and psychologically, was immense. I fell through the trapdoor with a resounding thud.

At the same time, however, I was blessed in a way I never could have imagined. I was given the "opportunity" of learning to see with more than my eyes; to hear with more than my ears; and to feel with more than my hands. I was given the chance to experience a veritable treasure chest of wonder: the veil of illusion, the peace of "nothingness," the power of dreams, the playground of coincidences, the natural rhythm of the dance of the Universe, the strength of a "natural" athlete, the vibrancy of being free from the chains of my past, the comfort of a reconnected family bond, the pure innocence of living from the core of my heart, the waltz to the "center" of things with a being-to-being connection, as well as the sheer magic of living in the *Bliss Zone* that I had known as a child.

There is still so much more to experience, so much more to learn, and so much more to unfold. But the foundation of who I am is now cast in gold, and eternally fired by a direct connection to my heart. Struggling for answers, and trying to use my will alone to demand "my place in the world," has been erased from the blackboard of my experience. In the long run, my efforts in that regard proved fruitless and empty. My "place," my piece of the puzzle, so to speak, is assured by my very existence on this Earth. And this is true for all of us.

There is a certain peace in knowing that you know, and a certain security in knowing that we all have been put on this Earth for a very special purpose. There is a magnificence about realizing that you are no longer alone, and that you are connected to everything that ever was, everything that is, and everything that ever will be. It is an absence of the consideration of time, an absence of the consideration of boundaries, and an absence of the consideration of fear. The energy from the Universe gives you "life," and that energy can be re-ignited within you in a heart-beat when you live in the *Bliss Zone*.

I believe that we all are born into this magical place, but unfortunately, are never taught the skills necessary to continue to live our lives within its realm. I certainly wasn't. Consequently, when our world becomes filled with challenges, heartbreak, and loss, we unwittingly disconnect from our natural core. We unconsciously go out of the *Bliss Zone* and into "reality" in an effort to overcome our adverse circumstances. At that precise moment, whenever it occurs, our world of innocence, joy, awe, and wonder, comes crashing headlong into what we now believe is the "real world." Unfortunately, this propels us further and further away from our true source of power, creativity, and wisdom.

We often believe that we are what we "do" in life, and that our joy comes from the results we have achieved. But that's only part of the story. In order to experience the full richness, depth, and magic in every moment, whether we are actually "achieving" anything or not, it is essential that we learn how to flow from the pure inner essence of who we are. This allows us to connect with the essence of everything, so we can join in the "dance," always open to the infinite possibilities existing within its natural rhythm.

Each of us has our own unique part to play in this puzzle called life, so there is actually no such thing as competition; only the challenge of learning to utilize every single ounce of who we really are to the fullest. Only you can fully realize *you.* When you understand this, your experience of life on a day to day basis will be one of magnificence, meaning, and indescribable bliss.

The challenge, as I see it, is to consciously remember that our *essential nature* is one of pure possibility, and that the magnitude of our destiny is awaiting us at every moment. This is the true game of life for those who are up for the adventure.

Our Divine task is for each of us to bring this ultimate creative force to the physical form. Therefore, I consider my life a gift, and how I live it, an art. By stepping into the energetic flow of the Universe and mastering your innate ability to shoot from the hip, you will soon be living in the realm of what you had only thought were your dreams. You will be on your way to the moon to play among the stars. And, you will realize that Heaven can also be right here on Earth.

The Universe is constantly unfolding before you, every gift you've ever needed or wanted. So, just awaken to this Energy, step into the "dance," embrace the coincidences that will naturally spring forth, have the courage to live from the core of your heart, and then, **Let the Magic Begin.**

> *. . . For me there is only traveling on the paths that have heart, . . . and the only worthwhile challenge for me is to traverse its full length . . . looking breathlessly . . ."*
>
> Carlos Castaneda

The Magician's Journey

Your Biographical Life Sketch

INSTRUCTIONS: Write down every major incident in your life, in chronological order as you remember it, from as early an age as you can recall. Describe what happened in as full detail as possible. Don't judge, and be truthful, this is for your eyes only.

Nutrition Tips

- One gram of fat = 9 calories
- One gram of carbohydrate = 4 calories
- One gram of protein = 4 calories
- If a food contains 1 gram of fat per serving, but each serving is only 35 calories, the food is actually 25 percent fat!
- Our body is 75 percent water. Keep it moving through you by drinking at least 8 glasses of water per day.
- Be aware of liquids that contain calories. Examples include Gatorade, Carbo Fuel and other sports drinks, fruit juices, and some flavored waters.
- Read labels! "Fat free" sometimes means "loaded with sugar."
- Sugar comes in many forms, including corn syrup, honey, sucrose, dextrose, and maltose. Be aware of foods ending in "ose."
- Fructose is the most natural form of sugar. Look for fruit-juice-sweetened items.
- Use fresh fruits and vegetables whenever possible. Frozen would be the second choice. When fruits and vegetables are canned, they can lose up to 90 percent of some vitamins and minerals.
- Cheese contains between 70 percent and 90 percent fat.
- One tablespoon of oil contains 13.5 grams of fat. Olive oil is no exception.
- One pickle has 833 mg of sodium.
- Green peppers have more vitamin C than oranges.
- Nonfat dairy products contain as much calcium as low-fat and whole-milk dairy products.
- Raisins are high in iron.
- Most canned soups and vegetables are high in sodium.
- Substitute fresh salsa or 2 tablespoons nonfat milk in baked potatoes for sour cream.
- Most muffins bought in the supermarket are very high in fat and sugar.
- One-half cup of nuts contains approximately 64 grams of fat.
- Avocados are 89 percent fat!

- Sweeten your oatmeal with sugar-free jam or unsweetened fruit juice.
- Spice up your air-popped popcorn with salsa or Mrs. Dash spices.
- Try nonfat versions of items such as sour cream, margarine, cottage cheese, cheese, or salad dressings on potatoes and steamed vegetables.
- Make tacos, burritos, pizza, lasagna, and other dishes, using nonfat beans, nonfat cheese, ground flank, ground turkey, and nonfat or low-fat ricotta cheese.
- Try sugar-free apple butter, fruit puree, or nonfat yogurt on pancakes instead of syrup.
- Use salsa or balsamic vinegar on salads and vegetables instead of regular dressings.
- Use sparingly: alcohol, coffee, and tea.
- Avoid the following: nuts, regular mayonnaise, salad dressings, butter, oils, and restaurant-prepared pasta sauces.
- When in doubt, order items on the side.
- Order Chinese, Thai, and Japanese food steamed.

Suggested Market List

COOKING AND CONDIMENTS

Parsley Patch Salt-free Spices
Mrs. Dash Salt-free Spices
Molly McButter or Butter Bud Products (3 tsp. servings)
Pam spray (regular, butter, or olive oil)
Rice vinegar (3 tbs.)
Salsa (sugar free)
Mustards
Nonfat mayonnaise, nonfat sour cream, and nonfat Miracle Whip (3 tbs.)
No-oil or nonfat salad dressing (2 tbs.) like Kraft Free or Trader Joe's
    oil-free salad dressing
Equal or Sweet 'n' Low
Simply Fruit or all-fruit jams (3 tsps.)
Tap 'n' Apple or no-sugar Apple Butter (1 tb.)
Powdered spices
Extracts
Worcestershire sauce—low salt
Soy sauce—low salt
Tabasco sauce

BEVERAGES

Diet soft drinks (preferably not colas)
Diet 5th Avenue seltzers
Diet Splash
Crystal Light products
Flavored sparkling mineral waters—sugar free
Teas and coffee (use sparingly)
Arrowhead & Schweppes flavored waters—sugar free
Nonfat milk, nonfat dry milk
Lactaid nonfat milk

Soy milk
Sugar-free hot cocoa
Juicy juice
Fresh juices (use sparingly)

CEREAL AND BREAKFAST FOODS

Quaker Quick Oats Oatmeal
Quaker Multi-Grain Oats
Quaker Instant Grits
Cheerios
Nutri-Grain Wheat cereal
Grape Nuts
Trader Joe's Muesli
Trader Joe's (or other brands) Nonfat Granola
Nature's Harvest Homemade Granola
Multi-Bran Chex
Health Valley Fruit Lites
Pritikin Hearty Hot Cereal
Orowheat Light Breads
Bagels (nonfat is best)
English crumpets
Nonfat Eggo "Special K" frozen waffles
Aunt Jemima or Log Cabin Lite Syrup
Aunt Jemima Lite Healthy waffles
Aunt Jemima Buckwheat Pancake mix
Arrowhead Mills Pancake mix
Estee or S & W Diabetic Syrup
Nutradiet Sliced Peaches
Dole Pineapple—fresh is best, but if unavailable, sugar free

LUNCH AND DINNER FOODS

Water-packed albacore tuna (canned)
Water-packed white chicken (canned)
Healthy Choice sliced turkey and chicken
Ground turkey (100% breast meat)
Imitation crab or lobster (whitefish)
Flank steak or very lean beef (ground for burgers or tacos)
Rosarita Nonfat or Vegetarian Beans
Heinz Vegetarian Beans
Wildwood Creations Wildfire Chili
Health Valley fat-free Chili
Taste Adventure Black Bean Chili
Mrs. Gooch's Vegetable Potstickers
Bean Cuisine soups
Healthy Choice soups
Healthy Choice, Trader Joe's Low Profile, and Le Menu Healthy frozen
    dinners
Pritikin soups
Trader Joe's Orange Szechuan Pasta
DiGiorno Lighter Varieties lowfat ravioli
Westbrae Natural Spinach Ramen
Soken Spinach Ramen
La Tortilla Factory Light Flour Tortillas
Basic Country Goodness French Fried Potatoes
Contadina Italian Style Tomato Sauce (no oil)
Trader Joe's Oil-Free Spaghetti Sauce
Campbell's Healthy Request Spaghetti Sauce
Robbie's Fat-Free Spaghetti Sauce
Tree of Life Fat-Free Pasta Sauce
Pomi Italian Tomato Sauce
Ci Bella Pasta Sauce
Pritikin Pasta Sauce

Healthy Choice Pasta Sauce
Dannon, Knudsen, Yoplait, light nonfat yogurts
Healthy Choice Nonfat cheese
Knudsen Free Light Sour Cream Substitute
Knudsen Free Cottage Cheese
Nonfat or lowfat ricotta cheese
Kraft "Free" American Slices
Borden Fat-Free Cheese Slices
Alpine Lace Fat-Free Parmesan
Heart D'Lite Fat-Free Cheese Alternative
Trader Joe's Fruit & Nut Duet

DESSERT & SNACKS (Use with Discretion)

Sugar-free popsicles or Crystal Light Bars (one bar)
Sugar-free Fudgecicles (two $\frac{1}{2}$ bars only)
Sugar-free Jell-O and Pudding ($\frac{1}{2}$ cup)
Welch's Fruit Juice bars
Sugar-free hot cocoa mix
Nouvelle Sorbet
Tree Top Apple chips
Simple Pleasures Light Frozen Dairy Dessert
Nonfat frozen yogurt
Sweet Nothings Fruit-sweetened nondairy dessert
Stars nonfat frozen yogurt
Health Valley nonfat cookies, muffins, crackers, and fat-free bars
Auburn Farms fat-free cookies
Auburn Farms fat-free Toast 'n' Jammers
Popcorn (air popped) e.g. Lapidus Popcorn Co. Life-Corn, Country
    Grown Pop-life, Featherweight
Rice cakes
Pretzels
Vera Cruz Baked Tortilla Rounds

Trader Joe's Baked Tortilla Chips
Health Valley Fat-Free Cheese Puffs
Childers Fat-Free Potato Chips
Pacific Grains "No Fries" Cheese Puffs
Valley Bakery "Hearts" Crackers
Kavli Hearty Thick Crackers
Premier Japan Rice Sembei Crackers
R.W. Frookie Gourmet Fat-Free Cookies
Burns & Ricker Crispini Oil-Free chips
Bearitos Baked Tortilla Chips
Matzos
Fat-Free Premium Crackers

Vitamins

Be sure to consult with your doctor and/or health practitioner before adding any supplements to your diet.

Under each listing, the numbers 1–4 indicate the following:

1. Uses for
2. Where to find
3. Signs of deficiency
4. Signs of excess

VITAMIN A

1. Tissue maintenance. Healthy skin, hair, and mucous membranes. Helps us see in dim light. Essential for normal growth and reproduction.
2. Liver, deeper yellow, orange, and dark-green vegetables and fruits (carrots, broccoli, spinach, cantaloupe, sweet potatoes), cheese, milk, and fortified margarines.
3. Night blindness, dry scaling skin, poor immune response.
4. Damage to liver, kidney, and bone; headache; irritability; vomiting; hair loss; blurred vision; yellowed skin.

VITAMIN B₁ (THIAMIN)

1. Helps body release energy from carbohydrates. Health of nerves and muscles, including heart. Helps prevent fatigue and irritability.
2. Pork, whole grains, dried beans and peas, sunflower seeds, nuts.
3. Beri beri (nerve changes, sometimes edema, heart failure).
4. None known.

VITAMIN B₂ (RIBOFLAVIN)

1. Helps body release energy from protein, fat, and carbohydrates. Good vision. Healthy hair, skin, nails. Necessary for normal cell growth.
2. Liver and other organ meats, poultry, brewer's yeast, fish, dried peas, beans, nuts, sunflower seeds, cheese, eggs, yogurt, milk, whole grains, green leafy vegetables, nori seaweed.
3. Skin lesions.
4. None known.

VITAMIN B₃ (NIACIN)

1. Energy metabolism. Important for healthy skin and digestive tract tissue. Stimulates circulation. (If taken by itself, may cause flushing.)
2. Liver and other organ meats, veal, pork, poultry, fish, nuts, brewer's yeast, dried beans, dried fruit, leafy greens, whole grains, milk, eggs.
3. Sensitivity to light, fatigue, loss of appetite, skin eruptions, and sore, red tongue.
4. Flushing of face, neck and hands, liver damage.

PANTOTHENIC ACID

1. Supports adrenal glands to increase production of hormones to counteract stress. Important for healthy skin and nerves.
2. Nuts, beans, seeds, dark green leafy vegetables, poultry, dried fruit, milk.
3. Fatigue, sleep disturbance, nausea, poor coordination.
4. None known.

Vitamin B$_6$

1. Helps body use protein to build body tissue and aids in metabolism of fat. Facilitates release of glycogen from liver and muscles. Helps in red-blood cell production, fluid balance regulation.
2. Sunflower seeds, beans, poultry, liver, nuts, leafy green vegetables, bananas, dried fruit.
3. Nervous and muscular disorders.
4. Unstable gait, numb feet, poor hand coordination, abnormal brain function.

Vitamin B$_{12}$

1. Important in formation of red-blood cells and building genetic material. Stimulates growth in children. Helps functioning of nervous system and in metabolizing protein and fat in body.
2. Animal protein foods, including meat, fish, shellfish, poultry, milk, yogurt, eggs.
3. Skin cell degeneration, and improper red blood cell formulation and elevated homeocysteine levels.
4. None known.

Biotin

1. Used in energy metabolism.
2. Widely distributed in foods, especially eggs.
3. Dermatitis, depression, muscular pain.
4. None known.

Folic Acid

1. Helps form red blood cells. Assists in breakdown and utilization of protein. Essential during pregnancy for its importance in cell division.
2. Dark, green leafy vegetables, nuts, beans, whole-grain products, fruit, fruit juices, liver.
3. Anemia, gastrointestinal disturbances.
4. Masks vitamin B$_{12}$ deficiency.

Vitamin C

1. Essential for connective tissue found in skin, cartilage, bones, and teeth. Helps heal wounds. Antioxidant. Stimulates immune system. Aids in absorption of iron.
2. Citrus fruits, berries, melons, dark green vegetables, cauliflower, tomatoes, green and red peppers, cabbage, and potatoes.
3. Scurvy (skin spots, bleeding gums, weakness), delayed wound healing, impaired immune response.
4. Gastrointestinal upset, confounds certain lab tests, poor immune response.

Vitamin D

1. Helps regulate calcium metabolism and bone calcification. Called the *sunshine vitamin* because it's manufactured in human skin when in contact with ultraviolet light. Wintertime, clouds, and smog reduce body's production.
2. Fortified and full-fat dairy products, tuna, salmon, cod-liver oil.
3. Rickets in children, bone softening in adults.
4. Gastrointestinal upset; cerebral, cardiovascular, and kidney damage; lethargy.

Vitamin E

1. Antioxidant to prevent cell-membrane damage.
2. Vegetables oils and their products, nuts, seeds, fish, wheat germ, whole-grain products, green leafy vegetables.
3. Possible degeneration of muscles or vascular abnormalities.
4. Possible anemia.

Minerals

Calcium

1. Maintenance of healthy bones and teeth. Muscle contraction and blood clotting. Nerve transmission.

2. Milk and milk products, tofu, dark green leafy vegetables, legumes, nuts (especially almonds), sunflower and sesame seeds, molasses.
3. Stunted growth, bone loss.
4. Depressed absorption of some other minerals.

PHOSPHORUS

1. Bone and tooth formation. Involved in formation of genetic material, cell membranes, and many enzymes. Involved in release of energy from fat, carbohydrates, and protein.
2. Meats, fish, poultry, milk, cheese, eggs, nuts, seeds, whole grains, brewer's yeast, wheat germ, many fruits and vegetables.
3. Weakness, demineralization of bone.
4. Depressed of some other minerals.

MAGNESIUM

1. Used in building bones, manufacturing proteins, releasing energy from muscle storage and regulating body temperature. Essential to good cardiovascular health.
2. Whole grains, dried fruit, dark green leafy vegetables, nuts and seeds, avocados, beans, tofu, fish, lean meats.
3. Neurological disturbances.
4. Neurological disturbances.

SODIUM

1. Body water balance, nerve function.
2. Salt, soy sauce, cured meats, pickles, canned soups, processed cheese, packaged gravies, olives, salted crackers and chips, seafood, beef, poultry, celery, beets, carrots, seaweeds, artichokes.
3. Muscle cramps, reduced appetite.
4. High blood pressure in genetically predisposed individuals.

POTASSIUM

1. Body water and electrolyte balance. Crucial to good cardiovascular health, nerve function. Important in releasing energy from protein, fat, and carbohydrates.

2. Widely distributed in foods, especially fruits and vegetables, beans, nuts, seeds, and lean meats.
3. Muscular weakness, paralysis.
4. Muscular weakness, cardiac arrest.

CHLORIDE

1. Formation of gastric juices.
2. Table salt, seafood, milk, eggs, meats.
3. Muscle cramps, reduced appetite, poor growth.
4. Vomiting.

IRON

1. Hemoglobin formation, essential oxygen carrying part of red blood cells. Gives energy and "glow" of good health.
2. Meats (especially pork), molasses, seeds, whole grains, fruits, dried fruits, beans, poultry, fish.
3. Iron-deficiency anemia, weakness, impaired immune function.
4. Shock, death, chronic liver damage, cardiac failure.

ZINC

1. Important in normal insulin activity, blood formation, wound healing and tissue maintenance. Helps maintain healthy skin. Supports immune system.
2. Whole grains, seeds, nuts, poultry, fish, shellfish, beans, lean meats.
3. Growth failure, reproductive failure, impaired immune function.
4. Nausea, vomiting, diarrhea. Adversely affects copper metabolism and immune function.

IODINE

1. Essential for normal thyroid function.
2. Marine fish and shellfish; seaweeds such as kelp, nori and dulse; dairy products; iodized salt; some breads.
3. Goiter.
4. Unknown.

FLUORIDE
1. Maintenance of teeth structure.
2. Fluoridated drinking water, tea, seafood.
3. Higher frequency of tooth decay.
4. Mottling of teeth, skeletal deformation.

CHROMIUM
1. Helps control blood sugar.
2. Brewer's yeast, beef, liver, seafood, whole grains, chicken, bananas.
3. Impaired glucose metabolism.
4. Lung, skin, and kidney damage (from occupational exposure).

SELENIUM
1. Antioxidant.
2. Seafood, meat, whole grains.
3. Muscle pain, heart-muscle deterioration.
4. Hair and nail loss.

MANGANESE
1. Helps activate enzymes.
2. Nuts, whole grains, fruits, and vegetables, especially alfalfa and spinach.
3. Abnormal bone and cartilage.
4. Neuromuscular effects.

MOLYBDENUM
1. Helps activate enzymes. May prevent dental cavities.
2. Legumes, lean pork, dark green leafy vegetables, tomatoes, milk, whole grains, wheat germ, carrots, winter squash, strawberries.
3. Disorder in nitrogen excretion.
4. Poor enzyme production, adversely affects cobalt metabolism.

Additional Beneficial Supplements

Be sure to consult your doctor or medical practitioner before adding any supplements to your diet.

1. *Antioxidants*—(Free-radical scavengers)—This includes a group of very important nutrients that, in their natural form, are reputed to be anticancer, anti-aging, antistress and immune-system builders. I use the starch-free, yeast-free variety by Allergy Research Group.

2. *Pycnogenol*—A grapeseed extract only recently discovered, that is reputed to be an extremely powerful antioxidant.

3. *Pure Synergy*—A natural food in powder, that combines the strength of algae, green juice, herbs, and natural antioxidants. I add 1 to 2 tablespoons a day to my diet.

4. *COQ10*—An additional antioxidant found in the body, that is extremely beneficial in terms of anti-aging, energy production, and fat metabolism.

5. *L-Carnitine*—A natural amino acid found in the body that is reported to be excellent for energy and fat metabolism.

6. *Gingko*—A natural herb reported to be excellent for memory enhancement and cognitive function.

7. *HCA* (hydroxy citric acid)—A natural plant extract which works to prevent sugar from turning into fat.

8. *DHEA*—(The mother hormone)—A newly discovered substance found naturally in the body. It is reputed to have strong age-reversing properties.

9. *Evening primrose oil*—A natural substance to be taken if you are on a low-fat diet to ensure the intake of enough essential fatty acids.

Bodybuilders Menu Plan

* This is a sample daily menu that professional bodybuilders use thirty days *prior* to a competition in order to maximize the leanness of their body, without depleting their energy or strength.

3 Meals = 1300 calories approximately
4 Meals = 1781 calories approximately

* Consult your doctor or medical practitioner before starting any diet.

Meal 1

Menu Selection	Cal	Pro g	Carbo g	Fat g
0.50 small banana	53	0.60	13.40	0.3
2.00 oz. oatmeal, Quick Oats	200	10.00	36.00	4.0
7.00 egg whites	119	25.20	2.10	0.0
	372	35.80	51.50	4.3

Meal 2

Menu Selection	Cal	Pro g	Carbo g	Fat g
1.00 mixed green dinnner salad	100	3.00	25.00	0.0
1.00 cup(s) rice, cooked	200	4.00	50.00	0.2
4.50 oz. chicken breast, baked	185	30.90	0.00	6.8
	485	37.90	75.00	7.0

Meal 3

Menu Selection	Cal	Pro g	Carbo g	Fat g
1.00 lrg. potato, baked w/skin	220	4.00	51.00	0.2
6.00 oz. tuna (water packed)	210	45.00	0.00	3.0
	430	49.00	51.00	3.2

Meal 4

Menu Selection	Cal	Pro g	Carbo g	Fat g
4.00 oz. mixed vegetables	44	2.50	10.00	0.2
9.00 oz. yams, cooked in skin	270	6.18	61.98	0.5
6.00 oz. turkey strips, boneless	180	40.02	0.00	2.0
	494	48.70	71.98	2.8

Eat *Meal 1* first, then arrange the remaining 3 or 4 (depending on your calorie needs) meals to fit your lifestyle and schedule. You may have water, coffee, tea or a diet drink with each meal. You may also choose a Meal-Substitute Drink for any meal.

MEAL-SUBSTITUTE DRINK
Do not substitute more than ⅓ of a day's calories unless medically supervised.

Drink Ingredients	Cal	Pro g	Carbo g	Fat g
1 cup orange juice	110	1.80	25.80	0.4
1 scoop Protein Powder	130	9.00	18.00	2.0
½ medium banana	53	0.60	13.40	0.3
½ medium apple	40	0.20	11.60	0.3
	333	11.60	68.80	3.0

Cathy Sassin Smith
Billy Smith

Basic Breathing

Lie on a flat surface, or sit comfortably in a chair. Relax your shoulders by lifting and dropping them a few times until they just hang. Keep your mouth and eyes closed. Breathe in to an even count of four through your nose and exhale to an even count of four through your nose as well. Find the proper rhythm that allows you to breathe fully and slowly without any strain, and then relax into the sensation. Do this for 1 minute a day in the beginning, and work up to 5 minutes, 2 times a day, until it becomes a natural part of your daily experience. Try to keep your mind free of all thoughts. If you begin to focus on any one problem or subject, let that thought drift away, and return your attention to your breath.

Dan Millman
(The Warrior Athlete)

Basic Aerobic Information

1. In order to achieve your body-fat goal, you need to start with 5 minutes of aerobic activity and work up to 30 minutes, 3 to 5 times a week.
2. To maximize your time spent doing aerobic activity, you need to be exercising within your target heart rate zone. Use the following equation to find it.

(220 − your age) × 60% = your low target
(220 − your age) × 75% = your high target

For example, if you are 40 years old:

220 − 40 = 180 × 60% = 108 beats/minute
220 − 40 = 180 × 75% = 135 beats/minute

Your Target Heart Rate Zone Is ___ − ___

3. Follow my program or any other aerobic program that has been approved for you by your doctor.

Cardiovascular Fitness

Cardiovascular fitness comes from aerobic exercise that strengthens the heart and lungs. Aerobic literally means "with oxygen," and such exercise places an emphasis on maintaining a good workout over an extended period of time.

Cardiovascular fitness represents the body's ability to take in oxygen and distribute it to the muscles and other parts of the body, including the brain. The heart is the core of the cardiovascular system. Exercise that conditions the heart improves cardiovascular fitness. Aerobic exercise causes the heart to pump harder, but should not make you short of breath. Take extra time to warm up before exercise and cool down after your workout.

Cathy Sassin Smith
Billy Smith

Cathy Lee Crosby's
Twenty Minute Beautiful Body Workout™

*Consult your doctor or medical practitioner before beginning any exercise program.

Warm up for 5 minutes.

Begin exercise program with 5 minutes of gentle aerobic activity. Choose from the following: walking in place, jumping rope, cycling, stairclimbing, dancing in place, jogging in place, and so on.

STRETCHES

DOORJAM: *Helps open chest cavity and assist with proper breathing.* Gently lean forward with hands about hip-high in a doorway and stretch for 5 seconds. Don't bounce, just gently stretch. Finally move your arms to shoulder level and stretch again for 5 seconds.

KNEE TO CHEST: *Helps loosen up spine, stretch gluteals, and release tension in lower back.* Lie on your back on a comfortable surface with legs stretched out in front of you. Keeping your head, shoulders, and buttocks on the floor, gently take one leg at a time and bring your knee to your chest. Hold for 10 seconds. Next bring both legs up and gently hold them to your chest for 10 seconds. Breathe evenly and fully.

FOOT TO BUTT: *Helps stretch the quadriceps, the hard-working muscles in front of the thigh.* Lie on stomach turning head to the side and letting your arms rest palms up. Pull one leg up to the buttocks with your corresponding hand. *Don't arch your back.* Hold for 5 seconds. Repeat with other leg. Do first leg again and hold, then switch again for 5 seconds. If you can't quite reach your foot, just bring your foot as close to your buttocks as you can.

HANG TEN: *Helps to relieve stress and provide a good overall body stretch.* Grasp the top of a doorjamb or hold onto a tension bar fitted securely in a doorway at a level that's comfortable. Stretch comfortably for 10 seconds, making sure that your feet remain on the ground.

TOUCH HANDS: *Helps to open chest, shoulder area, and upper back. Also, a great posture aligner.* Stand with knees slightly bent, looking straight ahead. Take both hands and touch them at the fingertips right in front of your nose, keeping your elbows back behind your shoulders and your head aligned with your spine. With your elbows out and your palms facing down, slowly move your hands behind your head, and touch your fingertips behind your head, palms facing forward. Make sure to keep your shoulders and head still. Do this 5 times very slowly.

TONING EXERCISES

ABDOMINAL SQUEEZE: *Helps to strengthen the abdominal muscles.* Lie on your back with knees bent and reach your hands straight up toward the ceiling. Concentrate on keeping the abdominal muscles firm and tight on the way up and down. Exhale on the upward movement, and inhale on the lower, down to the floor. Work up to 10.

INNER-THIGH CRUNCHER: *Helps to tone and firm the inner-thigh muscles and buttocks.* Lie on the floor with knees bent and feet flat, and then lift the pelvis without straining the back. Squeeze the buttocks and inner-thigh muscles and keep them tight throughout. Do 15.

FANNY FIRMER: *Helps to tone and firm the gluteal muscles in the buttocks.* With one knee on a bench or bed, support your weight on your hands. (Lower yourself down to your elbows and forearms for more back support.) Lift the extended leg straight up with your foot flexed and back down again without arching the back. Slowly lift by squeezing the gluteal muscles throughout the move, both on the way up and on the way down. Work up to 13 times.

TUMMY TONER: *Helps to tone the lower abdominal area.* Balance far enough back in a sturdy chair so that you feel secure. Bring your knees up as far as you can and then straighten your legs back down, touching your heels to the floor. Remember to do it slowly and with total muscle control. Keep your toes flexed. Do 15.

LEG-SHAPING LUNGES: *Helps to firm and tone the legs, hips, and buttocks.* Stand with your feet together, then step forward and lunge into a "sitting" position. Return to a standing position by tightening and pushing back with your leg muscles. If you need support, place your hands on your forward thigh, right above the knee. Do 10 with each leg.

ALTERNATIVE: If the above is too tough for beginners, stand with your back against a wall and slowly bend your knees to a semisitting position coming down 4″–10″ if you can. Hold it there as long as you comfortably can, rest, and then try again until you can work up to the total time allowed for this section.

HAMSTRING CURLS: *Helps to tone the back of the thighs.* Stand, holding onto a chair or a wall for support. With your toes flexed, slowly lift one foot up behind you as close to your buttocks as you can, and then return it to the starting position. "Resist" the movement in both directions, and be sure to keep the hamstring muscles tight throughout. Do 10 on each side.

LEG EXTENSIONS: *Helps to tone the quadriceps, the muscles in the front of the thigh.* Seated comfortably with your back straight, lean back and hold onto the sides of a sturdy chair or bench. With your toes flexed, slowly raise your lower legs until they are fully extended in front of you by tightening the quadriceps muscles. Then lower them back down to the starting position, keeping the muscles tight throughout the movement. "Resist" the movement in both directions as you lift and as you return. Do 10.

BACK BUILDER: *Helps to strengthen the back and shoulder muscles.* Stand with knees relaxed and arms bent at your side about shoulder high with fingers pointing up. Slowly press down with your arms as if something is resisting your arm movement. Then bring them back up again as if something is resisting this movement as well. Keep your upper body straight and your palms facing forward. Do 10.

PUSH-UPS: *Helps to strengthen the arms, shoulders, and chest.* With your legs extended, lie on the floor on your stomach. Balance on both your hands with your elbows bent, and on your knees (beginners) or on your toes (advanced athletes). Lower your body by bending the arms until your chest is within an inch or two off the floor. Then return to the starting position. Work up to 10.

BOSOM BUDDY: *Helps to strengthen the chest, shoulders, upper back, and arms.* Lie on a bench and put your hand weights together in an arc overhead. Slowly lower your hands down to shoulder level, and tighten your muscles to form a slightly rounded arc. Work up from 3 to 10 pounds in each hand. Make sure you breathe in when your arms lower down, and breathe out as you lift up. Keep your back flat. Do 10. If you don't have any weights, make tight fists.

POWER PULLS: *Helps to strengthen the biceps and arm muscles.* Lie under a sturdy desk firmly and pull yourself up. Keep your body as straight as possible. Beginners may only be able to pull the head and shoulders, but eventually you'll pull up the entire body. Work up to 8.

JIGGLE BE GONE: *Helps to tone the triceps area in the back of the arm.* With legs bent and slightly apart, hold on to a chair with one hand, and bend your working arm close into your side. Slowly straighten your arm out backwards behind you. Keep your elbow stationary and pinned to your side. Squeeze the tricep muscle on the way backwards and on the way back down again. Start with 2 to 3 pounds and work up to 10 pounds. Do 10 with each arm. If you don't have any weights, make tight fists.

ARM ROLLOVERS: *Helps to build strength and flexibility in the shoulder and upper-back area.* Stand comfortably with knees slightly bent and arms extended at shoulder level out to each side well behind your shoulders. Rotate the entire shoulder joint by turning your palms in a full circle, and then back around again. Keep your arms straight and strong. Move slowly and resist the action by keeping the muscles tight throughout. Do 10.

COOL DOWN

KNEES TO CHEST: Lie on back. Bring knees to chest, grabbing just under them and pull toward chest. Hold 10 seconds.

LYING HAMSTRING PULL: Bring one knee at a time to chest, grabbing just under knee with both hands. Rest other foot on your bent knee and slowly pull until a stretch is felt. Hold 20 seconds.

SITTING TOE TOUCH: Sit on floor with legs out straight and together. Extend arms forwards toward toes. Stretch, and hold for 10 seconds. Reverse position.

TRICEP STRETCH: Place one arm behind your head with your elbow pointing up and your hand flat toward back of your head. Hold for 10 seconds. Reverse arms.

WIDE CIRCLES: Stand, knees slightly bent and circle arms from shoulder joint in a wide slow circular movement. Do 4 in each direction.

SIDE STRETCH: Standing comfortably, raise one arm directly overhead and lean and stretch easily to the opposite side. Feel the stretch throughout side and waist. Hold for 10 seconds then switch sides. Continue to breathe evenly and fully.

CALF STRETCH: Stand facing a wall with your palms resting against it and your feet slanted back behind you about 4'–5' depending on your height. Place one foot in front of the other about 12". Point toes forward. Lean forward until a stretch is felt in the calf muscle. Hold for 10 seconds, then switch legs.

FINAL STRETCH:

THE EGG: This wonderful position not only promotes deep relaxation and stress reduction, but it's also very important in getting the most out of my 20-Minute Beautiful Body Workout. With your legs in a kneeling position, lower your trunk so that your butt rests as close to your heels as possible. Keep your arms at your sides, palms up. Focus your attention on your breathing, keeping it full and easy. Hold this position as long as you desire, but 1–2 minutes is recommended. Here is where you should create a picture in your mind of exactly what you want your body to look like and exactly what results you want to achieve. Take your time, let this powerful visualization technique work wonders for your new beautiful body.

Core of Your Being Picture Exercise

INSTRUCTIONS: Find a favorite nonposed picture of yourself between the ages of five and seven years old. If you don't have one, look for a picture of some other child in that age range that "feels" like who you are. In your notebook or journal, describe what you are doing, and write down as many details as you can about what you see (how are you holding your head, the look on your face, and so on). Describe how this photograph makes you "feel." Read your answers several times. Compile all your observations and then describe your "essence" as completely as you can. Keep your picture and your description close at hand for easy referral.

Personal Playground Blueprint

INSTRUCTIONS: Once you have completed your Biographical Life Sketch, using your paper, notebook, or journal, answer the following questions in as much detail as possible.

1. **Who are you at your essence?** What lasting character remains a continuing part of all that you value? Who are you in the dreams that wake you with joy? Who is it you would become if the choice had to be made for your next lifetime right now?

2. **What is it that you radiate?** We all communicate a great deal just moving about in our world. What would you guess your effect is on others by just being in their presence doing routine events? What is it of substance that you carry into the world with you each day?

3. **What is your gift?** We all have special and unique gifts. Most of them are invisible to us because we are them. Often our children know exactly what we're good at because they haven't been taught job descriptions or don't know what an IQ is. Wherein lies your true value to others?

4. **What is your relationship with yourself like?** Usually the person we speak with the most during the day is ourselves. In fact, our inner dialogue probably exceeds our outer dialogue by quite a large margin. To what degree is that dialogue useful? Is your witness (the other voice) a friend? Are you your own best champion?

5. **What is your higher purpose?** Is there a mission in life that you occasionally feel *called* upon to do? Is there a service to the world, or to something noble that emotionally touches you? Have you told anyone?

6. **When are you most alive?** Is there a kind of work, a place you go, or a circumstance that you find yourself in that boosts your capacity because it is sheer joy? Do you cause that circumstance to be repeated just because you enjoy it? Are you ever really able to rest or feel blissful?

7. **What is your bliss?** Is it having a quiet moment in a natural setting? Is it finishing a very challenging project? Is it a moment of heartfelt

intimacy with a new friend? Is it lying in the sun after a great swim in the ocean? Do you ever plan to have that bliss in your life on a regular basis?

8. **What are your three most unfulfilled or suppressed dreams?** Tell them as if they had already been attained. Was there a time you were watching television and you fell in love with the character because of their passion . . . or the time you had a dream of doing something you never imagined and noticed how wonderful it felt. What do you want to include in your future that you don't have now?

9. **Describe a moment in your life when you remember being filled with warmth and love.** Sometimes it occurs during a daydream, or sometimes it's simply a feeling . . . It's an occasion where you had an unbelievably full and delicious feeling. What you want here is, the event or activity associated with that great feeling, that's what you want to record.

10. **What is your ideal work?** The secret is to imagine the work that includes all of your gifts and skills. Don't be afraid to actually create a new job description that incorporates all of your best features.

11. **Your house is on fire, and you have thirty seconds to get out, if you only had time to choose three items, excluding people and animals, what would be the first three you'd grab?** This is a way to discover more about what is really important to you. Let your sentiments find a real place in your life. Don't let them just be squeezed in between compulsive activity.

12. **When was the last time you did something with your hands that excited you, and what was it?** Very often cognitive skills, brain work, overpowers very sensory, physical activities. Check your life and jot down times when you were manually doing things that satisfied and balanced other activities.

13. **What experiences in your life have really touched your emotions?** Notice specific times when you were particularly touched by an event. What was the event? And what was the emotion you were feeling at that time? Include such events in your schedule to keep an emotional immediacy in your life. This keeps you emotionally alive.

Creating Your Visual Action Map

INSTRUCTIONS: Make a copy of the Visual Action Map on page 264. Write your answers to the questions below in your notebook or journal and use them and your Personal Playground Blueprint as a starting point to create your own Visual Action Map. BE BOLD. BE CREATIVE.

I. FOCUS ON THE IMAGES OF YOUR ULTIMATE SELF

1. Where are you and what are you up to when you are feeling at your ultimate?
2. Write down specific situations with as much visual clarity as possible.
3. Take what you have written and connect it to specific images of people, past or present, fictional or real.
4. Find and cut out or draw these images and attach them at the top of your Visual Action Map.

II. THE "ELEMENTS" OF YOUR VISUAL ACTION MAP

1. *Your archetype*—These are classic characters from history: the king, the magician, the champion, the athlete, the fairy princess, Tinkerbell, the Angelic. Consider combinations or hybrids. Stand in the physical posture of that character and use that archetype to inspire your position in the world. Attach pictures or drawings to the top of your copy of the Map.
2. *Your dreams*—Be bold. Write down the visions you have regarding the ultimate place for you in the world, and write them on your copy of the Map.
3. *Your relationships*—Focus on the ultimate relationships you have/ could have. Include lovers, friends, mentors, coaches, etc. Also include those you would love to help. Add to your copy of the Map.
4. *Your health*—Get an image of yourself in peak form. Get a sense of how you feel. Now, stand in and experience the fullness of these attributes.

Describe the feeling and fill in the appropriate box on your copy of the Map.

5. *Your rhythms*—Don't be stuck in the forty-hour work week. Choose a pattern of indoor/outdoor, work/play, alone/together combinations that would strike you as a delicious way to live. Simplify your description and place it in the appropriate square of your copy of the Map.

6. *Your internal guidance*—What are the elements inside you that help make the choices in your life. Imagine that the Creator, a parent, or a good friend is inside you, choosing the very best for your life. What would be the key points of this guidance? Add to your copy of the Map.

7. *Your coach*—Where does your internal coach live? Does it come in the moment? Is it a small, inaudible voice? Is it a feeling in the pit of your stomach? Is it the voice of someone you know? Make contact with your inner knowing and write down in the appropriate square of your copy of the Map who it is.

8. *Ideal future events*—Take a walk in your mind into the future. Smell it, feel it, see it, hear it, and create it just the way you want it. Then walk through these scenes several times until they've registered deep in your subconscious. Pick some key words that will remind you of your ideal future and write them in the appropriate square of your copy of the Map.

9. *Your special skills*—Since birth, there have been things that you could always do. They just came easy. Whether big or small, take stock of them and include them as a direct force to propel you toward your dreams. Include them in your copy of the Map.

10. *Your calling*—Most people have felt a certain calling. Usually it's an unexplained pull to be a champion for some kind of service to a greater cause. Trust your thoughts and write them on your copy of the Map.

11. *Your power*—If you don't know what your "natural" power is . . . ask your close friends. Add it to your copy of the Map, and it's yours.

12. *Your reframing*—Make a list of your major weaknesses, and decide to redefine them as assets. Ask a friend to help. Just place them in a context where they can be of some value on your copy of the Map.

13. *Your awakening process*—Everyone can learn to read the subtle signals that tell them how their awareness is growing. Write down in which ways you are growing and add them to your copy of the Map.

14. *Your spiritual connections*—As you improve your own awakening process, you can improve the quality of your connection to the Universe. Find a way to improve the clarity of your gratitude and your ability to request and give thanks for support. Put some key words in the appropriate square of your copy of the Map that will remind you of this connection.

15. *Your presence*—In any given moment, be available to the situation around you. Listen, and observe. This will vastly improve the quality of your "presence." What is it you feel at these moments? And how does that allow you to be fully present at all times? Fill in the appropriate box on your copy of the Map.

PATH OF THE
Angel Warrior

TO BECOME ACTRESS TO BE REKONED WITH
DREAM

TO FIND/ACT/BE IN GENUINE FEMALE HERO ROLE.
DREAM

TO HAVE "ALL" OF THE CHILDREN AND A DIRECT EXPERIENCE OF LOVE WITH THEM
DREAM

TO BE IN CAHOOTS WITH STRATEGIC ALLIES "FULL OF THE DICKENS"
RELATION-SHIPS

LIVE AS A WARRIOR ATHLETE
HEALTH

RHYTHMS

3:5

5 RINGS

The Playground

DIRECT "CHECK IN" THEN GO...FROM THAT SPACE
INTERNAL GUIDANCE

C/V/C PRODUCTIONS

THE CHARACTER EMERGES

ABILITY TO "CHECK IN" JUST A BREATH AWAY

MY COACH

GOD THE UNIVERSAL ENERGY

PRODUCED BY

CELESTINE PROPHECY

SPECIAL SKILL

EMITING & BLOWING FULL HEART INTO OTHERS ...

GIVEN LOVINGLY, SIMPLY, AND HUMOROUSLY

Cathy Lee's
VISUAL ACTION MAP™

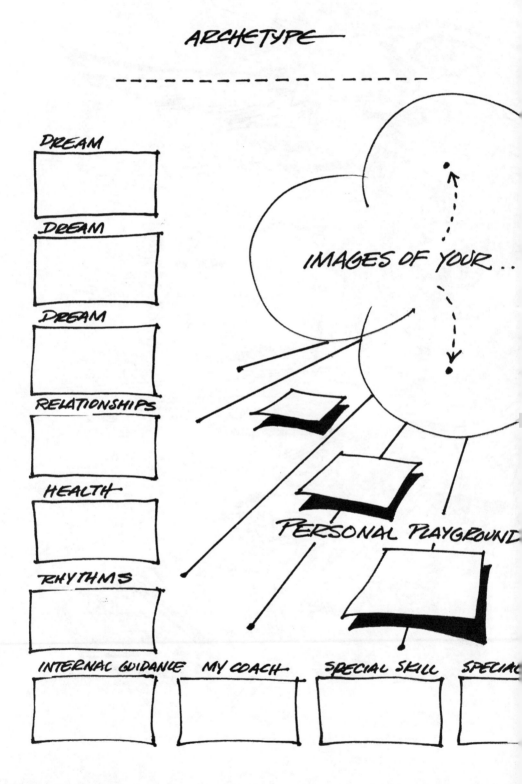

sample
VISUAL ACTION MAP™

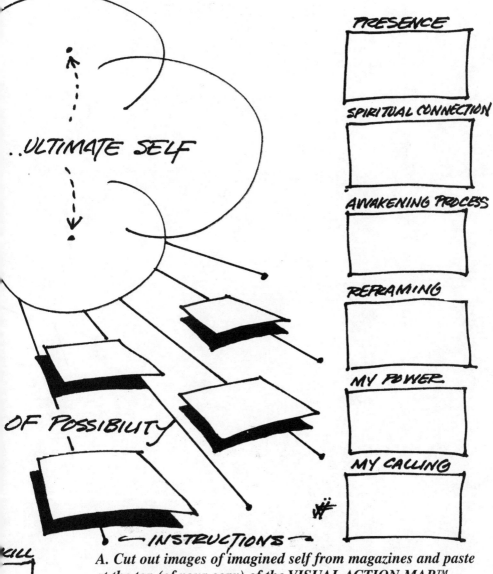

..ULTIMATE SELF

OF POSSIBILITY

PRESENCE

SPIRITUAL CONNECTION

AWAKENING PROCESS

REFRAMING

MY POWER

MY CALLING

KILL

← INSTRUCTIONS →

*A. Cut out images of imagined self from magazines and paste
at the top (of your copy) of the VISUAL ACTION MAP™.
B. Label the ideal elements of your possibility playground
in the flying boxes.
C. Write (on your own copy) key phrases for each of the
elements in the boxes around the border.*

Related Reading

Boyd, Doug. 1994. *Mad Bear: Spirit, Healing, and the Sacred in the Life of a Native American Medicine Man.* New York: Simon & Schuster.

Burton Goldberg Group. 1994. *Alternative Medicine.* Puyallup, Wash.: Future Medicine Publishing.

Cameron, Julia. 1992. *The Artist's Way: A Spiritual Path to Higher Creativity.* New York: G. P. Putnam's Sons.

Canfield, Jack and Mark Victor Hanson. 1993. *Chicken Soup for the Soul.* Deerfield Beach, Fla. Published by Health Communications.

Chopra, Deepak. *The Seven Spiritual Laws of Success.* San Rafael, Calif.: Amber-Allen Publishing.

Coelho, Paul. 1993. *The Alchemist.* San Francisco: Harper San Francisco.

Gawain, Shakti. 1986. *Living in the Light: A Guide to Personal and Planetary Transformation.* San Rafael, Calif.: Whatever Publishing, Inc.

———. 1993. *The Path of Transformation: How Healing Ourselves Can Change the World.* Mill Valley, Calif.: Nataraj Publishing.

Hendler, Sheldon Saul. 1989. *The Oxygen Breakthrough: Thirty Days to an Illness-free Life.* New York: Pocket Books.

Houston, Jean. 1987. *The Search for the Beloved.* New York: The Putnam Publishing Group.

Jackson, Phil. 1991. *Sacred Hoops: Spiritual Lessons of a Hardwood Warrior.* New York: Hyperion.

King, Serge Kahill. 1990. *Urban Shaman: A Handbook for Personal and Planetary Adventure Based on the Hawaiian Way of the Adventurer.* New York: Simon & Schuster.

Millman, Dan. 1979. *The Warrior Athlete: Body, Mind & Spirit.* Walpole, NH: Stillpoint Publishing.

———. 1980. *Way of the Peaceful Warrior.* Tiburon, Calif.: HJ Kramer, Inc.

————. 1991. *Sacred Journey of the Peaceful Warrior.* Tiburon, Calif.: HJ Kramer, Inc.

Neihardt, John G. 1939. *Black Elk Speaks.* Lincoln: University of Nebraska Press.

Norris, Chuck. 1988. *The Secret of Inner Strength: My Story.* Boston: Little, Brown and Co., Inc.

Pierrakos, Eva. 1990. *The Pathwork of Self-Transformation.* New York: Bantam Books.

Ragan, James. 1995. *The Hunger Wall.* New York: Grove Press.

Redfield, James. 1993. *The Celestine Prophecy.* New York: Warner Books.

Rilke, Rainer Marie. 1934. *Letters to a Young Poet.* New York: W. W. Norton Co.

Storm, Hyemeyohsts. 1972. *Seven Arrows.* New York: Ballantine Books.

Tzu, Ram. 1990. *No Way.* Redondo Beach, Calif.: Advaita Press.

Waterhouse, Debra. 1993 *Outsmarting the Female Fat Cell.* New York: Warner Books.

Welwood, John, 1990. *Journey of the Heart: Intimate Relationships and the Path of Love.* New York: Harper Perennial.

Williamson, Marianne. 1993. *A Woman's Worth.* New York: Random House.

Zwang, Moshe. 1995. *Palm Therapy: Program Your Mind through Your Palms.* Los Angeles: Ultimate Mind Publisher.